THE PHILOSOPHY OF HISTORY
NATURALISM AND RELIGION

THE PHILOSOPHY OF HISTORY
NATURALISM AND RELIGION

A HISTORIOGRAPHICAL APPROACH TO ORIGINS

JAMES STROUD

TATE PUBLISHING
AND **ENTERPRISES**, LLC

Published by Tate Publishing & Enterprises, LLC
127 E. Trade Center Terrace | Mustang, Oklahoma 73064 USA
1.888.361.9473 | www.tatepublishing.com

Tate Publishing is committed to excellence in the publishing industry. The company reflects the philosophy established by the founders, based on Psalm 68:11,
"The Lord gave the word and great was the company of those who published it."

Book design copyright © 2013 by Tate Publishing, LLC. All rights reserved.
Cover design by Joana Quilantang
Interior design by Joana Quilantang

Published in the United States of America

ISBN: 978-1-62854-480-0
1. Philosophy / General
2. History / General
13.09.13

ACKNOWLEDGMENTS

Special thanks to Casey Luskin and the Discovery Institute for corroborating with me to show why the subject of "Origins" belongs just as much to the field of history as it does science; the members of the Socratic Reform and Academic Freedom initiatives; philosopher Dr. William Lane Craig with whom my wife and I recently had the privilege of traveling to the Mediterranean with on an archaeological survey; Dr. Subodh Pandit of India whom I have worked with since 2008 on many of the topics covered in this work; my undergraduate history advisor at the University of Arkansas, Dr. Donald W. Engels; the employees at the Metropolitan Museum in New York City where I spent many hours of research 2010–11; and to all the professors and students I have worked with at various other philosophy, science, and history departments for help in compiling and critiquing this work. With such a consensus of various minds confirming that at least "most" of what I report in these pages to be accurate, I can at least rest assured that I am "mostly" accurate in my hypotheses and the conclusions that therefore follow.

Mr. Stroud, with whom I have worked with in the past, has chosen a good topic of discussion in the Philosophy of History because it is not a common one. While I as a doctor do applaud naturalism in the study of science;

the pitfall lies in the misuse and abuse of the principle. Most scientists mistake the philosophy of naturalism to be the same as science. But it is not. Naturalism is a philosophy which itself is not subject to the scientific method of inquiry. If we can clearly differentiate between science and the philosophy of science, we will be able to see that the claims from many scientists regarding the supernatural are not based on science but on the philosophy of science, and as such they become the conclusions of circular reasoning. It is at this point that naturalism is misused and abused both by the scientist as well as the historian. If we place both religion and naturalism on the same level as beliefs, we can now appeal to science and ask whether there are any indirect scientific evidences which could help us decide which is more credible when it comes to the whole of our existence. The masquerading of naturalism as science has driven most of the secular study of historical events and has falsely described religion as quite inferior in value. They falsely claim that science is opposed to miracles found in religions, while the truth is that it is naturalism, (not science), that opposes the idea of miracles. Science cannot oppose what it does not study and Mr. Stroud has done an excellent job in surveying this very concept in his work surrounding the very philosophy of what we call history today.

—Dr. Subodh Pandit, MD

James Stroud (MA Ancient and Classical History; BA Philosophy of Religion) worked on his first undergraduate in history at the University of Arkansas from 1996–2001 and later a bachelor of arts in philosophy of religion from APU in which he graduated cum laude. This book is a compilation of his revised masters of arts thesis on the philosophy of history. James is also a member of the Society of Collegiate Scholars, the Association of Ancient Historians (AAH), Society for Historical Archaeology (SHA), the Philosophical Research Society (PRS), and has personally visited many of the archaeological points of interest referenced in this book.

James has collaborated and cosponsored events with the Discovery Institute in Seattle, which is the "think tank" for the Intelligent Design Movement that seeks to establish "academic freedom" where students and teachers alike are allowed to hear and investigate both the pros as well as the cons for naturalism versus nonnaturalistic. James has hosted various speakers both domestically as well as internationally to speak at various universities and colleges on this topic. James insists that through examination of the evidence and open debate, that objective truth can be discovered as opposed to the yoke of intimidation and restrictions forced upon the majority of academia today which does not allow faculty or students to "follow the evidence wherever it leads."

James most recently returned to the Midwest from the New York City area where he and his wife, Gina, have spent the last two years.

CONTENTS

FOREWORD

BY CASEY LUSKIN

RESEARCH COORDINATOR AT DISCOVERY
INSTITUTE, SEATTLE WASHINGTON

> While such rhetoric may shut down discourse in the short
> term, optimists might hope that in the longer view—the
> one that matters the most—the evidence wins.
>
> —Casey Luskin, *Human Origins*

I first met James Stroud in 2010 when he approached me regarding the work I had done with Discovery Institute defending academic freedom in public education. My second encounter with James was in 2012, when he hosted myself and Dr. John West at three universities discussing modern scientific challenges to neo-Darwinian evolution.

I came to Discovery Institute in 2005 as Program Officer in Public Policy and Legal Affairs, and my main role was to assist teachers, school board members, and other educators and policymakers to discuss both the scientific evidence for and against neo-Darwinian evolution in a legal, accurate, and pedagogically effective manner. These efforts took me to many U.S. states to meet and assist educators and legislators, including Louisiana, Florida, Idaho, Oklahoma, Missouri, Alabama, California, Texas, and Pennsylvania. Pennsylvania, in fact, was my first assignment, as I started working at Discovery Institute just before a trial began in Harrisburg over a school district in Dover, PA which had required the teaching of intelligent design (ID) in its science instruction.

Long before I joined Discovery Institute, the organization had opposed mandating intelligent design in public schools. As the Institute's Science Education Policy Page states:

> As a matter of public policy, Discovery Institute opposes any effort to require the teaching of intelligent design by school districts or state boards of education. Attempts to mandate teaching about intelligent design only politicize the theory and will hinder fair and open discussion of the merits of the theory among scholars and within the scientific community. Furthermore, most teachers at the present time do not know enough about intelligent design to teach about it accurately and objectively. Instead of mandating intelligent design, Discovery Institute seeks to increase the coverage of evolution in textbooks. It believes that evolution should be fully and completely presented to students, and they should learn more about evolutionary theory, including its unresolved issues. In other words, evolution should be taught as a scientific theory that is open to critical scrutiny, not as a sacred dogma that can't be questioned.[1]

Unfortunately, the Dover Area School Board did not listen to our policy position, and chose to push ID into its curriculum. As a result, they faced a lawsuit which became the first case to assess the constitutionality of teaching intelligent design in public schools. The judge in the case, federal district court Judge John

E. Jones III, struck down the teaching of intelligent design and declared it unconstitutional to teach in public schools. The ruling was the subject of my first lecture hosted by Mr. Stroud at the University of Arkansas in 2010. In my talk, I pointed out that the ruling has numerous errors, including the facts that the judge:

- Employed a false definition of ID, presumed that it requires "supernatural creation"— a position refuted during the trial by ID proponents who testified in court;

- Ignored the positive case for ID and falsely claimed that ID proponents make their case solely by arguing against evolution;

- Overstepped the bounds of his role as a judge and engaged in judicial activism. Jones declared that ID had been refuted when in fact he had been presented with credible scientific witnesses and publications on both sides showing evidence of a scientific debate;

- Used poor philosophy of science, by presuming that being wrong precludes being scientific;

- Dangerously stifled scientific advance by taking the level of support for a theory as a measure of whether it is scientific or not;

- Blatantly ignored and denied the existence of pro-ID peer-reviewed scientific publications that were in fact the subject of testimony in his own courtroom;

- Blatantly ignored and denied the existence of pro-ID scientific research and data that was likewise the subject of testimony in his own courtroom;

- Made numerous inaccurate (or at least easily challenged) scientific claims about the evolution of the bacterial flagellum, the blood clotting cascade, and new genetic information;

- Adopted an unfair double standard of legal analysis where religious implications, beliefs, motives, and affiliations count against ID but never against Darwinism;

- Broke a cardinal rule of constitutional law by declaring a religious belief to be "false" from the bench of a U.S. court;

- Engaged in further judicial activism by presuming that it is permissible for a federal judge to define science, settle controversial social questions, settle controversial scientific questions, settle issues for parties outside of the case at hand so that his ruling would be "a primer" for people "someplace else."[2]

But perhaps the most disturbing aspect of the ruling was identified by a legal scholar who is also *a leading critic of intelligent design*: Boston University law professor Jay Wexler. Professor Wexler argues that "The part of *Kitzmiller* that finds ID not to be science is unnecessary, unconvincing, not particularly suited to the judicial role, and even perhaps dangerous both to science and to freedom of religion."[3] Wexler's point is that Judge Jones adopted a "rule" of science where only naturalistic causes may be investigated—all for the purpose of excluding nonnaturalistic causes from being considered by scientists, or mentioned in the science classroom. Thus, Judge Jones used his ruling in *Kitzmiller* to judicially canonize an arbitrary "rule" of science in order to restrict freedom of speech and academic freedom to investigate origins. But is this rule working?

In his work, Mr. Stroud makes potent arguments that both history and science ought to abandon the rule of "naturalism"—not to avoid explaining observed natural phenomena, but to reinvigorate science and history with the ability to "follow the evidence wherever it leads." This is probably why he was concerned about the *Kitzmiller v. Dover* ruling, and asked me to speak on it in 2010.

Like all proponents of naturalism, Judge Jones's powers were limited. Try as he might to restrict explanation to naturalistic causes, he could not change the nature of the evidence. As a result, even after the Dover ruling, the fine-tuning of nature—from the life-friendly settings architecture of Universe down to the specified and irreducible complexity in the smallest cell—still remained. Indeed, since the Dover ruling, the ID movement has made great strides in research advancing the case for design. In 2011, the ID movement published its 50th peer-reviewed research paper. These papers provide both theoretical arguments, and empirical data, which support the view that life and the Universe were designed by intelligence. These research advances served as the basis for my 2012 talks hosted by Mr. Stroud.

At those talks, I discussed the work of the BioLogic Institute, an ID-research lab headed by molecular biologist Douglas Axe. As a post-doc at the University of Cambridge, Axe performed mutational sensitivity tests on enzymes to measure the likelihood that a string of amino acids will generate a functional protein. In 2000 and 2004, he published this research in the *Journal of Molecular Biology* showing that functional protein folds may be as rare as 1 in 10^{77} amino acid sequences.[4] He describes the significant implications of those numbers:

> I reported experimental data used to put a number on the rarity of sequences expected to form working enzymes. The reported figure is less than one in a trillion trillion trillion trillion trillion trillion. Again, yes, this finding does seem to call into question the adequacy of chance, and that certainly adds to the case for intelligent design.

To put the matter in perspective, Axe's results indicate that the odds of unguided processes generating a functional protein fold are less than the odds of someone blindly firing an arrow into the Milky Way galaxy, *and hitting one pre-selected atom.*

If functional protein sequences are rare, then natural selection will be unable to take proteins from one functional sequence to the next without getting stuck in maladaptive or non-beneficial stages. This suggests that the evolution of new proteins might require many mutations before any benefit is gained—mutations which are unlikely to accumulate via unguided evolution alone. Other ID research has corroborated this conclusion.

In 2004, biochemist Michael Behe and physicist David Snoke published research in the journal *Protein Science* reporting results of computer simulations of the evolution of protein-protein interactions. Vital to virtually all cellular processes, these interactions require a specific "hand-in-glove" fit, where multiple amino acids must be properly ordered to allow the three-dimensional connection. Behe and Snoke's calculations found that for multicellular organisms, evolving a simple protein-protein interaction which required two or more mutations in order to function would probably require more organisms and generations than would be available over the entire history of the Earth. They concluded that "the mechanism of gene duplication and point mutation alone would be ineffective...because few multicellular species reach the required population sizes."[5]

In 2008, Behe and Snoke's would-be critics tried to refute them in the journal *Genetics*, but found that to obtain only two specific mutations via Darwinian evolution "for humans with a much smaller effective population size, this type of change would take > 100 million years." The critics admitted this was "very unlikely to occur on a reasonable timescale."[6]

In 2010, Axe published another peer-reviewed research paper which also seemed to confirm Behe and Snoke's results. He presented calculations modeling the evolution of bacteria evolving a structure which required multiple mutations to yield any benefit.[7] Axe's model made assumptions which were exceedingly generous toward Darwinian evolution. He assumed the existence of a huge population of asexually reproducing bacteria that could replicate quickly—perhaps nearly 3 times per day—over the course of billions of years. Despite the fact that bacteria have some of the highest known mutation rates, even here molecular adaptations requiring more than six mutations to function would not arise in the history of the earth.

The following year, Axe co-published a research paper with developmental biologist Ann Gauger which suggested that many features would be beyond the reach of Darwinism. Their experiments sought to convert one bacterial enzyme into another closely related enzyme—the kind of conversion that evolutionists claim can easily happen. They found that this conversion would require a minimum of at least *seven* simultaneous changes,[8] exceeding the six-mutation-limit which Axe had previously established as the boundary of what Darwinian evolution can accomplish in bacteria. Because this conversion is thought to be a simple one, this suggests many biological features would require more than six simultaneous mutations to give some new functional advantage.

These results show there is too much complex and specified information in many proteins and enzymes to be generated by Darwinian processes on a reasonable evolutionary timescale. But it's not just ID theorists who are identifying problems with materialistic explanations. Some evolutionary and / or atheistic scientists admit that we lack good explanations for key events in the history of the Universe—the very events which Mr. Stroud discusses as being best explained by intelligent design.

For example, in 2007, Harvard chemist George Whitesides was given the Priestley Medal, the highest award of the American Chemical Society. During his acceptance speech, he offered a stark analysis of origin of life research, reprinted in the respected journal, *Chemical and Engineering News*:

> The Origin of Life. This problem is one of the big ones in science. It begins to place life, and us, in the universe. Most chemists believe, as do I, that life emerged spontaneously

from mixtures of molecules in the prebiotic Earth. How? I have no idea.[9]

Similar problems exist for the abrupt appearance of animal life, which has been dubbed, the Cambrian explosion. A 2009 paper in *BioEssays* concedes that "elucidating the materialistic basis of the Cambrian explosion has become more elusive, not less, the more we know about the event itself."[10]

In fact, the history of life is riddled with such "explosions"— including an abrupt appearance of humans themselves. In 2004, the famed evolutionary biologist Ernst Mayr recognized the abrupt appearance of humans, without a transition from the fossil record:

> The earliest fossils of *Homo, Homo rudolfensis* and *Homo erectus*, are separated from *Australopithecus* by a large, unbridged gap. How can we explain this seeming saltation? Not having any fossils that can serve as missing links, we have to fall back on the time-honored method of historical science, the construction of a historical narrative.[11]

The same applies to the origin of human language and cognition. As MIT professor and linguist Noam Chomsky observes:

> Human language appears to be a unique phenomenon, without significant analogue in the animal world. If this is so, it is quite senseless to raise the problem of explaining the evolution of human language from more primitive systems of communication that appear at lower levels of intellectual capacity. ... There is no reason to suppose that the "gaps" are bridgeable.[12]

And finally, as for the origin of the Universe itself, Stephen Hawking and Roger Penrose admit that "almost everyone now believes that the universe, and time itself, had a beginning at the big bang."[13] As Mr. Stroud points out, Hawking believes the Universe requires no first cause. But some highly respected physicists feel otherwise, as Nobel Prize-winning physicist Charles Townes has stated: "Intelligent design, as one sees it from a scientific point of view, seems to be quite real. This is a very special universe: it's remarkable that it came out just this way. If the laws of physics weren't just the way they are, we couldn't be here at all."[14]

The point of this is that strictly materialistic/naturalistic explanations of nature are failing in many key areas. New approaches are necessary. In this regard, it is refreshing to see naturalistic Darwinism being tackled from the approach of philosophy of history, as Mr. Stroud has done here. It is also refreshing to see Mr. Stroud's compelling case that naturalism should not be a rule that is enforced upon academics to prevent them from following the evidence wherever it leads. Unfortunately, it seems that the more the evidence points away from naturalism, the more naturalists resort to strong-arm tactics to retain their cultural power.

In essence, the *Kitzmiller v. Dover* ruling represents the near endgame of what Mr. Stroud warns against: the judicial enforcement of naturalistic philosophy upon academic inquiry. This is something we too warned Judge Jones not to do, though he didn't listen to us. In an *amicus* brief I helped write for the court, we explained to Judge Jones that some highly successful pro-ID scientists were coming up for tenure, but that a judicial ruling that tried to enter into "dangerous" areas, like the definition of science, was inappropriate for a court to do, and could impact the academic freedom of scientists. Judge Jones didn't take those concerns seriously, and in fact one of the very scientists we mentioned was later denied tenure—with his opponents citing the *Kitzmiller v. Dover* ruling as justification for why his pro-ID views didn't belong in the academy. Unfortunately, this sort of discrimination is not uncommon, I say this based upon firsthand, as I have been involved in the defense of many pro-ID scientists and faculty whose academic freedom was being restricted because of their support for ID. To give just a few of many examples:

- In 2005, the president of the University of Idaho instituted a campus-wide classroom speech-code, where "evolution" was "the only curriculum that is appropriate" for science classes.[15] This was done in retaliation toward a professor at the university, Scott Minnich, who at the time was testifying in favor of intelligent design as an expert witness at the *Kitzmiller v. Dover* trial.

- In 2005, top biology professors at Ohio State University derailed a doctoral student's thesis defense by writing a letter claiming "there are no valid scientific data challenging macroevolution" and therefore the student's teaching about problems with neo-Darwinism was "unethical" and "deliberate miseducation."[16]

- In 2005, pro-ID adjunct biology professor Caroline Crocker lost her job at George Mason University after teaching students about both the evidence for and against evolution in the classroom, and mentioning ID as a possible alternative to Darwinism.

- In 2007, pro-ID engineer Robert Marks, Distinguished Professor of Electrical and Computer Engineering at Baylor, had his ID-research lab thrown off the Baylor campus after he did an interview supporting intelligent design.[17]

- In 2009, a high level computer technician at NASA's Jet Propulsion Lab was demoted and punished for sharing pro-ID videos with co-workers, and ordered not to do so again.

The list could go on, but the point is this: well-credentialed, qualified, and highly competent scientists and academics have faced negative repercussions to their careers directly due to their support of intelligent design. What is the response from ID-critics? When Mr. Stroud invited me to speak at a college in northwest Arkansas in 2012, a group of self-styled "skeptics" voiced opposition to these sort of examples, and denied that this persecution of ID proponents was taking place. I then asked them if they personally would deny a job to a scientist strictly because he or she supported ID. They unanimously said "yes." In reply, I said something along the lines of the following: "So you deny that ID proponents face discrimination, yet you admit you would discriminate scientists simply because they are pro-ID. Do you see the disconnect?" They didn't—but everyone else in the room did, as it burst into applause for exposing the intolerance of ID critics.

Indeed, it's not hard to believe that ID proponents face persecution. After all, leading evolutionary scientists have admitted they would try to keep ID proponents out of the academy. In 2006, a professor of biochemistry and leading biochemistry textbook author at the University of Toronto, Laurence A. Moran, stated that a major public research university "should never have admitted" students who support ID, and should "just flunk the lot of them and make room for smart students."[18] In 2011, Jerry Coyne, a leading evolutionary biologist at the University of Chicago, stated that "adherence to ID (which, after all, claims to be a nonreligious theory) should be absolute grounds for not hiring a science professor."[19] ID-critics in some arenas have become so intolerant that in 2007, the Council of Europe, the leading European "human rights" organization, adopted a resolution calling ID a potential "threat to human rights"![20]

These ID critics have every right to disagree with intelligent design. They should have every right to discuss and critique ID and publish their views. The problem, is that they don't extend such rights to those who dissent from their position. But if there is no freedom to dissent, then there is no academic freedom. In this regard, the plight of ID proponents should be concerning not just to those who support intelligent design but also those who disagree with it. Academic freedom is a precious value that underlies our entire society. When non-naturalists lose academic freedom to pursue their ideas, everyone else loses as well. And this is true not just in the hard sciences, but also in the social sciences like history and philosophy. In this regard, I applaud Mr. Stroud's argument that philosophy of history, like the natural sciences, should be "open" to the idea that naturalism is not necessarily true, and therefore free to take the evidence wherever it leads.

PREFACE

> The study of history is a study of causes. The historian continuously asks the question: "Why?" And, so long as he hopes for an answer, he cannot rest.
>
> —Edward Hallet Carr, *What Is History?*

All modes of knowledge are permeated by philosophy. Whether it is philosophy of the natural or social sciences all seem to stem simply from more ad hoc assertions and presuppositional beliefs than empirical evidence. Much of this stems from the way most of academia today is still permeated by the same Enlightenment philosophy following the French Revolution, which endorsed naturalism in all criterion of knowledge; however, just because the majority of academia hold to this philosophy, that in itself does not mean it is necessarily correct. This nineteenth-century paradigm is beginning to slowly come undone, and the philosophy to take its place is yet to be seen. What is exciting about this development is that it opens the academic door for multifaceted education as opposed to a type of education undergirded by a type of indoctrination of an Enlightenment-like paradigm. And what is this paradigm? By and large it could best be described as the philosophy of naturalism. Naturalism, though there are many subbranches of it, is essentially a worldview that takes account only of natural elements and forces while ruling out any nonnaturalistic ones. This in turn rolls over into metaphysical naturalism, which holds that there exists nothing but natural elements, principles, and relations of the kind studied by the natural sciences. Metaphysical naturalism holds that all properties related to the mind and consciousness is reducible to nature. More specifically, it rejects any supernatural concepts and explanations that are usually found in religious systems. The question is: "Is this a sound theory or not to base all modes of knowledge?" Moreover, this belief concludes that all phenomena are within the "laws of science" and that therefore all teleological explanations are without value. Since the Enlightenment, this philosophy of science has morphed into other branches of knowledge and inquiry to the extent that today almost all fields of inquiry (including history) are built on presuppositional beliefs that naturalism is true and that scientism is the superior and objective field of knowledge. Take for example the world-renowned physicist Stephen Hawking and Leonard Mlodinow in their 2010 book *The Grand Design* in which he ponders on the philosophical questions regarding the nature of reality and then concludes:

> Traditionally these are questions for philosophy, but philosophy is dead. Philosophy has not kept up with modern developments in science, particularly physics. Scientists have become the bearers of the torch of discovery in our quest for knowledge.[21]

As philosopher William Lane Craig remarked follow-ing this statement in his critique *Hawking and Mlodinow: Philosophical Undertakers:*

> The professional philosopher can only roll his eyes at the effrontery and condescension of such a statement. Two scientists who have, to all appearances, little acquaintance with philosophy are prepared to pronounce an entire dis-cipline dead and to insult their own faculty colleagues in philosophy at Cal Tech and Cambridge University, many of whom, like Michael Redhead and D. H. Mellor, are eminent philosophers of science, for supposedly failing to keep up. I couldn't help but wonder what evidence our intrepid authors have of Mr. Redhead's laggard scholar-ship? What recent works in philosophy have they read that form the basis for their verdict? Alas, they do not say. The professional philosopher will regard their verdict as not merely condescending but also as outrageously naïve. The man who claims to have no need of philosophy is the one most apt to be fooled by it. One might therefore anticipate that Mlodinow and Hawking's subsequent exposition of their favored theories will be underpinned by a host of unexamined philosophical presuppositions. That expec-tation is, in fact, borne out. Like their claims about the origin of the universe from "nothing" or about the Many Worlds Hypothesis to explain fine tuning, their claims about laws of nature, the possibility of miracles, scientific determinism, and the illusion of free will are asserted with only the thinnest of justification and little understanding of the philosophical issues involved.[22]

So not only has a naturalistic philosophy of science taken over the sciences, but naturalism has also sought to control the philosophy of the social sciences as well—including the phi-losophy of history. I understood that as my masters of history thesis (in which this book is a revision of), I would have been much better off by simply looking at a subject such as a specific facet of Byzantine culture or perhaps the history of daily life in ancient Persia as opposed to challenging the "status quo" of modern philosophy of history as many have warned me. But if I am restrained from following the evidence where it seems to lead then what is the purpose in doing history in the first place? Moreover, as long as I am restricted to a philosophy of history that I feel is unwarranted, then I simply cannot pursue any type of post-graduate degree simply because there would be no logical point in doing so. With that being said, the only logical thing for me to have focused my MA thesis on would be on the very area of philosophy of history that I feel should be challenged or at the very least investigated. My hypothesis that naturalism is a weak philosophy and should not be allowed to permeate the methodology of history *a priori* is either true or it is false. I am willing to be convinced that my hypothesis is false, but having undergraduate degrees in both history and philosophy, I simply have yet to see any reasons for believing naturalism to be plausible; and if it is not, I simply cannot accept it *a priori* nor can I follow a "closed philosophy" of history that appears unwarranted.

The vast majority of my entire academic career has been in a secular setting so this is by no means an attempt to challenge the way we do history based on myself studying at private or theologically minded schools. While any challenge to naturalism (per se) may have metaphysical or theological implications, this is not my purpose in analyzing and breaking down naturalism; my purpose is to show that any closed-philosophical paradigm that does not allow the inference to the best explanation should be abandoned or at least challenged, and I feel that naturalism is just such a philosophical viewpoint that is outdated and should not be used as a limiting factor for philosophy of history studies.

Note: I have chosen to use the traditional designations "BC" and "AD" for dating purposes throughout this book. I understand why many historians now choose to use the more politically correct terms "BCE" (Before Common Era) and "CE" (Common Era) to avoid seeing history from a Judeo-Christian reference point; but using these new modified terms while still basing them off of Jesus Christ's birth seem somewhat pointless.

INTRODUCTION

PHILOSOPHY OF HISTORY AS A SCIENCE

All historical events are unique; no historian has a right to a closed system of natural causation, for, as the Cornell logician Max Black has shown in a recent essay, the very concept of cause is a "peculiar, unsystematic, and erratic notion."

—John Warwick Montgomery, *History, Law and Christianity*

What is "history?" This question might strike you as an overly easy one at first glance; one that all professional historians agree upon in the recording of past events to the best of the historians' knowledge in methodological research. This is only part of the answer however. When I first began my undergraduate studies in 1996 in the field of history, I too believed that the definition of history was somewhat cut and dry. However, after my undergraduate studies in history, I began work on a degree in philosophy and what I found was that there is just as much philosophy in history as there is history per se. Philosophy of history is one of the least looked at components of history that concerns epistemological approaches to gaining knowledge of the past. It attempts to answer questions such as, "What does it mean to know something?" "How do we come to know something?" "Can we know the past and, if so, to what extent?" "What does it mean when historians say that a particular event occurred?"[23] With this in mind, science and history could be said to operate as a "first-order" discipline that simply looks at "X" set of facts (picture an archaeologist finding a city or burial grounds). Philosophy then acts as a "second-order" discipline to then "interpret" these facts (in the archaeology example it could be that this is the lost city of Troy or a particular peoples group). The point being, virtually every first-order discipline has a second-order philosophy linked directly to it. Whether it is biology inferring the origin of life or history inferring a linkage to ancient Sumerian and Egyptian cultures; philosophy plays a crucial role in how data is inferred and what conclusions are drawn.

The term "philosophy of history" at its core refers to the theoretical aspect of history. The term itself also suggests the ideas of human agency, change in human affairs throughout time, and the ability to learn from our own past history and what that in fact could mean. Though there can be several different ways to define the philosophy of history, it may help to break these into critical and speculative philosophy of history. Critical philosophy of history is more focused on the theory that deals with questions such as the nature of historical evidence itself or the degree to which objectivity is possible. Speculative philosophy of history is an area of philosophy concerning the overall significance of human history or if it in fact is devoid of any significance. Furthermore, it speculates as to a possible teleological end to its development; it asks if there is a design, purpose, directive principle, or finality in the processes of human history as a whole.

Speculative philosophy of history asks at least three basic questions:

- What is the proper unit for the study of the human past: the individual, civilization, culture, or entire species? Do there seem to be patterns of progress or cycles? Is history deterministic? Are there patterns we can see or is history holistically random? What is the place of religion in history?

- If history can indeed be said to progress, what is its ultimate direction? Is there objective meaning to history and what (if any) is the driving force of that meaning?

I will be taking a holistic approach encompassing both bullet points to gauge the type of open-philosophy of history that should (or should not) be used and "why" this is the case as the overlying thesis of my research.

There are numerous challenges to knowing the past. Since the past is forever gone, it can neither be viewed directly nor reconstructed precisely or exhaustively. Accordingly, historians cannot verify the truth of a hypothesis in an absolute sense. In this, however, the historian is far from being alone. Only mathematics seems to operate with any degree of objective truth whereas the vast majority of all branches of science as well as history run by the highest degree of "plausibility" but not anything in the sense of an "objective truth." This does not however mean that objective truth does not exist for the historian: either George Washington lived or he did not and either he was the first president of the United States or he was not. While the historian may not conclusively be able to prove either of these statements, it does not mean objective truth does not exist. Moreover, the earth is either flat or spherical in its shape—it cannot be both; therefore "relativism" is false even if the historian cannot empirically prove a specific something. Therefore, the historian should allow circumstantial evidence to point the way to the most plausible of objective truths and in so doing so "follow the evidence where it leads."

During my undergraduate years, I quickly began to see how one's personal philosophy and presuppositions guided one's interpretation of the available data, sometimes to an alarming degree. Moreover, I began to see the historian play the role of scientist and the biologist play the role of historian all with a type of universally "closed philosophy" in mind. This was summed up perfectly in my mind when Charles Hartshorne, one of the most recognized philosophers of religion and metaphysics, commented on a debate on the historicity of the resurrection of Jesus of Nazareth between philosopher Antony Flew and historian Gary Habermas: "I can neither explain away the evidences for the resurrection to which Habermas appeals, nor can I simply agree with the skeptical position. My metaphysical bias is against resurrection." Flew himself later said, "This is in fact the method of critical history. You try to discover what actually happened, guided by your best evidence, as to what was probable or improbable, possible or impossible and miracles are things that you just take to be impossible."[24]

These types of examples along with countless others, where ones' presuppositions and own personal philosophies are allowed to cloud their inference of data to the point that any competing alternative voice is immediately shut down *a priori*, moved me to question the philosophy of history as a whole. The more I began to discover this type of naturalistic philosophy that was undergirding my studies in history, the more I began studying in great detail the natural sciences to discover for myself whether or not this type of presuppositional belief had any place in directing how one "must" do history. What I found was that within the philosophy of science itself was a history book riddled by story after story of persons, acting in the name of "science" wanting to protect their particular paradigm (philosophy) even at the sacrifice of the very definition of "science." Moreover, I began seeing that many theories of science would be better categorized as "theories of history" in that they were unrepeatable events in the ancient past (the very definition of "history").

Two points to be made here are that science itself is often stepping on the toes of the historian and that the sciences themselves have attempted to enforce a type of "naturalistic" philosophy, not only in the biological sciences but also in cosmology/cosmogony, geology, anthropology, sociology, history, and basically all of the social sciences. From what has seemed like countless hours inside and outside of the classroom with various experts in their respected fields, I have become even more convinced not only that naturalism is untenable but also that it stagnates the philosophy of history as a whole, and therefore, I will argue that an "open philosophy" is needed not only in history and the social sciences, but of the natural sciences as well. I will attempt to show that an open philosophy will better help the social as well as natural sciences in allowing all tools to be used without confining one to a strict presuppositional interpretation of the data. Moreover, we will take a historiographical approach to origins, which envelopes the unrepeatable sciences to show why origins belong back into the historians' realm of expertise. Nonrepeatable events such as these are usually called "origin sciences," but I will make the case that they might better be called "origin histories" instead.

The case of origins has like so many other areas of inquiry been limited to a naturalistic paradigm that attempts to describe origins from arising by nature alone. This mode of thought first came into popularity shortly after the time of the Enlightenment and has grown ever since to the point that a strictly closed philosophy is held in most of academia that does not allow for nonnaturalistic hypotheses. Again, this is why it is important to spend the first few chapters not only breaking down the historiography of this changing paradigm up through today but also in order to differentiate between origins as science versus history. I am far from being alone in believing that an open philosophy should be openly endorsed as well as challenging that much of what is considered the "natural sciences" would really be better described as a combination of history with that of philosophy of science. Thomas Kuhn (1922–1996), who is one of the most influential philosophers of science of the twentieth century, would seem to agree with me. In his 1962 book *The Structure of Scientific*

Revolutions, Kuhn not only broke with several key positivist doctrines (which attempted to rule out the metaphysical from science) but also inaugurated a new style of philosophy of science that brought it closer to the "history of science."

Kuhn's influence within the philosophy of history may have been just as great if not greater than it was within the philosophy of science. The social sciences (specifically history) were taken up by Kuhn with enthusiasm, and Kuhn's impact cannot be underestimated. Kuhn's idea of science appeared to permit a more liberal conception of what science is than hitherto, one that could be taken to include disciplines such as sociology, anthropology and various branches of philosophy. Kuhn also rejected the idea of an *a priori* set of rules for determining scientific outcomes and had no problem in appealing to factors, external to science, in explaining why a scientific revolution took the course that it did.

A rather unique influence on social science was Kuhn's influence on the development of social studies of science itself, in particular the Sociology of Scientific Knowledge. A central claim found in Kuhn's work is that scientists do not make their judgments as the result of consciously or unconsciously following rules. Their judgments and conclusions are nonetheless tightly constrained during normal science by the example of the guiding paradigm of the day. Kuhn expressed concern over the very strong impulse to distort reality for it to "fit in" to what prevailing modes of scientific inquiry required. He also drew attention to the corporate aversion to novel findings—that square peg that refuses to be compressed into that ideological round hole. Men whose research is based on shared paradigms are committed to the same rules and standards for scientific practice. In this type of "rehearsal," one researcher shows the community that one has mastered the tricks of the trade and can use them to produce conventional copies of the standard fare. During a revolution, they are released from these constraints (though not completely). Consequently there is a gap left for other factors to explain scientific judgments. Such suggestions were taken up as providing an opportunity for a new kind of study of science, showing how social and political factors external to science influence the outcome of scientific debates.[25]

Though Kuhn's contributions to the philosophy of science can hardly be underappreciated, I agree with philosopher of science and logician Karl Popper who criticized Kuhn's reliance on the concept of ruling paradigms as "the myth of the framework." In other words, why should the "politics" or "elites" of academia enforce their own personal philosophies if there is no warrant for doing so? What I have found in my various studies is that time and time again in the natural and social sciences including history, it is a naturalistic philosophy that controls the paradigm and thus no alternative theories are accepted. Not only do I agree with Popper that such a paradigm makes academia a series of "myths" that has no objective basis, but I feel it retards the ability to follow Socrates' adage of "follow the evidence where it leads."[26]

For example, philosopher Daniel Robinson of Oxford concluded in a series of lectures that there are very few if any universal laws within science other than classical mechanics. In fact, even Newtonian Laws have been challenged based on relativity theory. So what then can be said for much of biology and psychology in fact of their "scientific status" given that neither of those disciplines can explain events by deducing them from universal laws known to be true? And why is that? It is because biology and psychology have no universal laws known to be true.

It was one of the objectives of the logical positivists to rid science of metaphysics and to some this meant doing away with all nonnatural events and possible causations. Nonetheless, it would strain credulity to believe that the lawful and time-ordered sequences in the natural world come about without the participation of just such forces. The struggle can be said to be between scientism versus nonscientism. The adherent of scientism believes that science itself can account for all of reality. I, along with almost all philosophers today, believe that scientism is not only inaccurate but overwhelmingly inaccurate. The famous philosopher C. S. Lewis often called this type of scientism "scientocracy" and was quite outspoken about the dangers to not only academia but humanity itself when we hand over the reins of power to an "elite" group of supposed experts claiming to speak in the name of science. In this type of philosophy of science not only is science "closed" but so are the other fields of academia that do not presuppose the superiority of naturalistic science; gone too is the free society in which one is allowed to follow evidences where they may (or may not) lead.[27] It is important to briefly breakdown this changing paradigm as well as its own history in the opening chapters in order to understand how and why naturalism became the dominant paradigm still held by many if not most historians today and how this then gave rise to scientism and thus academically persecuting those who challenged this philosophically closed system.

So in summary, the term history is not as easy to define as one may think at the onset as much of it depends on the paradigm that drives the philosophy of history itself. Within this definition, a naturalistic presupposition has carried over from science into the social sciences including history, whether one admits this or not; this presupposition forces history to thus have a "closed philosophy," which greatly limits the toolbox of historical methods at the historians' disposal, which I have and will continue to argue is unjustified. I am therefore contending for an "open philosophy" of history, and I will show why this is the most plausible theory for attaining the highest degree of historicity possible.

In order to break history free from the paradigm of naturalistic scientism that has at least partially ensnared it, it is important to briefly review why naturalism/scientism in and of itself has no strong basis within science and philosophy and therefore most definitely has no basis for being used in historic methodology. This will allow us to conclude that an open philosophy of history is completely warranted and the best option for inference to the best explanation of past events. Once this is completed we will review a series of four past events that fall into the realm of ancient history through this "new lens" and see how the mode of current "naturalistic science" compares to an "open philosophy of history" to demonstrate not only that an open-philosophy should be the replacement paradigm that does not restrict inference to the best explanation, but that much of what has traditionally been called "science" would be better described as "philosophy of history." The four areas we will be reviewing based on a closed-philosophy presupposing naturalism (which is espoused by virtually all of academia today) versus an open philosophy of history (as an origin science) will be:

1. Origin of the Universe and cosmological constants
   - A brief analysis of the origins of Information/Consciousness Theory and Morality

2. Origin of Animal Life—Cambrian Explosion (Fossil Record)
   - A brief analysis of Human Origins

3. Origin of Civilization and the Pre-Common Era—
   - A brief analysis of languages/writing, anthropology/sociology and the Old (Hebrew) Testament—Religious Myth versus Historicity

4. The Common Era of the Historical Jesus—
   - A brief analysis of the New Testament—Religious Myth versus Historicity

I chose these four areas predominantly because they offer not only a highly contestable naturalistic view offered in the vast majority of textbooks today, but they also are much more "historic" in their scope than they are accessible by the scientific method. Moreover, they also offer four examples of why the subject of "origins" belongs just as much under the umbrella of philosophy of history as it does that of science. If I can make a case for an open philosophy of history (as a science) being a stronger criterion that fulfills the four points outlined above better than that of naturalism this should at the very least beg the question— "How could this be true 'if' naturalism is true?" It is my belief that the evidence is strongly against the theory of naturalism especially when analyzing origins not only in plausibility, but also in explanatory power and scope, and if this is true then not only is there a great warrant to incorporate an open philosophical view of history but nonnaturalistic theories such as deism and theism are back on the table as live options to be broken down, reviewed and analyzed instead of prematurely dismissed. If my hypotheses are true, then the conclusion that naturalism is false logically and inescapably must follow. This should not, however, discourage historians who have long held to a closed philosophical methodology but instead should represent an exciting time in the study of history and philosophy.

POSITIVISM: ITS COLLAPSE AND RETURN?

> Our philosophy of science should incorporate all that we believe to be true about the world, including the allowance of divine revelation as well as reason and the scientific method as possible sources of information.
>
> —Alvin Plantinga, *Methodological Naturalism*

Why does anything at all exist instead of just nothing? This is the foundational question when it comes to any philosophy. Many persons who uphold metaphysical beliefs often link these to a transcendent being usually referred to as "God" while the strict naturalist following a strict scientism or physicalism, maintains the belief that all things can either be explained by science or natural processes. Each side (whether a closed or open philosophy) has an unverifiable belief in the ultimate uncaused cause in which everything originated. If scientism cannot answer some question(s), then it is false and should not be followed. Moreover, if it is false, then a historians' philosophy of history should not be limited to a strict naturalistic form of history omitting such phenomena usually referred to as "miracles" arbitrarily.

While both sides are unable to empirically verify their hypotheses, they can partake in reason and logic as in any other field of study to gain an inference to the best explanation and build a powerful cumulative case argument based on a great number of circumstantial evidences. Here is a simple example of applying logic to reach a conclusion:

1. Jon is taller than Scott

2. Scott is taller than Jane

3. Therefore Jon is taller than Jane

In this simple example, if premise 1 and 2 are correct, then 3 must logically follow. It is irrelevant how tall the persons in question are—"if" Jon is taller than Scott and Scott is taller than Jane, it is a logical necessity that Jon is taller than Jane. Arguments like this can either be deductive or inductive. An inductive argument makes it probable that the conclusion is true if the premises are true while a deductive argument *guarantees* that the conclusion is true if the premises are true. The argument must be sound, not question-begging, and all the premises leading to the conclusion must be more plausible than their denials. For an argument to be certain, we must have certainty in the premises leading up to its conclusion whether it is two premises as above or one hundred. If someone could provide evidences that Jon was on stilts when he was measured against Scott's height in the above example, then premise 1 could be false (if it was shown without the stilts that Scott was indeed taller) and therefore the entire argument would collapse. But so long as a statement is more plausible than its negation, we should believe it rather than its negation.

As I have stated earlier, the vast majority of persons already have a philosophy in place that alters their belief regardless of the evidences. This could be someone who wished naturalism to be false because of their belief in God or someone like Thomas Nagel who stated in *The Last Word*, "I want atheism to be true and am made uneasy by the fact that some of the most intelligent and well-informed people I know are religious believers. It isn't just that I don't believe in God and, naturally, hope that I'm right in my belief. It's that I hope there is no God! I don't want there to be a God; I don't want a universe like that."[28]

While there is of course nothing wrong with ones' own personal beliefs, beliefs like this should not be allowed to dictate in academia that naturalism/scientism must be true. This type of hypocrisy should not be allowed to permeate academia anymore than a church or Islamic law should be able to; if 1+1=2 then that is what should be concluded on *all* sides and by all parties. On a positive note, however, scientism as well as positivism (the belief that any talk concerning "God" or metaphysics is literally meaningless), has been increasingly in retreat as they have continually been torn apart by even the most basic of philosophers over the last part of the twentieth century and early twenty-first century. Positivism has not, however, gone quietly into the night; paradigms are not easily challenged once the "powers that be" have a firm grasp of the helm.

Ever since the eighteenth century following the French Revolution, a form of militant secularism began to permeate the landscape in place of a militant theocracy that had been in its place. At this time, historians also began to turn toward a more positivist approach for their historical methodology focusing on fact as much as possible but still with an eye on telling histories that could instruct and improve. Starting with Fustel de Coullanges and Theodor Mommsen, historical studies began to progress toward a more modern scientific form. Sadly, we went from one paradigm to the next without really stopping to analyze the evidence. We then saw a combination of the natural sciences and social sciences attempting to militantly remove any concept of "God/nonnaturalistic causation" from the landscape entirely. While many different persons such as Charles Lyell, David Hume in his attack on the miracles, and Charles Darwin were at the head of looking for a way to account for natural processes alone being able to account for all of reality—thus birthing "scientism" (the belief that all knowledge can be accounted for by the physical and biological sciences) we also saw this same level of scientism permeating into the histories. Many authors began attacking religion (mostly Christianity which was the predominate religion of the West) to the point of denying that someone like Jesus of Nazareth even existed. This also permeated over into anthropology, sociology, and psychology with each one following the notion of "naturalistic evolution" from simple to complex into their own philosophies. This was followed in the early 1920s by the attempt to remove metaphysical "God" talk from all of academia through "positivism"—in which talk about "God" was concluded as literally meaningless nonsense. The original members of this positivist movement were led by physicist Moritz Schlick, included mathematicians, physicists, sociologists, and economists but no professional philosophers. This omission was unfortunate because "united by their passionate dislike of the metaphysical—the realm beyond the physical world—the group developed a unified philosophy that embraced science and attempted to destroy philosophy."[29] Nevertheless, the ideas of the Vienna Circle on positivism were spread far and wide. The ghost of their attitude toward metaphysics in general (and God in particular) continues to haunt parts of Western academia to this day.[30]

On the positive side of the story almost all of these movements have collapsed entirely or are in the process of erosion. Positivism no longer has any followers, virtually no historian denies Jesus of Nazareth's existence today, and an increasingly growing number of philosophers of science are becoming skeptical of naturalism as a whole, and most all but deny scientism as being tenable since there are a great number of non-scientific truth claims.

THE RESURRECTION OF GOD-TALK[31]

I recently met philosopher Douglas Geivett in July of 2012. Geivett explained, chief among the woes of logical positivism was the fact that the verification principle was neither empirically verifiable nor tautological. That is, the verification principle was itself a metaphysical claim, a claim that therefore ruled itself to be meaningless: "It failed its own requirement for factual meaningfulness" and thus was self-refuting. On 8 April 1966, *Time* magazine ran a cover story about the then current "death-of-God" movement in American theology entitled "Is God Dead?" William Lane Craig explains that "according to the movement's protagonists, traditional theism was no longer tenable and had to be once and for all abandoned. Ironically, however, at the same time that theologians were writing God's obituary, a new generation of young philosophers was rediscovered His vitality." Only a few years later, *Time* carried a cover story asking, "Is God coming back to life?" Interest in the philosophy of religion continued to grow to the point where, in 1980, *Time* found itself running a story about "Modernizing the case for God," describing the contemporary movement among philosophers, putting new life into the arguments for God's existence:

> In a quiet revolution in thought and argument that hardly anybody could have foreseen only two decades ago, God is making a comeback. Most intriguingly, this is happening not amongst theologians or ordinary believers, but in the crisp intellectual circles of academic philosophers, where the consensus had long banished the Almighty from fruitful discourse. The reference to banishing the Almighty from fruitful discourse is a reference to logical positivism. Hence it is no surprise to find Tyler Burge, Professor of philosophy at UCLA, writing that the central event in philosophy during the last half-century was 'the downfall of positivism and the re-opening of discussion of virtually all the traditional problems of philosophy.'[32] The death of positivism meant that questions of metaphysics, including the existence of God, were once again live issues in the world of academia.[33]

Sadly, the infection of positivism and scientism still permeate academia with many now using the media and politics as its main weapon to keep its current paradigm in place. I have witnessed firsthand how the "powers that be" within academia come out in full battle gear when the paradigm of philosophical naturalism is challenged today.

THE COLLAPSE OF SCIENTISM

If positivism is false, as we have outlined and which virtually no scholar contests today, and scientism is as well, then there is no reason for either of these to continue to play a part in science, much less in the definition of history. To this I "hope" we can all agree. If something is known to be false, then why continue to hold on to it? Thankfully with the fall of positivism more and more are now beginning to abandon the philosophy of scientism (though the proponents of scientism are now turning to the media in a last ditch effort to win by popular opinion). One reason for this growing abandonment of scientism is simply that philosophers of science can easily see many things that scientism simply cannot account for, and if there is just one thing it cannot account for then it is false. Take the below conversation between a philosopher William Lane Craig and chemist and supporter of scientism Peter Atkins during a 1997 debate between the two that shows the limits of science and moreover naturalism:

> Atkins: "Everything in the world can be understood without needing to evoke a God. You have to accept that's one possible view to take about the world."
>
> Craig: "Sure, that's possible, but..."
>
> Atkins: "Do you deny that science can account for everything?"
>
> Craig: "Yes, I do deny that science can account for everything."
>
> Atkins: "So what can't it account for?"

Craig calmly said he would just name five:

1. Mathematics and logic—science cannot prove them because science presupposes them.

2. Metaphysical truths—such as, there are minds that exist other than my own. (Ex: The Matrix)

3. Ethical judgments—you cannot prove by science that the Nazis were evil because morality is not subject to the scientific method.

4. Aesthetic judgments—the beautiful, like the good, cannot be scientifically proven.

5. Science itself—the belief that the scientific method discovers truth cannot be proven by the scientific method itself.[34]

With this being said, we must dismiss our presuppositions and prejudices against such things as "miracles" (nonnaturalistic causations) prematurely. Though entire books have been written on the five points listed above in reference to the implausibility of scientism, I will not have the space to elaborate greatly on each of them but will include components of them in my breakdown of the four major events of the ancient past that we often infer *a priori* as science with a presuppositional belief toward naturalism, but as I will argue, that naturalism can simply not adequately account for but our modified definition of philosophy of history can. Having shown that the tenets of positivism (and likely scientism) to be false, if one can now show that the tenets of naturalism itself are also false, then there should not only be a consensus of agreement to change our definition of science to an "open philosophy" that does not retard its limits to natural causation alone, but history itself should continue to be looked at through this same lens and also not be limited to a type of naturalism that we have been discussing. To this, I hope, even the staunchest naturalist can agree. Philosopher and writer C. S. Lewis made a similar argument against scientism and since then many philosophers like Alvin Plantinga have tweaked and modified it, and it today remains unrefuted by proponents of scientism. Basically, the argument states that if scientism is true, we could never know it was, since if it were true and our minds are nothing more than evolutionary mental/brain (physical) events, then we could simply never trust them anyway, and therefore we could never know whether scientism were true or not. Lewis stated in his book *Miracles* that unless human reasoning is valid, no science can be true.[35] Lewis's argument reduces to this:

1. Naturalism entails determinism.

2. If naturalism is true, our beliefs are held on the basis of nonrational (deterministic) causes, and we would not be able to make inferences.

3. In that case we are not able to cite reasons to justify holding our beliefs.

4. But it is incontestable that we do in fact reach truths by logical inferences.

5. Therefore, we must either reject naturalism as false or stop taking for granted that we reach true beliefs by logical inferences.

6. We cannot stop taking for granted that our beliefs are generally true.

7. Therefore we must conclude that naturalism is false and that something else exists in addition to nature.[36]

While this is Lewis's original argument, which has since been strengthened and modified, its basic premises still remain true. If one argued against human beings being able to make inferences, they would be refuting the statement they just said and could therefore not know if what they just said was accurate or at all logical.

The belief that all causes can be attributed to natural processes alone therefore seems to be false; if it is false, then we should not allow it to affect how we do work in history or any other field by presupposing it to be true. By arguing through four of the most saturated hypotheses that naturalism holds to be true based on its own naturalistic philosophy, we should be able to determine whether this is true or false. Therefore we will compare naturalism against the open philosophy of history (as a science) we outlined earlier to determine which provides the best explanation and is therefore most likely to be true.

ACADEMIC FREEDOM AND HONESTY

> To limit teaching to only one idea is a disservice to students because it is unnecessarily restrictive, dishonest, and intellectually myopic.
>
> —Dr. Russell Carlson, www.DissentFromDarwin.org

History as well as the sciences has a long history of having its accounts being "written by the victors" so to say. A classic example of this could be the notion of the history of the Americas "beginning" when they were "discovered" by Europeans (not the Native American people groups already here). Obviously, we can look back now knowing this is blatantly false; however, for centuries this was the way in which this part of history was taught though it was not completely accurate. Moreover, the victors usually have a much more favorable view in recorded histories than do the losers.

This reinterpretation of the historical record is usually referred to as historical revisionism. In its extreme form, historical revisionism is called negationism. An example would be when Thomas Jefferson negated all the nonnaturalistic (or supernatural/miraculous) events in the New Testament based on his belief that naturalism (even if it was a deistic form) is true. Another example is how some Islamic textbooks deny that the Jewish Holocaust ever happened. Secular academia is no less guilty of such inconsistencies either. Whether it is recording the supremacy of Caucasian over black, positivism as fact, Darwinian naturalism as fact, etc., all have been enforced by the media; modern academia is far from an innocent defendant in all of this. The revision of previously accepted historical accounts is a constant process in which "today's winners are tomorrow's losers," and the rise and fall of present institutions and movements influence the way historians see the past.[37]

Obviously the victors do have advantages in promoting their version of events even if they do not erase their enemies completely from existence. In dictatorships, ruthless censorship allows only the state-approved version of events to be made public and much that happened remains secret if it proved hurtful to the ruling elite. Liberal democracies are not immune to this either however. In the West for example, the concentration of media into ever fewer hands has given the captains of major media and the public relations industry increased control over the parameters of public discourse that form the boundaries of debate each of us has in classrooms and with friends and coworkers on matters such as war and politics. I found this out firsthand when I began my work on academic freedom (in the context that anyone should be allowed the freedom to follow a line of reason/evidence wherever it leads both inside and outside of academia) and challenged the "status quo" of how an open philosophy should be the basis for all modes of study and inquiry.

A case could be made that ever since Plato's *Republic*, civic education has had a centralized role in politics and the constitution of a common identity. Science as well as history itself has at times become the target of propaganda leading to historical revisionist altering history in order for the history to record what a specified group wants it to. Public education is one of the largest areas that can be susceptible to such propaganda and pseudoscience/history. An easily assessable example would be when the former Soviet Union established atheism as the only scientific truth and any criticism of the government's stance could result in loss of job and imprisonment.[38] This tactic obviously meant one had to falsify evidences for textbooks used throughout the school systems to show that naturalism was an uncontested truth. While this is an obviously extreme example, it nonetheless shows how far propaganda can go if left unchecked even within a major world power. Similarly, history textbooks are one of the many ways through which this common history has always been transmitted. In most societies, schools and curricula are controlled by governments. As such, there is always an opportunity for governments to impose their own philosophies (good/bad/neutral). While in most cases government control parameters are setup in order to keep such things as hate-speech and dogma out of the textbooks, the power itself to impose is available for use in the education system to influence thought of malleable minds toward a version of truth it endorses. The question I have continually asked myself however is that even "if" the idea of the earth being spherical as opposed to flat offends people, should we therefore adjust our histories and sciences to accommodate them? Does the government (or anyone else) have the right to control inquiry and thus indoctrinate as they see fit? For example, let us look at the general definition for "science." Much like the definition of history, the definition of science is even more difficult to define with the definition "evolving" drastically over the last century.

General definitions of **Science:**

1. the state of knowing: knowledge as distinguished from ignorance or misunderstanding

2. *a*: a department of systematized knowledge as an object of study <the *science* of theology> *b* : something (as a sport

or technique) that may be studied or learned like systematized knowledge <have it down to a *science*>

3. *a*: knowledge or a system of knowledge covering gen-
    eral truths or the operation of general laws especially as
    obtained and tested through scientific method *b*: such
    knowledge or such a system of knowledge concerned with
    the physical world and its phenomena

4. a system or method reconciling practical ends with sci-
    entific laws <cooking is both a *science* and an art> b. The
    observation, identification, description, experimental
    investigation, and theoretical explanation of phenomena. c.
    Such activities restricted to a class of natural phenomena.d.
    Such activities applied to an object of inquiry or study.[39]

The definition that virtually no one will argue with is #1 or
simply the "state of knowing;" with the advent of the scientific
method we see this included in a subbranch to the definition as
well as a systematized set of knowledge. Where we really enter
into the "philosophy of science" and (like history) one that I
believe has no place in the definition of science is #4c: "Such
activities 'restricted' to a class of 'natural' phenomena." So #4b uses
the terms "experimental investigation" and "theoretical explanation" of phenomena but then in #4c anything other than natural
phenomena is ruled out *a priori*. Do you see a problem here?
Though positivism (the ruling out of metaphysics) has completely
collapsed and is no longer believed to be true, its effects on the
definition science still remain: metaphysics is ruled out no matter
the evidence. Is this really the best way to handle debate—to rule
it out in advance?

In 2008, I began working with Dr. Subodh Pandit of India
on just such criteria. I hosted Dr. Pandit at a small college and
invited several university faculties from the science departments.
During the discussion, we posited the notion that this "4c" part

of the definition of science should be discarded since its roots to positivism have long been shown fallacious. The science department stated in a unified voice that "this was impossible" and that anyone who would not limit their scope to only naturalistic explanations should not be allowed to teach. I was literally shocked when each one of them stated this in such a unified voice and followed up by adding that someone such as Dr. Pandit should not be allowed to teach if he denies #4c. So much for "inference to the best explanation" or "taking the evidence where it leads…"

The more I began to see that both our definitions of the sciences as well as the social sciences had this closed philosophy somewhat built into it, the more I began to see the "emperor indeed had no (or very few) clothes on." While I could have stopped right there and just "drank the Kool-Aid" along with the rest, I simply could not agree to alter/falsify my own findings simply in order to appease the status quo. The more I began to see how the philosophy of history had this undergirding of naturalism "lightly" though still built into it, the more that pointed me back to the philosophy of science. It was at this point that my wife and I flew to Seattle to explore the relationship of the philosophy of science to that of history to get a competing view over that of naturalism.

Having flown to Seattle to spend the weekend at the Discovery Institute hearing from scientist from Princeton, Cambridge, Oxford, and the like, I was amazed at how many of these scholars confirmed exactly what my concerns were. There has been documented case after case of PhD scholars who are ostracized, fired, and denied tenure for questioning this naturalistic paradigm. Upon my arrival back from Seattle, I decided to test my hypothesis firsthand in 2010 at the university level. If I was correct, merely challenging the paradigm of naturalism would result in the same type of ad hoc/ad hominem attacks with little to no refutations of the evidences. I contacted the Discovery Institute who then directed me to Casey Luskin (masters in science and

Juris Doctor in law), to set up an "academic freedom" day on the university campus. At the heart of this debate was a presuppositional belief that the philosophy of science/social sciences should only be guided by naturalistic phenomena regardless of the evidences.

What occurred was continued hate e-mail sent to my website and that it was an "outrage" that an event that challenged the philosophy of naturalism and supported the theory of intelligent design was being allowed onto "their" campuses. I had one professor attempt to stop me from putting on the 2010 event, but since I was paying for all expenses on my own as a private test, and thus not affiliated with the university, there was thankfully no way he could stop it. I personally sent out invitations to all collegiate departments and encouraged them to show why a closed philosophy of interpretation is superior to an open one; moreover, I encouraged them to literally "expose Luskin" during the Q&A and discussion time if we were as false in our analysis of the data concerning academic freedom and the theory of intelligent design as these critics were inciting. What we experienced were various professors saying that we were "false" but giving no reasons why we were false other than a presupposition that naturalism was true and therefore could not be challenged. I saw firsthand account after account of ad hominem attacks at a personal level and ad hoc assertions that since intelligent design "could" point to nonnaturalistic phenomena, then it is not "real science" by default and therefore false. Most of these attacks were so elementary it was sad to see at a university level. Straw men arguments were set up to point out that that since Luskin was a theist, that there was a hidden agenda, and therefore his arguments were false (genetic fallacy). At no time were there any sound arguments for the defense of naturalism or sound/plausible arguments against intelligent design; moreover, not one person even attempted to defend the reason why philosophy of science should be closed as opposed to open. These events as well as others have only strengthened the fact that limiting natural/social sciences to natural phenomena only is as outdated as positivism and limits our inference to the best explanation since oftentimes the inference may not be naturalistic.[40] (I repeated a similar test in 2012 with both Casey Luskin as well as social scientist Dr. John West and expanded it to two university campuses and one college, which resulted in the same type of attacks in each with no real substance or logic to the attacks on why naturalism is true or "real science").

Peter S. Williams (masters in philosophy) summarizes this point beautifully in his article "The Definitional Critique of Intelligent Design Theory."[41] When critics of intelligent design theory attack it as not being scientific, they necessarily presuppose the existence of a sound demarcation criteria able to distinguish between science and nonscience, just as positivists of the past assumed the existence of a sound demarcation criteria able to distinguish between the sense of science and the nonsense of metaphysics. (Of course, the failure of logical positivism means that even if ID is not science, it might nevertheless be a true philosophical claim.) The failure of logical positivism should, I think, give pause for thought to the definitional critics of ID. Indeed, just as the verification principle ruled either too little or too much "in" to the positivists' favored category of "science," so the demarcation criteria of ID's critics does the same.

On the other hand, if you decide to define science so that it excludes explaining anything with reference to *intelligence*, then of course ID is not science in that sense of the term. But then, neither is forensic science, archaeology, psychology, cryptography, or SETI (the search for extraterrestrial intelligence)! Just as the logical positivists failed to define their verification principle in such a way as to exclude religious claims whilst including 'scientific' claims so the definitional critics of ID fail to define science in such a way as to exclude ID whilst including claims that even they admit are scientific. Either both are in or numerous things that even ID's critics accept as scientific are out. As ID critic Bradley Monton argues, ID should not be dismissed on the grounds that it is unscientific.[42]

What matters in the final analysis is:

a. The existence of reliable design detection criteria (something already accepted by various sciences and even by many critics of ID).

b. The existence of evidence that warrants a design inference according to these criteria. If adequate criteria and empirical evidence both exist, then the conclusion of intelligent design follows.

Although an acceptance of ID does not automatically equate with an acceptance of supernaturalism, let alone theism, ID should lead one to ponder whether God might be the best candidate for the source of design, that possibility cannot be dismissed as nonsense simply because it is metaphysical and the same principle applies to the subject of history.[43]

WHAT ABOUT HISTORY?

Historic Scholars who would consistently implement such methodological skepticism when studying other ancient historical writing, as they do to religious texts, would find the corroborative data so insufficient that the vast majority of accepted history would have to be jettisoned.

—Craig Blomberg and Jennifer Markley,
A Handbook of New Testament Exegesis

It is very important for me to lay down a firm foundation outlining why the philosophy of history has naturalistic tendencies and that has required me to investigate not only where these tendencies come from within the philosophy of science but to investigate their plausibility. For me to just state: "Philosophy of History should not be limited to natural causation" without any warrant would make me guilty of the very presuppositional mind-set that I am making a case against. Therefore it is very important to carefully review the foundations in which the current philosophy of history paradigm is built and then show that "if" this foundation is weak or false, it should then be replaced. By arguing for an "open philosophy" I must therefore bear my own share of the burden of proof and show that the current "closed philosophy" is weaker and therefore in need of replacement.

As I have stated earlier, no historian holds to history in an absolute sense; therefore when historians say that "x occurred" in the past, they are actually claiming that based on the available data, the best explanation that we are warranted at this point in drawing is that "x" did in fact occur because this has the greatest of explanatory scope and is superior in this scope to competing hypotheses. Therefore, we do indeed have a "rational" reason for believing it happened; however, as new data may come into play in the future, this conclusion may indeed be changed. Science takes this same inference; it may look at the current state of geology and "infer" that the present is the key to the past (a.k.a. Uniformitarianism) which is the assumption that the same natural laws and processes that operate in the universe today have always operated in the universe in the past and apply everywhere else in the universe. Uniformitarianism has been a key principle of geology and virtually all fields of science, but many of naturalism's modern geologists no longer hold to such a strict version of it. Therefore uniformitarianism and geology as a whole is just as much "history" as it is science since it, like the existence of Alexander the Great, cannot be mathematically proven with any degree of certainty.

So is history a science? It has often been asked whether history is a science (and in my case I am at least in part asking if science is a history) since the majority of the sciences are faced with the same challenges as is history. Astronomers view distant galaxies that they must infer a great deal upon, the geologist theorizes to the geologic past, and the evolutionary biologist is unable to verify if a particular life-form evolved from another—in all of these there is a large amount of guessing involved. Even within a much stronger and mathematically developed science such as physics, physicists still are forced to posit numerous entities to which they have no direct access such as quarks and strings. J. H. Zammito in his work on the philosophy of history and theory commented that "an electron is no more immediately accessible to perception than the Spanish Inquisition. Each must be inferred from actual evidence, yet neither is utterly indeterminable."[44] Historian Mike Licona similarly states: "Historians often operate in a manner similar to physicists. Physicists determined that black holes exist by observing certain effects and positing the cause. They take what we can observe and posit what we cannot to explain them. Historians likewise consider observable data and posit the unobservable past."[45] It is historian Richard Evans, however, in his *Defense of History*, who makes the affirmative claim that history is by definition a science; a point that I believe to be accurate and that I will build upon throughout this work:

> History, in the end, may for the most part be seen as a science in the weak sense; an organized body of knowledge acquired through research carried out according to generally agreed methods, presented in published reports, and subject to peer review. It is not a science in the strong sense that it can frame general laws or predict the future. But there are sciences, such as geology, which cannot predict the future either. The fact seems to be that the differences between what in English are known as the sciences are at least as great as the differences between these disciplines taken together and a humane discipline such as history.[46]

So contrary to popular opinion, the idea that scientists always have direct access to the objects of their study whereas the historian does not is blatantly false. Neither the scientist nor the historian has direct access to their field of study in most cases and thus the scientists' understanding of the present is just as much a "theoretical" construction as is the historians' understanding of the past. So while the historian does not have direct access to the past, they do have access to things that really existed and that are accessible to them. The modern historian is not only dependent on earlier documentation evidences; for example, archaeological data furnishes direct access to the objects of the historian's investigation. The renowned English historian RG Collingwood states: "Scissors and paste is not the only foundation of historical method. Archaeology has provided a wonderfully sensitive method for answering questions to which not only do literary sources give no direct answer but which cannot be answered even by the most ingenious interpretation of them."[47]

Thus, the historian, like the scientist again, often has direct access to things he or she is investigating. As Old Testament scholar RK Harrison explains, modern historians are not so heavily dependent on subjective literary sources as before because the sciences of linguistics, sociology, anthropology, numismatics, and archaeology have become so developed.[48]

OPERATIONAL VERSUS ORIGIN SCIENCE?

It is important to note how some philosophers of science like Norm Geisler have broken up science into that of operational and origin sciences. It is very helpful to review how he differentiates these two branches of science to understand why I am defining history as a "weak science" and one that can therefore tell us more about "origin sciences" than can the current mode of scientific methodology that Geisler and others define as "operational science."

Operation Science	Origin Science
Studies Present	Studies Past
Studies Regularities	Studies Singularities
Studies Repeatable	Studies Unrepeatable
Re-creation Possible	Re-creation Not Possible
How Things Work	How Things Began
Finds Secondary Causes	May Find Primary Cause

As you can see based on the chart above, origin science is really "history" (or history as a weak science as mentioned earlier) whereas operation sciences are truly scientific in their scope adhering to and being testable by the scientific method. Origin sciences studies past singularities (events that are not reoccurring such as the instant of time or first life, etc.) rather than present and testable normalities covered in operation sciences. Therefore any singularities would best be reviewed by an origin scientist or a historian as opposed to an operation scientist as is the case today. Since the four events I will be covering fall into the category of singularities (beginning of the universe, life, civilization, religion) it is my belief and hypothesis that the historian is more capable of addressing questions of origin science with philosophy as an aid than the operation scientist. Moreover, once we shake free the shackles of naturalism that are presupposed by the operation sciences' closed philosophical system we can utilize an open philosophy that allows us to more holistically interpret the data. Origin science works on different principles than operation science does. Since the past events that it studies cannot be repeated today, it uses analogies between the kinds of cause/effect relationships that we see today and the kind of effect that is being studied. Also, origin science does not claim to give definitive answers but only plausible ones.[49] The below chart gives examples that fall into either origin or operation sciences:

	Origin Science	Operation Science
Universe	Cosmogony	Cosmology
Life	Biogeny	Biology
Humans	Anthropogeny	Anthropology

While much more could be said on this, I believe enough has been stated to at least give a credible reason for believing history does in fact fall into the categorization of a "weak science" in the same notion that most of the sciences are not within the realm of establishing "absolute truths," and they too are guilty of their own inferences that the data itself does not always lead to. Moreover, weaker sciences such as anthropology and sociology as well as linguistics all fall under the much larger umbrella of "history." Therefore, I believe we are well warranted to rereview what philosophy of history is and is not; it coupled with general philosophy can tell us more conclusively about the past than science can or ever will be able to. This may be a bold statement, but I believe it is one that needs to be stated just this boldly. I have debated many naturalistic scientists on just such a challenge to their scientism, and I have became increasingly confident of the truth to this statement the more I have seen them retreat from their own paradigm (scientism) as being untenable once the gauntlet was thrown down to challenge them. If I am wrong, then so be it; I should easily be refuted in the vast majority of the points I have made if I am wrong. If however my points are not refuted and it turns out that the majority of what I am stating is not only plausible but is also the inference to the best explanation, then why is philosophical naturalism held so firmly as being true? I highly encourage others to not settle for the "status quo" but to press for an open philosophy of history to include the possibility of nonnaturalistic causation and not rule it out *a priori* from the historians' toolbox of possibilities and thus relook at history as a science in and of itself.

MEASURES TO BE USED

Historians, like their scientist cousins, seek to reach a "probable truth." Optimally historians would like to identify a cause that is logically necessary in order for the evidence to be as it is. Would the effect have occurred as it did without the hypothesized cause? As historian Aviezer Tucker clearly spells out, we must remember that "historiography does not reconstruct events; it cannot bring Caesar back to life to reenact the battle of Actium. Historiography does attempt to provide a hypothetical description and analysis of some past events as the best explanation of present evidence. This knowledge is probably true, but it is not true in an absolute sense. The most that historiography can aspire for is increasing plausibility, never absolute truth. Most of history has left no lasting information-carrying effects after it. Therefore, most of history is and always will be unknown and unknowable."[50]

This however does not mean that we cannot make an inference to the best explanation about the past. The methodology that I found most helpful in my past historic studies is that of Christopher Behan McCullagh in his book *Justifying Historical Descriptions*. Though the vast majority of historians use a very similar method of establishing historical probability they may diverge on some points, but for the most part, Dr. McCullagh's methodology should make even the most skeptical historian happy. Dr. McCullagh of Cambridge University lists the factors which historians typically weigh in testing a historical hypothesis as follows:

1. The hypothesis, together with other true statements, must imply further statements describing present, observable data.

2. The hypothesis must have greater explanatory scope (that is, imply a greater variety of observable data) that rival hypotheses.

3. The hypothesis must have greater explanatory power (that is, make the observable data more probable) than rival hypotheses.

4. The hypothesis must be more plausible (that is, be implied by a greater variety of accepted truths, and its negation implied by fewer accepted truths) than rival hypotheses.

5. The hypothesis must be less ad hoc (that is, include fewer new suppositions about the past not already implied by existing knowledge) than rival hypotheses.

6. The hypothesis must be disconfirmed by fewer accepted beliefs (that is, when conjoined with accepted truths, imply fewer false statements) than rival hypotheses.

7. The hypothesis must so exceed its rivals in fulfilling conditions 2–6 that there is little chance of a rival hypothesis, after further investigation, exceeding it in meeting these conditions.[51]

While these seven steps are not exhaustive and still form no absolutes when referencing a historic event in the past that cannot be repeated, it will suffice for our purposes in weighing out the four events of the past that are usually pulled into the realm of "science" when they should in fact be reviewed by the historian as well. Again, the four areas we will be reviewing based on a closed naturalistic philosophy versus an open philosophy of history (as an origin science) will be:

- Origin of the Universe and cosmological constants
- Origin of Life—Cambrian Explosion (Fossil Record)
- Origin of Civilization and the Pre-Common Era
- The Common Era of the Historical Jesus

If I can make a case for an open philosophy of history (as a science) being a stronger criterion that fulfills the four points outlined above better than that of naturalism (with Dr. McCullagh's seven points of establishing historicity in mind) this should at the very least beg the question: How could this be true "if" naturalism is true?

WHAT ABOUT NATURALISM?

> As far as I can see, no strong arguments at all exist for naturalism but there are strong arguments against it. I therefore suggest that naturalism, like logical positivism, should be consigned to the scrap heap of philosophical history.
>
> —Alvin Plantinga, *Philosophia Christi*

As one of the most accredited scholars of the late twentieth century, Alvin Plantinga stated the above in the spring 2012 issue of the philosophy journal *Philosophia Christi*—one of the largest reasons why positivism, scientism, and now naturalism as a whole is beginning to lessen its grip on academia and thus allow an open philosophy that is not strictly naturalistic, is because of naturalism's increasing implausibility. Moreover, Plantinga has stated and provided many arguments why "naturalism" is not only false but that it falls much more into the categorization of "religion" than it does "science," which should really cause all within academia to ponder "why" we use naturalism as a mode in which all natural and social sciences must adhere to?

One type of naturalism that is often adhered to by naturalists is that of materialism. Materialism holds that the only thing that exists is matter or energy; that all things are composed of material and all phenomena (including consciousness) are the result of material interactions. Naturalism, on the other hand, is any of several philosophical stances wherein all phenomena or hypotheses, commonly labeled as supernatural, are either false or not inherently different from natural phenomena or hypotheses. So for the most part (though not entirely)—all materialist are naturalists but not all naturalists are necessarily materialists (though most are).

So what if naturalism (as a whole) is false as more and more philosophers like Plantinga are beginning to conclude? While most of academia endorsed positivism at the beginning and middle of the twentieth century, virtually none do now; similarly most of academia still endorses a form of naturalism today even though, as Plantinga stated above, it too may need to be consigned to the scrap heap of philosophical history like positivism was. This has enormous implications for today as well as the future. What this basically means is the modes in which we are currently doing the vast majority of inquiry and study today could in fact be "wrong" just as positivism is now known to be "wrong" and self-defeating.

Moreover, if naturalism is false, then it definitely strengthens the case for theism and deism, which would have theological implications; again, even if there are theological implications, this should not be a reason to avoid coming to grips with the points I am making. While an "open philosophy" would by no means necessitate the use of "nonnaturalistic" criteria, it would not be limited to them as is the case today in those fields which take a naturalistic paradigm as a default and necessary truth. Therefore, I will be taking the earlier mentioned four areas of established historicity per se, and I will give the traditional naturalistic "closed" philosophical view point of it and compare the same data with an "open philosophy of history (as a weak science)" as outlined above to show the strengths of this approach compared to the growingly out-of-date form of naturalistic materialism. If I can adequately show that in all four of these examples that this mode of thought is stronger than that of naturalistic materialism, then it should beg the question why we are still using what I believe to be a limiting form of philosophical thought that not only retards the study of history but the thought process itself that we use in reasoning and logical inferences to the best explanations of data. Finally, if these conclusions are logically valid, then I pray that this will help pry free the cage in which post-Enlightenment thinkers have locked nonnaturalistic philosophy into and thus allow an open philosophy of history in both the social and natural sciences. There is no coincidence that the naturalistic paradigm is beginning to lose its grip from many fields of academia in which it once ruled; moreover, if one does not want to retard or stunt Socrates' adage of "take the evidence where it leads," then all should welcome such a revolution in thought. Moreover, if I am wrong in my analysis, then I should easily be refuted and shown why a competing or standard naturalistic hypothesis is stronger than the one in which I have outlined and thus provide a case "for" continuing to limit history to the confines of the closed philosophy of naturalism in which it is currently locked.

As previously mentioned, if naturalism turns out to be false, then it does strengthen the philosophical and historical position of theism and deism. Deism is the notion that a being beyond space and time (God) does exist based on the evidence of reason and nature but not through any type of "religious revelation" such as the Bible whereas theism is the notion that (like deism) there is a creator God but this same God has revealed itself through possible revelation (such as the Torah, New Testament, Quran, etc.). It should be pointed out that while I am a Christian theist, I have debated many forms of Christianity in which I usually refer to many as church-ianity since many doctrines/dogmas are built more on popes and prelates than on the Christian origins themselves. With this being said, I am no supporter of any "church" infrastructure per se; however, I will be using Christian theism as a measuring tool for how a specified branch of "theism" competes (or does not) in these four areas of history in which we will be reviewing. I pick Judaic-Christianity partly because it is arguably the oldest religion today (along with Hinduism) and by far the most historically assessable also because it is the largest religion in which the second largest religion (Islam) is a direct offshoot. The cosmological argument from the beginning of the universe, the teleological argument from the fine-tuning of the universe for intelligent life, the moral and ethical argument for a personally embodied "good" (that we will be looking at in the next chapters) requires in its own way the existence of a personal deity (or nonnaturalistic being that transcends space/time/matter if you prefer not using the term "deity"). Each of these arguments is incompatible with the existence of an impersonal God, such as is featured in pantheistic religions like Taoism, Hinduism, and Buddhism. This would narrow down the options of the world's major religions to the great monotheistic faiths of Judaism/Christianity with Islam (much like Montanism in the second century and Manichaeanism in the third century) being a direct sixth-century offshoot that later claimed the Bible as its core but added a new prophet (Muhammad) and book (Quran). I exclude Islam due to the fact it is approximately six centuries later and is based more on divine revelation than it is historicity, which places it outside the confines of historic methodology; nonetheless, it has its base built upon Judaism and Christianity, which predominantly leaves us with only the Hebrew and New Testaments as being testable by the historic method. Moreover, Christianity is the only religion (per se) that adequately seems to cover a complete and coherent alternative answer to naturalism.

The most distinctive claim about Christianity in relation to other world religions is that Christianity says that God has revealed himself in history. As British theologian Alan Richardson has stated: "The Christian faith...is bound up with certain happenings in the past, and if these happenings could be shown never to have occurred, or to have been quite different from the biblical-Christian account of them, then the whole edifice of Christian faith, life and worship would be found to have been built on sand."[52] As many historians have pointed out, history itself is crucial to Christianity because it keeps the Christian faith from degenerating into mythology. Unless the Bible is rooted in actual historical events, there is no reason to think that Jesus of Nazareth should be any more determinative for my life today than so-called gods like Thor, Odin or Zeus or any other mythological deity as skeptics today espouse. History is the vital component in Christianity because it grounds faith in fact and keeps it from being mere myth in the sense of "fictional myth."

Christianity is not a code for living or a philosophy of religion; rather, it is rooted in real events of history which makes it testable by historic methodology. The reason it is scandalous is because it ties up the truth of Christianity with the truth of those historical facts. This means that if these historical events are shown to be fraudulent or fictional, then the whole basis of Christianity is removed. To put it as simply as possible: the truth or falsity of Christianity stands or falls with individual events within history which makes it a historically based religion that either has historical credibility or it does not but that first and foremost depends if your philosophy of history is "open" or "closed." This interrelatedness between a branch of nonnaturalistic "theism" with that of history makes it a prime candidate to test by the same standards we would test naturalism against; this is predominantly why I chose to break it down along with naturalism in assessing our philosophy of history.[53]

While I readily acknowledge that my comparisons may have theological implications, this is once again not my purpose; my point is to show why an origins researcher or historian should not be concerned with what is "off-limits." We are told challenging naturalism or supporting the Bible as history are both "off-limits"; therefore, I wish to show as an open philosophy of history why this should not be the case and how limiting both of these paradigms are. Popular historian Dr. Susan Bauer is of the opinion that that there is much good history in the Bible and has used it in her writings on the history of the world despite critics' attacks. These attacks are not in the form of a critique or break down of how or where her incorporation of biblical history is wrong and thus are either simple *a priori* or ad hominem attacks for her and other "amateur" historians like myself who challenge the currently historic methodology in place. For these reasons and more, I feel Christian theism provides a good explanatory challenge to naturalism when we review our philosophy of history and the closed versus open philosophy that surrounds it.

Philosopher and senior research fellow at Oxford University Ravi Zacharias often states that a coherent worldview must be able to satisfactorily answer four questions: that of origin, meaning of life, morality, and destiny. He says that while every major religion makes exclusive claims about truth, the Christian faith is unique in its ability to answer all four of these questions. He routinely speaks on the coherency of the Christian worldview, saying that Christianity is capable of withstanding the toughest philosophical attacks.[54] This coupled by the fact that it is steeped in history, as opposed to poetry or simply wise sayings, makes it a logical religion that can be tested for its own accuracy and thus makes the most logical sense to use as a specified theistic example. I, of course, have my own biases as does everyone else, but the "facts" are what count and if one can neither give a refutation for a claim nor supply their own alternative, then the claim must stand as true until a possible future event may or may not overturn it. With that being said, we will review four moments in history from the lens of the contending paradigm that the vast majority of textbooks in all branches of academia claim to be "true" based on a closed philosophy and compare the same points from a deistic/theistic viewpoint to that of a more specified Christian theistic point of view to see which worldviews best adheres to McCullagh's seven criteria for establishing historicity. It is strongly my hypothesis that an open philosophy will trump any closed one though it may be debatable whether that can plausibly lead to the specified Christian theistic worldview or not of course.

So why do so many persons believe in naturalism, and why does it continue to permeate not only the sciences but also the social sciences if it is at least highly probably wrong? Philosopher Jay Richards puts it well when he too was first indoctrinated with naturalism in the collegiate setting:

> The closest thing to an argument for naturalism that I encountered was along these lines: "Primitive peoples, including the ancient Jews and Christians, believed in all manner of spiritual beings that could act in the world. They supposed that angels could give messages to the faithful and that God could cause a virgin to become pregnant, raise Jesus from the dead, turn water into wine, and so forth. In our day and age, however, what with telephones and radios and microwave ovens, we can no longer believe such nonsense." As a philosophical argument, this isn't impressive. But it still had sociological force for a defenseless college student. The last thing you want to be, as a college freshman, is intellectually unfashionable. If all the smart people around you believe that the moon is made of green cheese, you may find yourself entertaining the green cheese hypothesis, even if you've never encountered any evidence for it.[55]

We can keep yelling that *"naturalism is true and history must conform to it"* all we want, but we must do it knowing that we are simply deluding ourselves. It then logically begs the question "why" are we deluding ourselves? To this question I have not been able to decipher an adequate explanation or reason and therefore must conclude that there is no good reason other than "that is simply what we have been indoctrinated to believe." If this is true, then it definitely should come as a legitimate challenge to the way one does not only the sciences but also the social sciences such as history. Before rushing ahead too far though, let us review these four supposedly naturalistic phenomena of the ancient past in order to give naturalism a fair chance as being a worthy hypothesis that is strong enough to be ruled as fact *a priori*.

HISTORIC EVENT 1:

ORIGINS OF THE UNIVERSE AND COSMOLOGICAL CONSTANTS

There is neither need nor excuse for postulation of non-material intervention in the origin of life, the rise of man, or any part of the long history of the material cosmos. Yet the origin of that cosmos and the causal principles of its history remain unexplained and inaccessible to science. Here is hidden the First Cause sought by theology and philosophy. The First Cause is not known and I suspect it will never be known to living man. We may, if we are so inclined, worship it in our own ways, but we certainly do not comprehend it.

—George Gaylord Simpson· *The Meaning of Evolution*

Human beings are currently understood as the only contingent beings capable of abstract thought, a perception of time coupled with a manipulation of thought concerning the past/present/future; an inquiry into the nature of history is based in part on some working understanding of time within the framework of human experience. History as we normally understand it tends to follow an assumption of linear progression: "this happened first, then second, then third, etc." This is in part based on the law of causality or cause and effect. Most ancient cultures held a cyclical instead of linear view of time that would have repeating dark and golden ages. Similarly, the Greeks believed that not only mankind had a cyclical basis of time (dark/golden ages) but so did governments. The story of the Fall of Man from the Garden of Eden in Judaism and Christianity can be seen in a similar manner with the existence of God creating a global explanation of history as a whole with the belief in a Messianic Age. Such theodicies claimed that history itself had a progressive direction leading to an eschatological end given by God. Augustine of Hippo, Thomas Aquinas, or Bossuet in his Discourse on Universal History (1679) formulated similar theodicies, but it was the famous philosopher Leibniz who created perhaps the most coherent theodicy. Leibniz based his explanation on the principle of sufficient reason, which states that anything that happens does happen for a specific reason.

This ultimately leads to the question based on principle of sufficient reason, namely "what is the ultimate or prime reality of existence?" Or to put it a different way, "what is the first cause from which all other things are derived?" Or even better yet, why does anything at all "exist" as opposed to just "nothing"? How does "being" come from "nonbeing"? From the naturalistic closed philosophic view, there are a few quite random viewpoints that we are informed are factual despite the lack of any evidence to that point. Not to lump all naturalists into the same bucket, but most naturalists (and the textbooks academia controls) usually accounts for the origin of the universe as one of two explanations: (1) The universe simply popped into being uncaused out of nothingness by the laws of physics. Their #2 answer is that neither we nor the universe really exist at all so it is a pointless question. Prominent physicist Lawrence Krauss holds the first view and the prominent chemist Peter Atkins holds the second (just to name two).

To the second question of "Why does the universe exist and why does it at least appear fine-tuned for life?" Naturalist's predominant answer: Blind chance—if our universe had not beyond all probability just came into existence, then we would not be here to ponder it. Followed closely by: If there were an infinite number of other universes, then some must by necessity come to be life permitting on a razor's edge and ours happens to be just such a universe. Information theory surrounding the pre-big bang as well as life itself are usually inferred to be due to chance as well and morality is simply subjective without there being any real definition of "right/wrong" or "good/evil" since these are inventions of the human mind.

While I readily admit that to lump all "naturalists" into the same bucket is not completely fair, I will do the same with theists and Christian theists, many of which might object I am sure; I simply do not have the space to postulate every detail of naturalism or theism. However, I can assure you that from years of study and debate these cover the vast majority of the naturalists' position. Therefore, the naturalist maintains that "if" we really do in fact exist, the universe simply popped into being uncaused out of nothingness (or another universe that itself popped into being from nothing). Following this popping into existence usually referred to as the "big bang" approximately 13.7 billion years ago the various galaxies began spreading out farther and farther away with our own Milky Way galaxy forming along with the laws of physics and prechemistry elements and much later our earth forming about four billion years ago. Our earth fell into a range beyond all probability to allow for life to come into existence from possible inorganic chemical systems in the early earth. Once this life came into being, it then evolved over hundreds of millions of years into all the various phyla, genus, species, etc., we see today and that is how we are here today in the year 2013.

I have tested the above statement with some naturalistic colleagues and friends and they mostly concur that this is a "mostly" accurate, though simplified, version of what they believe. They mostly agree that this is quite a fantastical theory, but they still agree that it is stronger than a metaphysical position that posits something transcendent or miraculous (such as God) for the ultimate reality or causation of reality. Fair enough. The more I began to see the very shaky foundation that all of these theories simply postulate "being" coming from "nonbeing" the more I began to wonder why naturalism is taught as if it is a mathematical truth, and moreover, why are the social sciences such as history based on such questionable "naturalistic" presuppositions?

The two premises on which the various theories of naturalism are based:

1. Naturalistic formula for making a universe:

   Nothing + nothing = two elements + time = ninety-two natural elements + time = all physical laws and a completely structured universe of galaxies, systems, stars, planets, moons, etc.

2. Naturalistic formula for making life:

   Dirt/inorganic materials + water + time = living creatures.

While I simply cannot elaborate on each naturalistic theory in any great scope, I would simply encourage all parties to read up on both sides (naturalistic and nonnaturalistic) and analyze each. One thing both a strict naturalist and nonnaturalist can agree is that there is an underlying order in nature and that it is intelligible. While people normally take this for granted, they should take note that the universe could have been nonorderly and nonintelligible, but it is not; the vast majority of everything we know concerning the universe is that it is incredibly intelligible and orderly, but this begs the question *why*?

ORIGINS OF THE UNIVERSE

Looking at the first point of origins, concerning the universe, should cause us to ask if there is a warrant in following a naturalistic "historic" frame of reference or not. For example, is Peter Atkins accurate when he posits in his new book, *On Being*, that to understand how something can come out of nothing, you simply have to appreciate the fact that "there probably isn't anything here anyway"—that "at a deep level there is nothing in the universe really" (that nothing really exists). The substrate of existence, he argues, "is nothing at all." Consider electrical charge. In our universe, there are positively and negatively charged particles. How did all that charge come into being out of nothingness? It did not, Atkins writes, since "the total charge is zero." The big bang merely separated out a uniform state of chargelessness into many individual instances of charge, positive and negative. The same goes for matter and energy generally: the total amount of matter and energy in the universe seems to be balanced out by huge amounts of "dark matter" and "dark energy," which express themselves in terms of gravitational attraction. The big bang did not create all that energy as such. Instead, it seems to have turned an initial nothingness into a "much more interesting and potent" nothingness—a "nothing that has been separated into opposites to give, thereby, the appearance of something." How much, if anything, does that explain? "The separation of nothing into opposites still needs explanation," Atkins concedes. Still, he writes, "It seems to me that such a process, though fearsomelessly difficult to explain, is less overwhelmingly fearsome than the process of positive, specific, munificent creation."[56]

As touched on earlier, Lawrence Krauss supports the fact that the universe simply popped into being uncaused out of absolutely nothing. Of course, Dr. Krauss simply is making an ad hoc assertion that has no basis for believing it. To his credit, he does admit that when he says "nothing," he does not necessarily mean "nothing" in the sense of "no-thing" but of a mostly "nothing." This is quite problematic as well and what is interesting is when philosopher William Lane Craig debated Dr. Krauss on the problems of his theory Dr. Krauss backed into a corner finally said: "Okay, we don't understand the beginning of the universe. We don't understand if the universe had a cause. That is a fascinating possibility."[57] So do these two theories (or a variation of them) provide the greatest explanatory scope/power with fewer assertions than any other view concerning the origin of the universe?

The first question is do these theories give an accurate assessment of what we know concerning cosmology and cause-and-effect relationships; and secondly, how can history, as a weak science/philosophy, help shed light on this subject? The absolute origin of the universe of all matter and energy in the big bang singularity contradicts the perennial naturalistic assumption that the universe has always existed. One after another, history has shown that the models designed to avert the initial cosmological singularity—the Steady State model, the Oscillating model, Vacuum Fluctuation models—have come and failed. Current quantum gravity models, such as the Hartle-Hawking model and the Vilenkin model, must appeal to the physically unintelligible and metaphysically dubious device of "imaginary time" to avoid the universe's beginning. In an oral presentation of his paper at a recent conference in Cambridge, Vilenkin was however quite clear: "There are no models at this time that provide a satisfactory model for a universe without a beginning."[58] Note that he did not say that there are "few" models, he said there are "no models" that show the universe without a finite beginning. Even Stephen Hawking said you cannot escape a finite beginning in "real" time but in "imaginary" time you possibly can. The contingency implied by an absolute beginning ex nihilo points to a transcendent cause of the universe beyond space and time it would seem. Likewise, if a transcendent being exists (a.k.a. God), it is more probable that contingent beings would exist than on naturalism because on naturalism there is no explanation for the existence of contingent beings.

The discoveries in the twentieth century that the universe did indeed have a beginning in the finite past has continued to be verified by a testing of the "history" of the universe's vast past utilizing very similar points of history as mentioned above including explanatory power, scope and less contrived. The big bang model in its most simplistic form represents a point in the unrepeatable past where not only space, but time and matter itself came into being at a singular point. The implications of this finding are enormous, and unfortunately, the ramifications are rarely spelled out to students or the public as a whole. Even though it does not necessarily stipulate "God" per se, it does point to a transcendent Intelligent Designer of the cosmos. I believe the late agnostic astronomer Robert Jastrow who sat in the same chair as Edwin Hubble summed it up well in his book *God and the Astronomers*: "This religious faith of the scientists is violated by the discovery that the universe had a beginning under conditions in which the known laws of physics are not valid, and as a product of forces or circumstances we cannot discover. When that happens, the scientist has lost control."[59]

The discovery that the universe had a beginning was not met with pleasure. Many scientists rebelled against the notion because it implied a beginner. Sir Arthur Eddington admitted that "the notion of a beginning is repugnant to me." Yet the evidence was there. Jastrow puts his finger on the problem: "Many scientists have a 'religious' commitment to the assumption that everything has a natural, scientifically accessible and quantifiable explanation. Just when they were becoming confident in this assumption, seemingly explaining everything from the formation of stars to the formation of species, they ran into something which in principle cannot be explained scientifically: that first instant of creation, when the universe began as a singularity, a point inaccessible to investigation."[60] Both naturalist and nonnaturalist recognize that the universe did have a first cause by a type of creation where not only space and matter, but time itself came into existence. As the below picture demonstrates, origin scientist/historians coupled with findings from physics and philosophy are in near universal agreement today that the universe—space/time/matter all came "into being" in the finite past in an event collectively referred to as "the big bang."

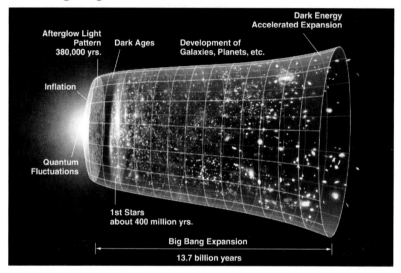

When we see light traveling to us, it is traveling from the distant past and so we are seeing the radiation echoes of the beginning of the universe. The historian therefore does not begin doing "history" at the time of human beings but anytime we discuss the past as a nonrepeatable event. This historic event can then be tested by philosophy in and of its own or incorporated into its own philosophy of history. Such an example is the historic cosmological argument. A simple version of this argument can go as follows:

1. Whatever begins to exist has a cause.

2. The universe began to exist.

3. Therefore, the universe has a cause.

Now if we stop right here, "most" of even the most ardent naturalists are forced to agree with all three premises. While there are still a few speculative theories, such as pre-big bang inflationary scenarios, which have been crafted to try to avoid this absolute beginning; none of these theories has succeeded in restoring an eternal past. At most they just push the beginning back a bit. But then the question inevitably arises: Why did the universe come into being? Unless you are willing to say the universe just popped into being uncaused out of absolute nonbeing (like Krauss suggests) there must be a transcendent cause beyond space and time, which created the universe. And while my point here is not to argue for "God's existence," clearly, God's existence is more probable given the beginning of the universe than it would have been without it; and if God does exist, then not only is naturalism obviously false, but this would most definitely alter philosophy of history as a whole.

Why are some such as theorist Lawrence Krauss so insistent on denying that the scientific evidence points to the beginning of the universe? That is *not* a supernatural conclusion; it does not imply the existence of God in and of itself. If we follow the scientific evidence where it leads, all of the evidence that I am aware of points to the fact that the universe is not past eternal. If we have any evidence that the universe *is* past eternal, I would love to hear Dr. Krauss or anyone present it. Philosopher William Lane Craig, who has spent the majority of his career researching this argument and the cosmological implications thereof breaks these premises down quite simply in his critiques on naturalism.[61]

Consider the three premises above—The first premise (anything that begins to exist has a cause) seems obviously true—at the very least more so than its negation. It is rooted in the metaphysical intuition that something cannot come into being from absolutely nothing. If something could really come into being uncaused out of nothing, then it becomes unexplainable why just anything does not come into existence uncaused. Moreover, we have never witnessed any type of event or causation that came from nothing; there is always a cause behind anything that begins to exist. In common usage, causality is the relationship between a set of factors (causes) and a phenomenon (the effect). The conviction that an origin of the universe requires a causal explanation seems quite reasonable, for on the naturalistic view, if the universe began at the big bang, there was not even the *potentiality* of the universe's existence prior to the big bang since nothing (not space/time/matter) is prior to the big bang. But then how could the universe come into being if there was not even the potentiality of its existence? It makes much more sense to say that the potentiality of the universe lay in the power of a being that lies beyond space/time/matter (God) to create it. Finally, the first premise is constantly confirmed in our experience. Atheists who are scientific naturalists thus have the strongest of motivations to accept it.

Premise two (The universe began to exist), the more controversial premise, may be supported by both deductive, philosophical arguments and inductive, scientific arguments. Even the most ardent of critics to the argument contend that an infinite temporal regress of events cannot exist since the existence of an actually infinite, as opposed to merely potentially infinite, number of things leads to intolerable absurdities. One of the best ways to support this claim is still by way of thought experiments, like the famous Hilbert's Hotel.[62] The idea is this: If there are an infinite number of rooms in Hilbert's Hotel, and they are all occupied, you can still double or triple the amount of new occupants and although you are once again "infinitely" filled you can continue to add more. Moreover, you can divide the number in half yet are still infinitely full. This is why within the laws of mathematics "infinity" oftentimes leads to contradictions.

This leads directly into a second argument for the beginning of the universe since a temporal series of past events cannot be an actual infinite because a collection formed by successive addition cannot be actually infinite. Sometimes the problem was described as the impossibility of traversing the infinite, so while one may talk about a "potential" infinite an "actual" infinite is not possible. In order for us to have "arrived" at today for example, temporal existence has, so to speak, traversed an infinite number of prior events. But before the present event could arrive, the event immediately prior to it would have to arrive; and before that event could arrive, the event immediately prior to it would have to arrive and so on *ad infinitum*. No event could ever arrive since before it could elapse there would always be one more event that will had to have happened first. Thus, if the series of past events were beginningless, the present event could not have arrived and in that case neither could "today," which is absurd. So to say that the infinite past could have been formed by successive addition is like saying that someone has just succeeded in writing down all the negative numbers, ending at -1.

A third argument for the universe's beginning is an inductive argument based on contemporary evidence for the expansion of the universe. The standard big bang model does not describe the expansion of the material content of the universe into a preexisting empty space but rather the expansion of space itself. This has the astonishing implication that as one extrapolates back in time, space-time curvature becomes progressively greater until one arrives at a singularity at which space-time curvature becomes infinite. It therefore constitutes an edge or boundary to space-time itself.

> The history of twentieth century cosmology has, in one sense, been a series of failed attempts to craft acceptable non-standard models of the expanding universe in order to avert the absolute beginning predicted by the standard model. While such theories are possible, it has been the overwhelming verdict of the scientific community than none of them is more probable than the big bang the-

ory. There is no mathematically consistent model which has been so successful in its predictions or as corroborated by the evidence as the traditional big bang theory. For example, some theories, like the Oscillating Universe (which expands and re-contracts forever) or the Chaotic Inflationary Universe (which continually spawns new universes), do have a potentially infinite future but turn out to have only a finite past. Vacuum Fluctuation Universe theories (which postulate an eternal vacuum out of which our universe is born) cannot explain why, if the vacuum was eternal, we do not observe an infinitely old universe. The No-Boundary Universe proposal of Hartle and Hawking, if interpreted realistically, still involves an absolute origin of the universe even if the universe does not begin in a singularity, as it does in the standard big bang theory. Recently proposed Ekpyrotic Cyclic Universe scenarios based on string theory or M-theory have also been shown, not only to be riddled with problems, but, most significantly, to imply the very origin of the universe which its proponents sought to avoid.[63]

Of course, scientific results are always provisional, but there is no doubt that one rests comfortably within the scientific mainstream in asserting the truth of premise two. Take for example the late agnostic astronomer Robert Jastrow of NASA and professor of Dartmouth College in an interview with Christianity Today. Jastrow said: "Astronomers now find they have painted themselves into a corner because they have proven, by their own methods, that the world began abruptly in an act of creation to which you can trace the seeds of every star, every planet, every living thing in this cosmos and on the earth. And they have found that all this happened as a product of forces they cannot hope to discover. That there are what I or anyone would call supernatural forces at work is now, I think, a scientifically proven fact."[64]

An additional argument for the finitude of the past is also an inductive argument, appealing to thermodynamic properties of the universe. According to the Second Law of Thermodynamics, processes taking place in a closed system tend toward states of higher entropy as their energy is used up. Already in the nineteenth century scientists realized that the application of the law to the universe as a whole (which, on naturalistic assumptions, is a gigantic closed system since it is all there is) implied a grim eschatological conclusion: given sufficient time, the universe would eventually come to a state of equilibrium and suffer heat death. But this apparently firm projection raised an even deeper question: if, given sufficient time, the universe will suffer heat death, then why, if it has existed forever, is it not now in a state of heat death? The advent of relativity theory altered the shape of the eschatological scenario predicted on the basis of the second law but did not materially affect this fundamental question. Astrophysical evidence indicates overwhelmingly that the universe will expand forever. As it does, it will become increasingly cold, dark, dilute, and dead. Eventually, the entire mass of the universe will be nothing but a cold, thin gas of elementary particles and radiation, growing ever more dilute as it expands into the infinite darkness, a universe in ruins. But this raises the question: if in a finite amount of time the universe *will* achieve a cold, dark, dilute, and lifeless state, then why, if it has existed for *infinite time*, is it not *now* in such a state? If one is to avoid the conclusion that the universe has not in fact existed forever, then one must find some scientifically plausible way to overturn the findings of physical cosmology so as to permit the universe to return to its youthful condition.[65] But no realistic and plausible scenario is forthcoming. Most cosmologists agree with physicist P. C. W. Davies that whether we like it or not we seemed forced to conclude that the universe's low entropy condition was simply "put in" as an initial condition at the moment of creation.[66]

We therefore have good philosophical and scientific grounds for affirming the second premise of the cosmological argument. It is noteworthy that this premise is a religiously neutral statement, which can be found in any textbook on astrophysical cosmology so that accusations of "God-of-the gaps" theology find no value since this is in no way a simple ad hoc assumption that "God did it." Moreover, since a being which exists by a necessity of its own nature must exist either timelessly or sempiternally (otherwise it's coming into being or ceasing to be would make it evident that its existence is not necessary), it follows that the universe cannot be metaphysically necessary, which fact closes the final loophole in the contingency argument above.

It follows logically that the universe has a cause. Conceptual analysis of what properties must be possessed by such an ultra-mundane cause enables us to recover a striking number of the traditional divine attributes, revealing that if the universe has a cause, then an uncaused, personal Creator of the universe exists, who sans the universe is beginningless, changeless, immaterial, timeless, spaceless, and enormously powerful.[67]

So if the three below premises below are logically coherent and true the question remains, "What is the cause?" I have proceeded to add two additional:

1. Whatever begins to exist has a cause.

2. The universe began to exist.

3. Therefore, the universe has a cause.

4. The cause of the universe must transcend the universe itself since it is outside of it and therefore must be non-temporal, nonspatial, nonphysical, and self-directing (not acting out of necessity so therefore personal).

5. Any being that has these properties is nonnaturalistic.

6. Therefore naturalism is false.

Though cosmology will not get you entirely to a theistic concept of a "God," it does force one to reject naturalism. One could conclude that therefore the concept of "God" is also much more plausible than naturalism but for our purposes it should be noted that cosmology is definitely a huge mark against naturalism and moreover it falls into the historic branch of "origin science" not the natural science of "operation science." If this is true, then the historians' philosophy of history should dictate an open philosophy to sciences dealing with nonrepeatable events as opposed to the other way around where history is held in check by the closed philosophical presupposition of naturalistic science.

PROBABILITY THEORY

One area that both scientist and historian utilize on a regular basis is that of probability theory. For example, in the origin sciences, what is the probability of our universe occurring by chance alone or the chance of life occurring through undirected natural processes based on what we know today? Similarly, what is the probability of the cosmological constants being fine-tuned for life to even be a possibility and to what degree do we mean by "fine-tuned?" Though I have been informed quite frequently that though probability theory equates that the chances of the universe or life forming by chance to be effectively zero, we are not supposedto use such probabilities, because if we happened to "win the lottery" (as some naturalist have put it), we should expect to exist regardless of probabilities against it. Just to spell that out in vivid detail, this would be like one thousand trained marksman at ten feet away all missing a person who was to be shot by them via firing squad. Should the person who just survived such an ordeal simply shrug their shoulders and assume they survived by pure naturalistic processes (such as the guns jamming, bad bullets, etc.), being responsible for their good luck? I would think not and that is why ever since the advent of probability theory it is at least good to look at a few of these scenarios to see just what the odds are.

Probability theory can take many forms and faces (only a handful of which will be touched on here). Imagine a coin is tossed, and you wish you find the probability of getting tails. There are two ways in which it can turn up (assuming the coin will not stand on its edge) therefore there are only two outcomes. If the coin is balanced the two outcomes (head/tails) are considered equally likely. Therefore the probability of obtaining tails when a fair coin is tossed, denoted by P(H), is 1 out of 2. That is, P(H) = ½. Activities such as tossing a coin, drawing a random card from a deck, or throwing a dice are called experiments. The set of "U" of all possible outcomes for an experiment is called the sample space for the experiment. There are many various ways in which to arrive at different probabilities such as drawing an ace from a 52 card deck (1 to 51) versus drawing 4 aces (C(48,1)/C(52,5)), thus drawing 4 aces in poker is 1 in 54,145. So even though it is highly unlikely that we will draw 4 aces in poker it is definitely not impossible.

LAYMAN'S TERMS PLEASE

To provide a much more easily assessable way of interpreting probability theory let me break it down without the equations involved. We use chance/probability analysis every day in some way. For example, if we hear a weather forecast that there is a 90 percent chance of rain versus a 10 percent chance of no rain, it is a fairly high probability that it will rain. Science likewise calculates such subjective statistics to determine whether something might or might not occur. In day-to-day life, we can say that an event that has only one chance of occurrence in 10^8 (100 million) is considered an impossibility; to break it down, if you picked up a rock and dropped it 100,000,000 times and each time it fell to the ground, we have established that gravity is very highly probable. In scientific evaluations, the number goes up to 10^{15} (quadrillion). When it comes to stating a scientific law, we are told that the number is 10^{50} (I, of course, realize that this number varies between parties, but 10^{50} is a mostly agreed to number in which anything greater than $1:10^{50}$ is considered "most likely" impossible). In other words, if there is a mathematical probability of something occurring 10^{50} times, with only one chance of failure, the event is said to have been established by law, meaning it will always occur. Conversely, if there is only one chance of occurrence and 10^{50} chances of failure, the event is considered to be utterly impossible.[68] (Keep these probabilities in mind.) Just to put this in concrete terms, if I were to write the number 1 on a piece of paper every second 10^{20} times, it would take me 1.5 trillion years (100 times the age of the entire universe); so I think it is safe to say these are huge numbers. So the next question is, "Is there reason to believe there is nonnaturalistic design in the universe?" If naturalism is true, then the answer should be a resounding "no."

The fine-tuned universe is the idea that the conditions that allow life in the universe can only occur when certain universal cosmological constants lie within a very narrow range so that if any of several fundamental constants were only slightly different the universe would be unlikely to be conducive to the establishment and development of matter, astronomical structures, elemental diversity, or any life as it is presently understood. Christian philosopher Alvin Plantinga argues that "random chance," applied to a single and sole universe, only raises the question as to why this universe could be so "lucky" as to have precise conditions that support life at least at some place (the earth) and time (within millions of years of the present).

According to the vast majority of cosmologists and astronomers today, the laws and constants of nature are so "finely-tuned," and so many "coincidences" have occurred to allow for the possibility of life, the universe must have come into existence through intentional planning and intelligence. In fact, this "fine-tuning" is so pronounced, and the "coincidences" are so numerous, many scientists have come to espouse "The Anthropic Principle," which contends that the universe was brought into existence intentionally for the sake of producing mankind. Even those who do not accept the Anthropic Principle admit to the "fine-tuning" and conclude that the universe is "too contrived" to be a chance event. This apparent fine-tuning of the universe is cited by theologian William Lane Craig as an evidence for the existence of a non-naturalistic intelligence capable of manipulating (or designing) the basic physics that govern the universe. Craig argues, however, that the postulate of a divine Designer does not settle for us the religious question.

The degree of fine-tuning is difficult to imagine. Dr. Hugh Ross gives an example of the least fine-tuned of the cosmological constants in his book, *The Creator and the Cosmos*:

> One part in 10^{37} is such an incredibly sensitive balance that it is hard to visualize. The following analogy might help: Cover the entire North American continent in dimes all the way up to the moon, a height of about 239,000 miles. Next, pile dimes from here to the moon on a billion other continents the same size as North America. Paint one dime red and mix it into the billions of piles of dimes. Blindfold a friend and ask him to pick out one dime. The odds that he will pick the red dime are one in 10^{37}. The nature of the universe reveals that a purely naturalistic cause for the universe is extremely unlikely and, therefore, illogical. One cannot say that a miraculous naturalistic event is a scientific explanation since miracles are only possible when an immensely powerful Being intervenes to cause them. When a model does not work, scientists must be willing to give up their model for a model that fits the facts better. In this case, the supernatural design model fits the data much better than the naturalistic random chance model.[69]

If the universe is indeed designed and with purpose it would then seem to lead to a teleological explanation of its existence. Teleology is the philosophical study of design and purpose. A teleological school of thought is one that holds all things to be designed for or directed toward a final result that there is an inherent purpose or final cause for all that exists. Therefore, another hypothesis that is derived from a teleological argument, or argument from design, which is an argument for the existence of God or a creator based on perceived evidence of order, purpose, design, or direction—or some combination of these—in nature. This argument was strongly supported by Plato, Aristotle, Cicero, Averroes, Thomas Aquinas, and many others, but William Paley summed it up in a more modern translation of his book *Natural Theology* in 1802 when he used his watchmaker analogy. The watchmaker analogy is basically a teleological argument for the existence of God and thus nonnaturalistic causation. The heart of the argument states that design implies a designer. The analogy has played a prominent role in natural theology and the "argument from design" where it was used to support arguments for intelligent design in the universe as well as life itself.

Consider the slightly revised argument below:

1. The complex inner workings of a watch necessitate an intelligent designer.

2. If the watch is magnified to be as large as a universe it still necessitates an intelligent designer.

3. Therefore the universe (and fine-tuning thereof) necessitates an intelligent designer.

In most formulations of the argument, the characteristic that indicates intelligent design is left implicit. Now let us fast forward to the late twentieth century and what we see is the teleological argument taken to an unimaginable level.

A modern variation of the teleological argument is built upon the anthropic principle. The anthropic principle is derived from the apparent delicate balance of conditions necessary for human life to exist in the first place. In this line of reasoning, speculation about the vast range of possible conditions in which life *could not* exist is compared to the speculated *improbability* of achieving conditions in which life *does* exist and then interpreted as indicating a fine-tuned universe specifically designed so life in general is possible. I cannot emphasize enough how incalculable the odds are for a universe (like ours) being life-permitting is verses if it was not. This view is shared in great detail by John D. Barrow and Frank J. Tipler in *The Anthropic Cosmological Principle* where they discuss in great detail how incalculable the odds are for the fine-tuning of our universe to have come about by chance alone.[70]

The extent of the universe's fine-tuning makes the anthropic principle one of the most powerful arguments for the existence of some type of creator. There are more than one hundred constants that strongly point to an Intelligent Designer, so we are just scratching the surface, but one example would be if gravity was 0.00000000000000000000000000000000001 percent altered, our sun would not exist and, therefore, neither would we. (And this is just *one* constant of many) As *Discover* magazine's November 2002 issue put it: "The universe is unlikely. Very unlikely. Deeply, shockingly unlikely."[71] So when there is virtually zero chance of a universe (much less a life permitting universe), occurring by chance, how then can anyone still hang on to the chance hypothesis? Physicist and mathematician Robin Collins summarizes this same point when interviewed by Lee Strobel:

> In light of the infinitesimal odds of getting all the right dial settings for the constants of physics, the forces of nature, and other physical laws and principles necessary for life, it seems fruitless to try to explain away all of this fine-tuning as merely the product of random happenstance. 'As long as we're talking about probabilities, then theoretically you can't rule out the possibility—however remote—that this could occur by chance,' Collins said. 'However, if I bet you a thousand dollars that I could flip a coin and get heads fifty times in a row, and then I proceeded to do it, you wouldn't accept that. You'd know that the odds against that are so improbable, that it's extraordinarily unlikely to happen. The fact that I was able to do it against such

monumental odds would be strong evidence to you that the game had been rigged. And the same is true for the fine-tuning of the universe—before you'd conclude that random chance was responsible, you'd conclude that there is strong evidence that the universe was rigged. That is, designed. In a similar way, it's supremely improbable that the fine tuning of the universe could have occurred at random, but it's not at all improbable if it were the work of an intelligent designer. So it's quite reasonable to choose the design theory over the chance theory. We reason that way all the time. Were the defendant's fingerprints on the gun because of a chance formation of chemicals or because he touched the weapon? Jurors don't hesitate to confidently conclude that he touched the gun if the odds against chance are so astronomical."[72]

As mentioned earlier, I have had the honor of working with philosopher and medical doctor Subodh Pandit of India since 2008. In one of our first philosophy of science meetings, we had several proclaiming naturalistic professors come to debate why a naturalistic philosophy should be the "default" position for all modes of academic inquiry. During this time, one professor explained that a nonnaturalistic/metaphysical position (which we agreed to call "God"), must be ruled out unless it spelled out in the stars the word *believe*, then he would accept that naturalism is false. But would he? Or would he simply extrapolate a theory on how those stars *"looked"* designed, but somehow they naturalistically came together to *"look"* like the letters to spell *believe* and thus they would dismiss it as yet another naturalistic occurrence. In the same seminar, an atheist philosopher stood up when I commented on the chance of their "chance hypothesis" being so weak to account for a design inference. His comment (from a PhD professor) almost floored me when he commented that though he admitted that the chances of something like Mt. Rushmore being formed strictly by chance over thousands of years of wind, rain, and erosion to look like the presidents is extremely improbable, it is still a chance while nonnatural causation is zero chance. I was aghast; this was what his reason and logic concluded in order to maintain his paradigm?

There is no plausible explanation for the anthropic principle other than some type of "cosmic designer" it would seem. Naturalists must take extreme measures to deny the obvious. When they dream up theories that are not supported by any evidence—and in fact are actually impossible by their own standards—they have left the realm of reason and rationality and entered into the realm of blind faith. Believing without observation is exactly what naturalists accuse religious people of doing; but ironically, it is the atheists who are pushing a religion of blind faith. Theists actually seen to have a plausible reason (such as the big bang and anthropic principle) for believing what they believe while naturalists for the most part really do not. This blind faith of the naturalist reveals that the rejection of a Designer is not a head problem—it is not as if we lack evidence or intellectual justification for a Designer. On the contrary, the evidence is impressive. What we have here is a will problem—some people, despite the evidence, simply do not want to admit there may be a Designer. Just as science has been hindered throughout its history by atheists, not wishing to acknowledge such events as the big bang because of its theistic ties, one such scientist spoke of the Anthropic Principle in the *NY Times*, October 2003 edition, and blatantly said his real objection was *"totally emotional" because "it smells of religion and intelligent Design."*[73] So much for scientific objectivity it would seem…

TO DESIGN OR NOT TO DESIGN—THAT IS THE QUESTION?

As philosopher and friend William Lane Craig continually stresses in his published writings and talks, it is very important when discussing design to distinguish between creation versus design. The first argument was specifically on creation but now it is important to review where design and what we usually refer to as "fine-tuning" can lead. Though one may argue that the fine-tuning conditions of the universe and life itself do seem to rest on a "razor's edge" for anything at all to exist, it too will not in its entireness get you all the way to theism, but it does once again force one to reject naturalism. Moreover, our point in discussing these points is not to "prove" God's existence per se; it is to show that naturalism is not only quite implausible but that it should not be forced into our philosophy of history, especially if it is false.

The teleological argument in a modified form may be formulated as follows:[74]

1. The fine-tuning of the universe is due either to physical necessity, chance, or design.

2. It is not due to physical necessity or chance.

3. Therefore, it is due to design.

The average reader might think that if the constants and quantities had assumed different values, then other forms of life might well have evolved, but this simply is not the case. By "life" scientists mean that property of organisms to take in food, extract energy from it, grow, adapt to their environment, and reproduce. The point is that in order for the universe to permit life (so-defined above), whatever form organisms might take, the constants and quantities have to be incomprehensibly fine-tuned. In the absence of fine-tuning, not even matter or chemistry themselves would exist, not to speak of stars or planets where life might evolve. It has been objected by some naturalists that in universes governed by different laws of nature, such deleterious consequences might not result from varying the values of the constants and quantities. The teleologist need not deny the possibility, however, for such universes are irrelevant to his argument. All he needs to show is that among possible universes governed by the same laws (but having different values of the constants and quantities) as the actual universe, life-permitting universes are extraordinarily unlikely.

Now premise one (the fine-tuning of the universe is due to necessity, chance or design) states the three alternatives in the pool of live options for explaining cosmic fine-tuning. The question is which the best explanation is. On the face of it the alternative of physical necessity seems extraordinarily implausible. As we have discussed, the values of the physical constants and quantities are independent of the laws of nature. If the primordial matter and antimatter had been differently proportioned, if the universe had expanded just a little more slowly, if the entropy of the universe were marginally greater, any of these adjustments and more would have prevented a life-permitting universe, yet all seem perfectly possible physically. The person who maintains that the universe must be life-permitting is taking a radical line, which requires strong proof. But as yet there is none, this alternative is put forward as a bare possibility. Philosopher of Physics Robin Collins puts it in readily assessable terms when he states:

> Imaginatively, one could think of each instance of fine-tuning as a radio dial: unless all the dials are set exactly right, life would be impossible. Or, one could think of the initial conditions of the universe and the fundamental parameters of physics as a dart board that fills the whole galaxy, and the conditions necessary for life to exist as a small one-foot wide target: unless the dart hits the target, life would be impossible. The fact that the dials are perfectly set, or the dart has hit the target, strongly suggests that someone set the dials or aimed the dart, for it seems enormously improbable that such a coincidence could have happened by chance.[75]

Sometimes physicists do speak of a yet to be discovered theory of everything, but such nomenclature is, like so many of the colorful names given to scientific theories, quite misleading. A "theory of everything" actually has the limited goal of providing a unified theory of the four fundamental forces of nature, but it will not even attempt to explain literally everything. For example, in the most promising candidates for this type of theory to date, super-string theory or M-Theory, the physical universe must be eleven dimensional, but why the universe should possess just that number of dimensions is not addressed by the theory. M-Theory simply substitutes geometrical fine-tuning for fine-tuning of forces. Furthermore, it seems likely that any attempt to significantly reduce fine-tuning will itself turn out to involve fine-tuning. This has certainly been the pattern in the past. In light of the specificity and number of instances of fine-tuning, it is unlikely to disappear with the further advance of physical theory.[76]

What, then, of the alternative of chance? As mentioned earlier, teleologists seek to eliminate this hypothesis either by appealing to the specified complexity of cosmic fine-tuning (a statistical approach to design inference) or by arguing that the fine-tuning is significantly more probable on design (theism) than on the chance hypothesis (naturalism). Common to both approaches is the claim that the universe's being life permitting is highly improbable simply because the far greater chance (almost incalculably high) is that the universe would not be fine-tuned and thus not life permitting.

In order to save the hypothesis of chance many naturalists have offered an alternative explanation, which is usually referred to as the many-universes or many-worlds hypothesis. According to this hypothesis, there are a very large, perhaps infinite, number of universes with the fundamental parameters of physics varying from universe to universe. Of course, in the vast majority of these universes the parameters of physics would not have life-permitting values. Nonetheless, in a small proportion of these universes there could be some that are life permitting (if there are an infinite number of other universes the probabilities increase), and therefore there would now be an explanation how our universe is, beyond all probability, life permitting to a incalculably high degree. Is the many worlds hypothesis as good an explanation as the design hypothesis? It seems very doubtful. In the first place, as a metaphysical hypothesis, the many worlds hypothesis is arguably inferior to the design hypothesis because the latter is simpler and according to Ockham's razor, we should not multiply causes beyond what is necessary to explain the effect. But it is simpler to postulate one Cosmic Designer to explain our universe than to postulate the infinitely bloated and contrived ontology of the many worlds hypothesis. This theory simply is a "what if there were an infinite number of other universes" type of question that has no reasons for believing it to be true other than an *a prior* inference to naturalism. Only if the Many Worlds theorist could show that there exists a single, comparably simple mechanism for generating a World Ensemble of randomly varied universes would he be able to elude this difficulty.[77]

Similarly Douglas Geivett explained in detail to myself and a large group of other inquirers in July of 2012: "The cosmological argument [and teleological] sets the stage for a fuller inquiry into the nature of a transcendent cause. The evidence of design, of moral responsibility, beauty, consciousness, or patterns in history including human inquiry for the transcendent and so forth, all acquire a compelling cumulative force pointing to a fuller composite description of a ultimate transcendent cause of the universe."[78] Once again, even if this argument does not necessitate "God's" existence per se, it does force us to reject naturalism since only design (not chance or necessity) qualifies as an explanation for the fine-tuned universe and cosmological constants. Similarly agnostic philosopher Paul Draper states: "Granted this argument doesn't quite get all the way to God's existence; accepting its conclusion does require rejecting naturalism."[79]

WHERE DOES "INFORMATION" COME FROM?

Design is obviously not only limited to the universe but can readily be seen in life and contingency itself. Take for example Aristotle who commented in his work *Physics*: "If the ship-building art were in the wood, it would produce the same results by nature. In other words, if raw pieces of wood had the capacity to form ships, we would say that ships come about by nature."[80] While this example may seem common sense to us today, this does convey an adequate point in the fact that the information needed to build a ship "from" wood is outside of the wood. The same could be said in concerns about random letters versus Romeo and Juliet or random notes versus Beethoven's symphony; information and matter are two separate entities though by naturalism the two must be one in the same. This too is yet another mark against naturalism.

Have you ever asked yourself where "information" itself comes from or what its source is? (Source meaning the origin of something.) An information source is a source of information for somebody—anything that might inform a person about something or provide knowledge to somebody. Information sources may be observations, people, speeches, documents, pictures, organizations, and so on. Different epistemologies have different views regarding the importance of different kinds of information sources. Empiricism regards sense data as the ultimate information sources while other epistemologies have different views. So what is the "information source" for the blueprint found in all things; from the universe and the pre-big bang to the cell? Example—before a building (or a universe or cell) comes together there has to be a blueprint on "how" the building will come together in the first place—so not only "how" but "where" is the construction of the building coming from, but where does the information that leads to the building come from?

In *Signature in the Cell*, philosopher of science Stephen C. Meyer discusses in great detail how the digital code in DNA points powerfully to a designing intelligence behind the origin of life. Unlike William Paley's previous arguments (the Watchmaker Analogy) for intelligent design, *Signature in the Cell* presents a comprehensive new case, revealing the evidence not merely of individual features of biological complexity but rather of a fundamental constituent of the universe: information. For far too long have naturalists evaded the question on where information itself comes from, and Dr. Meyer makes a powerful case for an intelligence that stands outside nature and directs the path life has taken.

The universe is comprised of matter, energy, and the information that gives order to matter and energy, thereby bringing life into being. In the cell, information is carried by DNA, which functions like a software program. The signature in the cell is that of the master programmer of life. In his theory of evolution, Charles Darwin never sought to unravel the mystery of where biological information comes from. For him, the origins of life remained shrouded in impenetrable obscurity. While the digital code in DNA first came to light in the 1950s, it wasn't until later that scientists began to sense the implications behind the exquisitely complex technical system for processing and storing information in the cell. The cell does what any advanced computer operating system can do but with almost inconceivably greater suppleness and efficiency. Drawing on data from many scientific fields, Stephen Meyer formulates a rigorous argument employing the same method of inferential reasoning that Darwin used. In a thrilling narrative with elements of a detective story as well as a personal quest for truth, Meyer illuminates the mystery that surrounds the origins of DNA. He demonstrates that previous scientific efforts to explain the origins of biological information have all failed, and argues convincingly for intelligent design as the best explanation of life's beginning. In final chapters, he defends ID theory against a range of objections and shows how intelligent design offers fruitful approaches for future scientific research.[81]

From recent works, such as Dr. Meyer's, more and more researchers are beginning to conclude that the complexity of information itself is far too complex to be attributed to undirected/naturalistic causation alone. Therefore I feel confident that the following conclusions are both logically consistent and coherent concerning the philosophy of information:

I had the privilege of meeting William Dembski in 2009 and who taught at Northwestern University, the University of Notre Dame, and the University of Dallas and has done postdoctoral work in mathematics at MIT, in physics at the University of Chicago, and in computer science at Princeton University. What he is probably best known for though is his theory of complex specified information that cannot be accounted for by naturalistic processes. If his theory is correct, then naturalism (at least in part) would be false. His analysis covered in a variety of books but only touched on here basically quantifies the shear odds against information arising by mere chance.

> For example, how do we recognize that an intelligent agent has made a choice? A bottle of ink spills onto a sheet of paper; someone takes a pen and writes a message on a sheet of paper. In both instances ink is applied to paper and in both an almost infinite set of possibilities is realized. Yet in one instance we ascribe agency, in the other chance. What is the relevant difference? A random ink blot is unspecified; a message written with ink on paper is specified. To be sure, the exact message recorded may not be specified. But orthographic, syntactic and semantic constraints will nonetheless specify it. Actualizing one among several competing possibilities, ruling out the rest and specifying the one that was actualized encapsulates

how we recognize intelligent agency, or equivalently, how we detect design.[82]

This type of specified design is not foreign to the historian who must cipher through manuscripts as well as archaeological artifacts to determine authenticity as well as accuracy. An easily assessable example could be pottery shards or stone weapons such as arrowheads. Is there a difference between a flint stone with and without chiseling that has flaked it into a usable form for weapons? Is there a difference between clay that has hardened as opposed to clay that has been hardened in the shape of an animal? Of course there is and in the field of ancient history this type of realization is critical as it is in origin science. As Stephen Meyer as well as William Dembski has alluded, there is no difference in origin sciences. If the information in DNA (or fine-tuning) itself is specified and complex, then it must be the product of intelligence and not naturalistically accounted for since the only two sources of information are physical processes or intelligent agency. Another way (amongst countless more) to postulate beyond information theory in contemplating information theory via mental events themselves (consciousness) could be as philosopher of mind J. P. Moreland puts it:

1. Mental events are genuine nonphysical mental entities that exist.

2. Specific mental and physical event types are regularly correlated.

3. There is an explanation for these correlations.

4. Personal explanation is different from natural scientific explanation.

5. The explanation for these correlations is either a personal or natural scientific explanation.

6. The explanation is not a natural scientific one.

7. Therefore, the explanation is a personal one.

8. If the explanation is personal, then it is theistic.

9. Therefore, the explanation is theistic, which entails that naturalism is false.

Dr. Moreland goes on to conclude: "The truth is that naturalism has no plausible way to explain the appearance of emergent mental properties in the cosmos. Ned Block confesses that we have no idea how consciousness could have emerged from non-conscious matter: 'we have nothing—zilch—worthy of being called a research program…Researchers are stumped.' John Searle says this is a 'leading problem in the biological sciences,' and Colin McGinn observes that consciousness seems like 'a radical novelty in the universe.'"[83]

What is important to discuss here concerning "information/mind/consciousness" is that from a naturalistic philosophy there is no way to account for a naturalistic evolution of consciousness. In other words, there is no such thing as a "simple consciousness" as famous philosophers of mind like Thomas Kuhn have pointed out. Human beings alone have developed consciousness, and there is no real way to account for consciousness evolving by chance. Similarly, there is no way to account for the origin of information itself; where did the information specifications of the singularity of the big bang originate? Where did the information of the cell come from? How does information evolve from noninformation, how does being from nonbeing, or life arise from nonlife? All of these questions remain a mystery but from a naturalistic presupposition they should all be explainable through natural processes, yet as of 2013 even the most ardent naturalist will say empirically we do not have a clue. While this may not mean naturalism is completely false as a hypothesis, it does mean that it is severely implausible and most certainly counts as yet another mark against naturalistic philosophy undergirding the way one does philosophy, whether of history or science.

SPECIFIED COMPLEX INFORMATION

So based on what we have covered thus far, we are faced with two choices as to where the specified complexity in all life originated, much like that of the archaeologist ciphering through ancient remains. Specified complexity in all things either evolved through millions of lucky accidents, which even according to naturalists is highly unlikely, or it was created. A type of creation is the only rational choice because naturalism fails to explain why specified complexity would arise spontaneously again and again and again. For the naturalist, the spontaneous appearance of specified complexity cannot be ignored because information is the centerpiece of life. You can have all the molecules for life available, but without information, or if the information is lost, life does not happen. The three major elements of naturalistic evolution (natural selection, variation, mutation) do not aid in any way in the creation of information.

> Natural Selection: only maintains what information is created by variation and mutation. It cannot act on any information that does not exist. Observational science has actually shown that natural selection only slows the erosion of information in life, and this function is due only to the way life is designed. So natural selection is not the source of specified complexity in life. Variation: is based on existing information, that is, specification that already existed. And while it can create many new combinations of this information, it does not create "new" information. Variation is not the source of specified complexity in life. Mutation destroys information and reduces specified complexity. Geneticists have known for quite some time that mutations are generally not beneficial; they are either neutral or harmful. And even neutral mutations build up over time to become harmful. Random changes, mistakes, misplacements in DNA do not generate information, they destroy it. Mutation therefore cannot be the source

of specified complexity in life. There is only one known source of specified complexity: intelligence. Life was intelligently designed. There should be no question about it.[84]

However, if we knew that life was designed and that there was a "God" for lack of a better word, would this affect our philosophy of history? I believe that all historians (as of 2013) would agree that it most certainly would affect the very methodological restraints currently in check on the study of history and would at least leave open the possibility that nonnaturalistic processes are a possibility when all naturalistic theories have been exhausted. This is the entirety in which my work is directed; that we should follow an open philosophy of history (that carries over into anything deemed origin science), instead of ruling out such criteria *a priori*, especially if it is unwarranted.

The Design Inference[85]: On the basis of his analysis, Dembski outlines a ten-step Generic Chance Elimination Argument:

1. One learns that some event has occurred.

2. Examining the circumstances under which the event occurred, one finds that the event could only have been produced by a certain chance process (or processes).

3. One identifies a pattern, which characterizes the event.

4. One calculates the probability of the event given the chance hypothesis.

5. One determines what probabilistic resources were available for producing the event via the chance hypothesis.

6. On the basis of the probabilistic resources, one calculates the probability of the event occurring by chance once out of all the available opportunities to occur.

7. One finds that the above probability is sufficiently small.

8. One identifies a body of information, which is independent of the event's occurrence.

9. One determines that one can formulate the pattern referred to in step (3) on the basis of this body of independent information.

10. One is warranted in inferring that the event did not occur by chance.

This is a gross simplification of Dembski's analysis, which he develops and defends with painstaking rigor and detail, but one can begin to see more and more with each level in the "rabbit-hole" that naturalism is increasingly unlikely and implausible. As the last fifteen years of studies have shown this, the more I have been dumbfounded by the way I was inclined to practice philosophy of history, which necessitated that I take a naturalistic viewpoint as opposed to a more teleological one. I have therefore found myself in increasing agreement with German philosopher and founder of the term historicism, G. W. F. Hegel who in many ways represents the epitome of a teleological philosophy of history. Hegel's teleology was also taken up by Francis Fukuyama in his *The End of History and the Last Man*. Hegel believed that history was moving man toward a complete "civilization." In his *Lessons on the History of Philosophy*, he explains that each epochal philosophy is in a way the whole of philosophy; it is not a subdivision of the whole, but this whole itself apprehended in a specific modality. Hegel's focus on historicism may be contrasted with reductionist or naturalistic theories of history, which suppose that all developments can be explained by fundamental principles or theories that posit historical changes as result of random chance. The historicist position by Hegel suggests that any human society and all human activities such as science, art, or philosophy are defined by their history so that their essence can be sought only through understanding that. The history of any such human endeavor, moreover, not only builds upon but also reacts against what has gone before; this is the source of Hegel's famous dialectic teaching usually summed up by the slogan "thesis, antithesis, and synthesis." Hegel's famous aphorism, *Philosophy is the history of philosophy*, describes it bluntly, and I am inclined to agree.

MORAL THEORY

Closely tied to information theory would be that of the objectivity or subjectivity of ethics and/or moral values. While book after book has been written on the objectivity of moral value and worth outside of a transcendent reality that constitutes as a basis in which to ground a foundational belief in "right/wrong" or "good/evil," it is important to simply point out that like information theory, there is simply no grounds in which to base something as right or wrong from a naturalistic viewpoint. In other words, if everyone believed that rape was "good," then it would be subjectively good on the naturalist viewpoint. There would be no such thing as objective moral values since by the very definition of naturalistic evolution our morals and ethics could have evolved a different way in which rape or torture was a "good" thing in our mind-set. All worth, purpose and morality/ethics on the naturalistic viewpoint is simply relative to the person. If person "A" believes torture to be a good thing and person "B" believes it to be a bad thing, then it simply is true to each of them, but there is no "objective truth" to either of their claims. We can define "kind" and "compassionate" independent of naturalism or supernaturalism of course; that is a question of *moral semantics*. My question however is concerning *moral ontology*, that is to say, not the *definition* or *meaning* of terms but their *grounding in reality*.

Now many philosophers believe that at least some branches of morality fall into the field of "properly basic beliefs" that are justified as objectively true even if we have no ways of proving them to be true. For example, most philosophers do not believe that the world was created ten minutes ago with the appearance of age or that our brains may be in vat hooked up to electrodes (such as portrayed in the movie *The Matrix*) feeding us false memory or imagery even though we cannot prove either one of these scientifically. We simply have to assume that we really do exist and that the outside world seems old because it really is and this is what is meant by "properly basic beliefs." Moreover, science itself presupposes mathematics and logic, so if the naturalist attempts to argue against logic, they are arguing in a circle since science presuppose math and logic. With this being said, many naturalists believe that morals and ethics are objectively true, but if they are objectively based then naturalism is false:

1. If God does not exist, then objective moral values do not exist.

2. Objective moral values exist.

3. Therefore God exists.

4. If God exists then naturalism is false.

5. God does exist (premise 3).

6. Therefore naturalism is false.

Now it is easy enough to simply get out of this point by denying the objectivity of morals and settle for subjective worth, but most of the most ardent naturalists have a problem with this. For example, naturalistic philosopher Michael Ruse has made the comment that while he appreciates people following the motif of *"Do unto others as you would like done to yourself,"* he says. "Morality is a biological adaptation no less than our hands and feet and teeth. Considered as rationality a justifiable set of claims about an objective something, ethics is illusory...Morality is just an aid to survival and reproduction and any deeper meaning is illusory."[86] However, he later argues that someone who tortures a small child for fun is just as objectively wrong as the person who says 2+2=5; some things are truly wrong/evil.[87] So you can see the paradigm; it is easy to simply argue for subjectivity/relativity of morality until you are faced with a black and white example of evil/good, but if you admit to the objectivity of right/wrong, you must by default reject naturalism. To give one last easily assessable example think about the Holocaust that was responsible for the genocide of over six million Jews. If Hitler would have won the war and killed everyone who said what the Nazis did was "evil" so that every person on the face of the earth said it was a "good" thing—would it therefore be "good"? On the naturalist view, it either would be good based on consensus with an "asterisk" acknowledging that there is no such thing as good/evil so that it would be subjectively good but objectively neither good nor bad. If naturalism is false, however, the problem becomes much easier to address—it would be evil regardless of whether anyone at all believed it to be evil or not (hence the definition of objectivity) since there would be a transcendent reality responsible for ethics and moral worth. This transcendent reality so far would account for everything we have brought into question that naturalism simply cannot even begin to provide the simplest answer for which "should" beg the question: "*Why?*"

CONCLUSION

Though the question "Why is there something rather than nothing?" can be a little like opening Pandora's Box, we have seen that whether discussing modern cosmology and the origin of the universe, naturalism simply does not have the explanatory power or scope to account for "being" coming from "nonbeing" in any form. Moreover, the idea that the universe simply came into being uncaused out of nothingness is much more ad hoc than nonnaturalistic theories such as theism and therefore does not adequately adhere to McCullagh's seven steps for establishing historicity. Similarly, when we look at the anthropic principle that displays a specified complexity of fine-tuning for our existence and when measured against the same probabilities we use for calculating the likelihood of an event occurring we discover that the universe is indeed "fine-tuned" for our very existence. Whether this fine-tuning can be explained by a theory postulating an infinity of other universes remains to be seen, but it definitely is much more ad hoc and contrived than a nonnaturalistic theory such as theism. The theory of "what if there are a plethora of other universes and ours is just one of many thus reducing its fine-tuning to only 'apparent' fine-tuning" not only seems quite implausible, but it still begs the question "why" our universe is the one that did fall into the precise range for existence and contingency to be possible? Finally, information theory and with it moral value seems to be unexplainable through naturalistic processes. Therefore we can conclude that naturalism does not best match McCullagh's steps for determining historic credibility when they are scrutinized by a rigorous observation of the facts and therefore should not be implored when discussing the origins of being.

1. Naturalism does not have great explanatory scope in its account of being, space, time, matter, information, or morality.

2. Naturalism does not have great explanatory power in its account of being, space, time, matter, information, or morality.

3. Most of the naturalistic accounts of being coming from nonbeing are simply not plausible.

4. Naturalism must evoke many contrived or ad hoc assertions in regard to the origins of the universe and being.

5. Naturalism is not in accord with accepted beliefs concerning being only comes from being; its presupposition that the universe popped into being uncaused out of nothing is not what we experience or see today.

6. Nonnaturalistic theories can philosophically outstrip naturalism in meeting conditions 1–5.

HISTORIC EVENT 2:

ORIGIN OF LIFE—CAMBRIAN
EXPLOSION AND HUMAN ORIGINS

To the question why we do not find rich fossiliferous deposits belonging to these assumed earliest periods prior to the Cambrian system, I can give no satisfactory answer. The case at present must remain inexplicable, and may be truly urged as a valid argument against the views here entertained.

—Charles Darwin, *Origin of Species*

Now that we have moved from the ancient history of the origins of the universe, cosmological constants and information itself— compared through the lens of both the naturalist's philosophy versus that of origin science as a history; I hope we can begin to see that a naturalistic view of origins is quite problematic and thus gives us no warrant so far in taking this view into how we do history. So far we have seen zero warrant in incorporating naturalism into our philosophy of history, and moreover, we have seen some good reasons why not to. If we move closer up the history time line however does a warrant "for" naturalism increase? Social naturalism became a popular conception in the nineteenth century. Auguste Comte's (1798–1857) positivist conception of history, which he divided into the theological, metaphysical, and the positivist stage, brought upon by modern science, was one of the most influential doctrines of progress. This gave rise to the later "Whig interpretation" of history, as it was later called, which began looking at human history as progress from "savagery and ignorance" to "prosperity and science." This was followed by the publication of Darwin's *The Origin of Species* in 1859, which popularized the theory of human evolution to an unprecedented scale and thus provided a possible warrant for naturalism via Darwinian evolution. However, this Darwinian form of naturalism was quickly transposed from its original "biological field" to the social science field with "social Darwinism" theories. Herbert Spencer, who coined the term "survival of the fittest," or Lewis Henry Morgan in *Ancient Society* (1877) developed evolutionist theories independent from Darwin's works, which would later be interpreted as social Darwinism, and thus history too was incorporated into this umbrella of "naturalistic evolution" theory. These nineteenth-century unilineal evolution theories claimed that human societies start out in a *primitive* state and gradually become more civilized and advanced over time, and this is where the social sciences are still "stuck" today in dire need of further "evolution"...

As history has taught us, this notion did of course lead to a type of "scientific racism" with the most "advanced" civilization being thought to be the most "elite" and the philosophy of history and historiography began to incorporate this same methodology and still does to a large degree today. After World War I, and even before Herbert Butterfield (1900–1979) harshly criticized the notion of scientific racism and insisted that the Whig interpretation was antiquated and false. However, the notion itself did not completely disappear. *The End of History and the Last Man*

(1992) by Francis Fukuyama proposed a similar notion of progress, positing that the worldwide adoption of liberal democracies as the single accredited political system and even modality of human consciousness would represent the "End of History." It was however Tim Ingold who suggested that history is a movement of self-creation in his work *On the Distinction between Evolution and History*.[88]

History is a movement of "self-creation"? The "End of History" and the "The End of Philosophy" are reoccurring themes in this postmodern type of philosophy and adds further credit to my point that this naturalistic philosophy retards the methodology and interpretation/conclusions of history. The critical underexplored question is less about history as content and more about history as process. We have already reviewed various reasons for being skeptical of the closed philosophy of naturalism when reviewing origins, but let us review the highly contested venue of human origins to see if naturalism fairs any better. Philosopher of Science J. P. Moreland summarizes how intelligence qualifies as the inference to the best explanation when it (along with naturalism) is allowed into the pool of live options (including those of human origins) in his contribution to the work *Philosophical Foundations*:

> The neo-Darwinian theory of biological evolution is a good example of inference to the best explanation. Darwinists recognize that the theory represents a huge extrapolation from the data, which support micro-evolutionary change but do not provide evidence of macro-evolutionary development. They further freely admit that none of the evidence, taken in isolation, whether it be from microbiology, paleogeography, paleontology and so forth provides proof of the theory. But their point is that the theory is nonetheless the best explanation, in virtue of its explanatory power, scope and so on. By contrast, the charge leveled by critics of the neo-Darwinian synthesis like Philip Johnson that the theory presupposes naturalism is best

understood as the claim that the explanatory superiority of the neo-Darwinian theory is a function of the pool of live options' being restricted by an unjustified methodological constraint [closed-philosophy], namely, the philosophical presupposition of naturalism. Johnson argues that once hypotheses positing Intelligent Design are allowed into the pool of live options, then the explanatory superiority of the neo-Darwinian theory is no longer apparent, [when discussing human origins].[89]

So what is the account given by naturalism when concerning the origins of the first life as well as animal life in general in which human beings evolved? *Origin of first life and animal life*—Naturalists' predominant answer: "Given enough time life will come from non-life from natural processes and though we do not fully understand how this happened nor can we replicate it today, that is the only possible explanation." The second answer much further back in the running is "panspermia" or that life was seeded on earth by possible extra-terrestrial beings (this theory however does not account for where these beings were derived or why they seeded life on earth). As far as how animal life came to its present state from this first life, the naturalists accounts for the Cambrian explosion (what biology often refers to as the "big bang" of life in which nearly all major phyla of animals just appear fully formed and unevolved from previous life-forms) by concluding that though we see no animal fossil records leading up to these phyla, they must either be there or they simply have disappeared over time and that is why we do not see any evidences of evolution leading up to the origin of the phyla. While the nonnaturalist can be open to the naturalistic ideas mentioned above concerning evolution the naturalist with a closed philosophy in mind simply cannot. No matter what the odds and evidence against the first life happening by chance and then evolving by chance over millions of years, it simply has to be true because naturalistic causation presupposes it to be.

FIRST LIFE

Origin of life hypotheses are quite elaborate and bizarre but to date even the most adamant proponents of naturalism, such as Oxford biologist Richard Dawkins, admits we simply do not have a solid understanding of how life arose on earth to begin the naturalistic evolutionary processes that would lead to the modern life-forms we see today. The reason for the most staunch of naturalists still having skepticism on the origin of life by spontaneous chemical generation (that life came from nonliving chemicals naturally over time) is first of all because we cannot as of 2013 with all of our "intelligent"-based systems create life. The other problem with this is that we are "intelligent creations" attempting to set the conditions for life by our own design and still cannot create life. Moreover, under the conditions required for life to have arisen spontaneously, it is much more likely that these initial elements would have been destroyed quicker than they could have been reproduced. Even if these chemicals in the right combinations could be produced, there is no satisfactory answer as to how they could have been arranged accurately within a cell wall; this would require yet again another set of conditions all together.

Dr. Michael Denton is considered one of the first to statistically challenge the idea of spontaneous generation of life. He looked at the simplest cell that could possibly live and function. What were the chances that one hundred proteins (the smallest number required), could come together by sheer coincidence? His calculation showed a probability of one in $10^{2000.}$ (Remember that 10^{50} is considered a scientific impossibility). Ralph Muncaster, in his book *A Skeptic's Search for God*,[90] stated that the chances of getting 10,000 amino acids with left-sided links (which is absolutely necessary), and 100,000 nucleotides with right-sided links together in one cell, was one in 10^{33113}. Harold Morowitz calculated the odds of a whole cell randomly assembling under the most ideal circumstances to be on in $10^{100,000,000,000}$, and this does not consider various other factors such as the exact function of each molecule, division of that cell, increasing biological complexity, life from some unknown source injected into the organism, etc. If the list itself is endless, what would the combined chances be for all components to come into existence and then come together spontaneously by sheer coincidence? Statistically, an absolute impossibility.[91]

As touched on earlier, William Dembski allows those in favor of "chance" an even larger area for "chance" to be a chance; but he still argues convincingly that there is a statistical limit to this improbability. Anything that is less than 1×10^{150} is essentially statistically impossible within our existing universe. He arrives at this number by multiplying the total number of elemental particles estimated to exist in the entire universe (1×10^{80}) times the number of transitions that each elemental particle can make in a second (1×10^{45}) times the supposed age of the universe, assuming the universe is a billion times older than twenty billion years old (1×10^{25} seconds) = 1×10^{150}. While this is a huge number, it is not large at all when contemplating very complex systems. Hubert Yockey, a highly regarded information theorist, has calculated the amount of information content in the minimum genome for life to arise and the probability of that occurring by chance as something less probable than $10^{186,000}$. So let us be honest for a moment—who has the most faith—the naturalist or non-naturalist?[92]

The only real game in town for the naturalist is that of spontaneous generation and chance which would then, through mutation and natural selection via Darwinian evolution, account for everything that "exists" today. Darwinian Evolution is, however, an incredibly slippery word to define because it can mean so many different things. Therefore, one could break it into the following categories to make it more assessable:

1. Cosmic Evolution

2. Chemical Evolution

3. Organic Evolution

4. Macroevolution

5. Microevolution

Of these terms, only microevolution (change over time), has been verified (cosmic/chemical have already been discussed in the previous chapter concerning the origins of the universe). The concept of microevolution was never really controversial in the first place and the concept existed well before Darwin. An example would be Eskimos having a higher fat content because they live in colder climates than someone who lives on the equator; different kinds of cats, dogs, etc. There are some changes notable as the generations have come and gone, but that is where it stops. We have big dogs and little dogs, but they are always dogs. This is an example of microevolution, which no one to my knowledge contests.

The other theories are 100 percent speculative and must be followed by extreme faith. Macroevolution contends that at some point everything can be traced back to a single cell that was created by complete chance as mentioned above. Modern evolutionary trees have slowly "evolved" to include three "domains" of life: bacteria, archaea, and eukarya (which includes all plants and animals). This is related to the term we hear called "common descent," which is generally accepted that all living organisms on earth are descended from a common ancestor or ancestral gene pool. In "layman's terms," this basically means that somehow beyond all probability, life came about from what is often called "primordial soup" from the early earth and then it somehow came to life and basically went through a series of drastic evolutionary changes/mutations followed by natural selection to account for all the phyla, classes, genera, species, etc., we have today.

There is an incalculable number of problems with this theory. First of all, it cannot be tested; therefore, it sets itself up as unfalsifiable. We cannot test origin science so we must remember (as history), cosmic, chemical, and organic evolutions are conjectured based off the evidence; the question is—is it the best inference of the data? We do not see any of these changes happening at present (because it would take at least millions of years), we cannot duplicate any of these experiments, so we are left with conjecturing and theorizing, but there is no data available for us to have any real confidence in these speculations. We also do not have any reason to believe that macroevolution is plausible. Though we have never seen this happen (because once again it would take millions of years) there should be a plethora of transitional intermediary fossils found in the "historic" fossil record just like archaeology, but there is not; moreover, the metamorphic changes required are grossly neglected by the vast majority of supporters to this idea. In a nutshell, what this means is that we never see any type of transition of one animal evolving into another, so in theory "if" evolution were true, then we should see transitional fossils such as a "cow" then another one a little less like a cow and another one less and less and less as each one is progressing toward let us say a whale (since the cow to whale evolution model is one that the evolutionist say are there "strongest" evidences). But the facts are that we have none of these; we have a few fossils that may look like a land mammal then one that looks like a little more aquatic, and one that looks like a whale so the evolutionist "infers" that this means that Darwinian evolution is true. The problem is that math tells us there would have to be at least fifty thousand transitional intermediate stages between the cow and whale so there should be a plethora of fossils confirming this; even if there were (which there is not), it would still be an "interpretation" of the fossils.

With this type of lack of evidence coupled with the fact that our oldest fossils of beavers, dogs, trees, insects, even animals like the platypus, etc., all look exactly like they do today with the exception of minor changes and larger overall size, we begin to see why more and more people are abandoning Darwinism for intelligent design; the cow to whale transition as mentioned above is supposed to be one of the stronger evidences in favor of evolution, but mathematician David Berlinski has calculated at least fifty thousand metamorphic changes would be required to go from the cow to the whale. We do not see any evidence for this today. We do not see any evidence for this in the fossil record nor would the fossils even be able to give us a great picture because they are untestable themselves. (In fact, we are not able to prove by looking at a seal fossil and a walrus fossil that one "changed" into the other). Once again, it is a speculation, which everyone is entitled to make; but this is a relatively weak theory since all that has been proven since well before Darwin is that all we see are variations within a given genus.

So to what degree has naturalistic "Darwinism" been ingrained into modern history and culture? William Dembski and Sean McDowell comically summarize the impact on modern culture in their book *Understanding Intelligent Design*: "Darwinism is one of the few subjects that popular culture holds in awe. In the television program called 'Friends,' there was an episode that displayed Darwinism in society; Phoebe and Ross discuss the merits of Darwinian evolution. Shocked to find that Phoebe rejects it, Ross says: 'Uh, excuse me. Evolution is not for you to buy Phoebe. Naturalistic Evolution is scientific fact, like, like, like the air we breathe, like gravity.'"[93] This quote provides us with a picture perfect example of how naturalistic philosophy undergirds the majority of not only what are normally referred to as the "natural sciences" but also the social sciences as well. Because if "Ross" is correct, naturalism is a fact just like "the air we breathe," and therefore, it is only logical to see the philosophy of history through this same Darwinian Naturalistic lens. But are supporters of Darwinism giving us a fair picture here? Is it just plain silly to deny Darwinism? What if there is a better explanation for the origin and structure of the universe than Darwinian naturalism? What if the world has been designed for a particular purpose?

If so, the attempt to understand all reality within a Darwinian perspective would be a colossal mistake. Darwin's theory of evolution, often referred to as "Darwinism," inspires the best-known form of naturalism. In *Darwin's Dangerous Idea*, philosopher Daniel Dennett says *all* reality should be understood within a Darwinian naturalistic framework. Why? Because Darwinism tells us our creation story, and such a story always controls how we interpret reality. Given how widely Darwinism is accepted, we should not be surprised that virtually every field of study is now being "Darwinized" including the philosophy of history.[94]

BIOLOGY'S BIG BANG

In 2009, I had the privilege of visiting the Discovery Institute in Seattle, Washington, where I was able to confirm many of the questions and lack of evidence concerning a strictly naturalistic/evolutionary beginning. My visit ended with being allowed to preview an upcoming documentary on the Cambrian Explosion, which is often referred to as "biology's big bang" since all major animal phyla simple appear fully formed and functional. This major documentary, the third in Illustra Media's internationally acclaimed intelligent design series, probes one of the great mysteries of science, the Cambrian explosion, when in a moment of geological time complex animals first appeared on earth fully formed, without evidence of any evolutionary ancestors.

Charles Darwin viewed this as an inexplicable mystery. He had envisioned the evolution of life through a multitude of small undirected steps. Yet the fossil record reveals no such supporting pattern of gradual development. Instead, early in the Cambrian period compound eyes, articulated limbs, sophisticated sensory organs, and skeletal systems simply burst into existence seemingly out of nowhere. "The big question that the Cambrian Explosion poses is where does all that new information come from?" says Dr. Stephen Meyer, a scientist featured in the documentary and author of the book *Signature in the Cell: DNA and the Evidence for Intelligent Design.* "We know that new information can only come from intelligence, and so the burst of genetic information during the Cambrian era provides compelling evidence that animal life is the product of intelligent design rather than a blind undirected process like natural selection."[95]

One of the most remarkable pieces of evidence calling into question biological naturalism (a.k.a. Darwinian Evolution) is the "Cambrian explosion." Many textbooks never even mention it, and the ones that do relegate it to a short phrase or paragraph as if it is some insignificant detail. This phenomenon is so pronounced in the fossil record that *Scientific American* called it "life's big bang." "When Darwin wrote the *Origin of Species*, the oldest known fossils were from a geological period known as the Cambrian, named after rocks in Cambria, Wales. But the Cambrian fossil record does not start with one or a few species that diverged gradually over millions of years into genera, then families, then orders, then classes, then phyla. Instead, most of the major phyla—and many of the major classes within them—appear together abruptly in the Cambrian, fully formed."[96] Moreover since the 1990s through today the Cambrian explosion has been verified on every continent; all major body plans and enormous varieties of each all coexist in this layer. This has caused many reputable and highly accomplished scientists at major accredited universities worldwide say it is an insurmountable challenge to Darwinian naturalism.

> Remarkably the layers below the Cambrian have practically nothing with regard to fossilized specimens. The few creatures that are found in pre-Cambrian strata are all soft-bodied organisms like worms. So essentially you have nothing along the lines of organic complexity and diversity pre-Cambrian, and then suddenly everything. But wait, it gets even more interesting. To compound this huge problem the number of species fossilized in the lay-

ers above the Cambrian period gradually decrease with each successive layer. Once you reach the most recent layers approximately 98% of everything that has ever lived is extinct. Have you ever heard that 98% of everything that has ever lived is extinct? This is where that saying came from—hard scientific fact. A reasonable and honest person must conclude from the evidence that the fossil record is diametrically opposite to what would be predicted by evolutionary theory. Nevertheless, it is a belief held among scientists world-wide.[97]

Even the late and famous evolutionist Stephen Jay Gould stated: "The history of most fossil species include two features inconsistent with gradualistic evolution—1) Stasis: Most species exhibit no directional change during their tenure on earth. They appear in the fossil record looking much the same as when they disappear; morphological change is usually limited and directionless. 2) Sudden Appearance: In any local area, a species does not arise gradually by the steady transformation of its ancestors; it appears all at once and fully formed."[98] Of course many naturalistic biologists like Ken Miller and Francisco Ayala will infer that it is possible that we may have simply not found transitionary fossils yet, but this is becoming a less and less plausible hypothesis since searches for answers to transitionary fossils as well as the Cambrian have been going on for over 150 years and are still no closer to answering these questions naturalistically than they were then. Moreover, some naturalists such as the late Stephen Gould mentioned above have attempted to answer this by the hypothesis that while gradual naturalistic evolution may be false, punctuated equilibrium might provide the answer. In a nutshell punctuated equilibrium states that as opposed to gradualistic naturalism, there could be short bursts of change and this is why we see nothing in the fossil record supporting naturalistic evolutionary processes today. Though this does seem much more possible than gradualism based on the evidence it is not very plausible because there is no explanation "why" punctuated equilibrium would be happening or what mechanism would be driving it; there should still be more evidences in the fossil record than there are today, and it still would not adequately address the Cambrian explosion. Lastly, we are beginning to see a few speculative philosophers of science such as Michael Ruse speculate the theory of "panspermia" once again (that life was seeded by possible extraterrestrial beings). While panspermia does at least show that naturalistic philosophers of science are beginning to look outside of the confines of naturalism, it still just pushes the question to "where did the aliens come from." On the other hands there are a few theistic-minded philosophers of science such as astronomer Hugh Ross and biochemist Fazale Rana who feel that biology's "big bang" (like the universe's big bang) are all best understood from the biblical story of creation ex nihilo (out of nothing) followed by life's creation "ex nihilo" since this does seem to be where the evidence points at least to some degree.

The famous philosopher Aristotle stated in his *History of the Animals* that "it is clear that certain fishes come spontaneously into existence, not being derived from eggs or from copulation. Such fish as are neither oviparous nor viviparous arise all either from mud or from sand and from decayed matter that rises thence as scum; for instance the so-called froth of the small fry comes out of sandy ground."[99] Modern readers would of course think this quote is quite amusing; how could anyone ever have believed such thing—right? However, the vast majority of thinkers over time have agreed with Aristotle that spontaneous generation seemed to best fit the data and to suggest otherwise was to invite ridicule and scorn. Similarly, theologians through time have adapted their theology to best fit the mainstream "status quo" of academia. Though many doubted spontaneous generation, it was not until Louis Pasteur that such ideas were (mostly) laid to permanent rest as a hypothesis no longer plausible and thus thrown into the trash heap of false theories.

In our own era, academia and thus culture is most comfortable with naturalism and its philosophical relatives. Thousands of scientists, theologians, historians, and philosophers have spent the last century with almost the full backing of the Western cultural apparatus, accumulating data filtered through this limited point view. This is not to postulate there is some "grand conspiracy theory" of course; it is just to show how once a paradigm is in place the "holders/protectors" of the paradigm will build protective forts/filters around the paradigm including the changing of definitions, rules, and laws of inquiry to limit competing hypotheses. This has always been the case with human history and most likely always will be (and the church in general has a history showing they are just as guilty so do not think this is just the secular entities). The bottom line though is do we want a paradigm (perhaps as bad as the "emperor has no clothes"), or do we want truth as far as we can comprehend it? We are all seeing the same evidences, and we agree with them for the most part so how can our conclusions be so different? A growing number of scientists and philosophers from prestigious universities have since the 1990s began demonstrating that philosophical naturalism may be retarding the advancement of science. If this is even possible then it should seriously concern even the most devout naturalist.

Noted philosopher of science J. P. Moreland similarly concludes: "Philosophical naturalism is used to argue both that evolution is science and creation science (or intelligent design) is religion, and that reason is to be identified with science. Thus, the empirical evidence for or against evolution is just not the issue when it comes to explaining why so many give the theory unqualified allegiance. There is a second reason for the current overbelief in evolution: it functions as a myth for secularists. By myth I do not mean something false though I believe evolution to be that but rather a story of who we are and how we got here that serves as a guide for life. Evolutionist Richard Dawkins said that evolution made the world safe for atheists because it supposedly did away with the design argument for God's existence. Why is it that evolution is so widely embraced with such certainty in a way that goes well beyond what the evidence justifies?"[100]

More and more we are seeing what would seem to be a "reverse" trend in the naturalist appealing to the theologians and media for popular support; this in and of itself seems illogical if naturalism is on such empirically sound footing. National Center for Science Education (NCE has repeatedly made the affirmation: Science posits that there are no forces outside of nature. Science cannot be neutral on this issue. All educated people understand there are no forces outside of nature.[101] But at the same time their spokeswoman Eugenie Scott has reached out to many theology schools and theological leaders in an attempt to endorse "theistic evolution." I was quite surprised myself to see an ongoing video recording in New York's Natural History Museum playing clips from vocal naturalists stating that naturalism and nonnaturalism (such as theism/deism) are compatible as long as you accept the tenets of philosophical naturalism. Why would naturalist resort to media and theology centers for support if naturalistic theory is as sound as "gravity" as I have heard many naturalists state? While much more could be said on this particular subject, I simply refuse to be categorized as "noneducated" as the NCE words it so eloquently, for not simply accepting an ad hoc assertion that naturalism is true even though there seems to be no basis for believing it to be so.

While peer reviewed articles and popular books are growing at an alarming rate on the weaknesses of naturalistic theory (while at the same time the naturalist are franticly placing fingers and gum in the increasing numbers of holes in the dam in a last attempt to keep the dam from collapsing and convince themselves the emperor does indeed have clothes); mathematician and philosopher of science David Berlinski draws similar conclusions on the philosophy of science:

The idea that science is a uniquely self-critical institution is of course preposterous. Scientists are no more self-critical than anyone else. They hate to be criticized...Look, these people are only human, they hate criticism—me too. The idea that scientists are absolutely eager to be beaten up is one of the myths put out by scientists, and it works splendidly so they can avoid criticism. We're asking for standards of behavior that would be wonderful to expect but that no serious man does expect. A hundred years of fraudulent drawings suggesting embryological affinities that don't exist—that's just what I would expect if biologists were struggling to maintain a position of power in a secular democratic society. Let's be reasonable...the popular myth of science as a uniquely self-critical institution, and scientists as men who would rather be consumed at the stake rather than fudge their data, is okay for a PBS special, but that's not the real world; that's not what's taking place...One of the reasons that people embrace Darwinian orthodoxy with such an unholy zealousness is just that it gives them access to power. It's as simple as that: power over education, power over political decisions, power over funding, and power over the media.[102]

If Dr. Berlinski is correct, it is at least possible that following a closed philosophy of science or history can only be justified in the name of power, popularity, and funding; if this is true, then how could we ever trust the current modes of academia that are following a closed philosophy as opposed to an open one?

So in conclusion, the origin of life and the big bang of biology (like that of cosmology) are simply unexplainable by naturalistic processes and even the most ardent naturalist will admit to this fact. Does this mean therefore that theism or deism must be true? Perhaps not, but it does mean that they as well as panspermia are much more plausible than naturalism. Moreover, we can see that the approach I have taken as a historian processing origin science is much more logically coherent than a naturalistic scientist attempting to explain origins through the processes of operational sciences since these are not testable and simply adhere to ad hoc and *a priori* inferences that goes against the evidences and limits history as well as science from taking the evidence where it leads (even if that is in the opposite direction of naturalism).

HUMAN ORIGINS

Having briefly looked at the origin of life as well as the chain of events within the Cambrian and what that means in lieu of animal life, we now turn to the origin of humans themselves from this same animal life much further down the naturalistic time line. How does naturalism account for the *origin of humanity*? Most naturalists maintain that over several million years of the evolutionary process mentioned earlier, the first humanlike members of the genus of Homo evolved (approximately 2.5 million years ago) and eventually gained consciousness and self-identity to the modern *Homo sapiens* of today. With that, the first languages, literacy, and civilization began to evolve from grunts and groans to form a basic language approximately ten-thousand-plus years ago and then evolved scribbling and pictograms into a writing system and thus quickly developed from nomadic existence to form the first major civilization in the Mesopotamian area of the Fertile Crescent approximately six thousand years ago. The question again is: "Is this a sound hypothesis?"

I had the privilege of meeting and talking with Dr. Jonathan Wells of Discovery Institute in Seattle in the summer of 2009. Dr. Wells has PhDs from both Yale and Berkeley universities with one being in cell and molecular biology. It is interesting that he has confirmed many historic frauds used to attempt to prove Darwinian history as being true. Like me, he is dumbfounded why so many adhere to a theory that has developed into an ideology. In his book, *Icon of Evolution*, he goes through a list of repeated hoax and outright lies that have been used to support evolution in textbooks, magazines, museums, and so on for the last century. In regard to human evolution, he references Henry Gee, a senior editor for *Nature*: "The conventional picture of human evolution as lines of ancestry and descent is a 'completely human invention created after the fact, shaped to accord with human prejudices.' Putting it even more bluntly, Gee concludes: 'To take a line of fossils and claim that they represent a lineage is not a scientific hypothesis that can be tested, but an assertion that carries the same validity as a bedtime story—amusing, perhaps even instructive, but not scientific.'"[103]

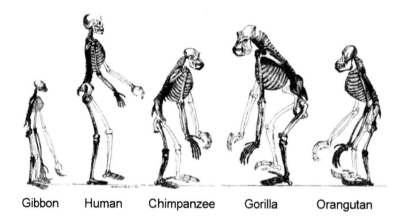

Gibbon Human Chimpanzee Gorilla Orangutan

When asked further about this type of information being given to the general public, Dr. Wells states:

> The general public is rarely informed of the deep-seated uncertainty about human origins that is reflected in these statements by scientific experts. Instead, we are simply fed the latest version of somebody's theory, without being told that paleoanthropologists themselves cannot agree over it. And typically, the theory is illustrated with fanciful drawings of cave men, or human actors wearing heavy makeup. Whether the ultimate icon is presented in the form of a

picture or a narrative, it is old-fashioned materialistic philosophy disguised as modern empirical science.[104]

After taking years of evolutionary theory courses ranging
from biology, anthropology, geology, sociology, and yes, history;
I took "biological anthropology" in 2001 with hopes of understanding how human evolution worked. Obviously, I did not find
the answers I was looking for. This was hurt further when much
of what we discussed in the chain of human evolution was overturned as soon as I completed the class by discoveries within the
alleged human fossil record that overturned the then chronologi-
cal order in which our textbook and professor had taught human
evolution had transpired. What it, as well as genetics, did help
me to see however was that the history of the human race was
anything but "clear."

Human genetic diversity seems to leave a straight-forward
understanding of evolutionary history in a quagmire since generally any two people have very similar DNA sequences, especially within protein-coding DNA. Within this however, some
may have the DNA base chemical "G" while members of another
family may have "C" instead even though thousands of bases from
that position are identical. Geneticists recently analyzed human
gene differences as was recorded in the leading publication *Science*
magazine in an article titled "Evolution and Functional Impact
of Rare Coding Variation from Deep Sequencing of Human
Exomes." In this article, they compared the placement of the four
DNA chemical bases positioned within thousands of genes in
over two thousand people and focused on various differences in
the protein-coding genes. These comprise less than 2 percent of
the total human DNA, but they hold a more reliable "historic"
record of past DNA changes than other more highly variable
DNA. The research team investigated the amount of diversity
among today's human genes and how long it would have taken
to reach the current amount of diversity. They concluded that

human genes diversified recently. Geneticist Brian Thomas concluded that "the maximum likelihood time for accelerated growth was only 5,115 years ago."[105] This is an incredibly small fraction (0.2 percent) of the 2.4 million years of humanity that naturalists account for in which genetic diversity supposedly evolved. The explosion of human genetic diversity has occurred in parallel with, and because of, human population growth. With each new person comes another opportunity for DNA differences to arise, either by designed genetic shuffling processes or mutations as naturalism presupposes. As a readily accessible example, if the evolutionary historic time line is true, then human population growth and genetic diversity have remained miraculously unchanged for a few million years before suddenly exploding in just the last few thousand years in the areas of the Fertile Crescent. What are the odds of the life-to-death ratios being almost perfect for replacement for approximately two million years as well as the fossil evidence showing practically none of these remains? While the historian can hypothesize on the pre-Sumerian civilizations, yet again, there should be no reason at all to presuppose a naturalistic interpretation of the data when no plausible reason for doing so exists.[106]

GENEALOGY OF MANKIND?

For all intent purposes, the field of study tracing a family line known as genealogy falls into the category of history as an origin science as well. The history of the races of mankind is an incredibly fascinating subject in itself. Race does not apply to skin color alone of course; the superficial distinction is actually quite false since all humans are the same "color" per se. Skin shade is simply due to the amount of melanin in the skin; the more melanin, the darker the skin. Modern genetics has shown that when a large interbreeding group is suddenly broken into many smaller groups which then breed within those smaller groups, different racial "characteristics" can arise. We can see this today in drastic measures where a 100 percent African American male (black) has a child with a 100 percent Caucasian female (white) and the child may be 100 percent black or white. Though the vast majority would be of course "mixed," genetics can take different roles with individuals and groups. Geneticists predominantly claim that the origin of lineages were derived from known people groups that first appeared in the Middle East (many now support the African origin followed by a quick migration to the Middle East), areas known as the Fertile Crescent near the areas of Sumer/Mesopotamia. This information is derived from DNA haplogroups, which are used in DNA tests for markers that give a broad or regional picture; this data comes from either Y-chromosomes passed down from a father or mitochondrial from a mother. Both can be used to define genetic populations from one generation to the next and though the majority of geneticists had traced all mitochondrial DNA to a single female and the Y-chromosome to a single male some since the mid-1990s have challenged this hypothesis.

Ann Gauger (PhD in developmental biology University of Washington, post-doctoral fellow Harvard), Douglas Axe (PhD Caltech, postdoctoral research scientist Cambridge), and Casey Luskin (MS earth sciences and JD in law) recently published a book on human origins in which they make a strong case for the plausibility of two original parents to the human race. Dr. Gauger is quite honest when she states:

> When evaluating explanatory causes for beings such as ourselves, we need to choose a cause that is up to the task. I personally am convinced that unguided, unintelligent processes can't do the job, not only because the neo-Darwinian mechanism is utterly insufficient, but also because we are beings capable of intelligence and creativity. These qualities are what makes us human, and together with our capacity for empathy and our desire for goodness and

beauty, they point toward the kind of cause that is sufficient to explain our origins.[107]

Dr. Gauger goes on to state that the models associated with
genetic diversity models and equations must take many "assumptions" to simplify the mathematics; some of these assumptions
are actually presuppositions.

> The use of tree-drawing algorithms begs the question of
> whether or not a tree exists. Similarly, the assumption that
> random processes are the only causes of genetic change over
> time is an assumption drawn from philosophical natural-
> ism. Geneticists therefore have developed ways of looking
> at sequence data to make these estimates. They use SNP
> data to draw evolutionary trees for the DNA sequences in
> and around the gene in question, and from those trees and
> assumed mutation rates they can estimate at what point
> in time the trees coalesce to a single allele. Once that has
> been determined, they can also estimate what must have
> been when the allele first arose, to explain the observed
> allele frequency of the lactase persistence gene today. These
> estimates depend on an awful lot of assumptions that may
> not be justified, and on estimates that may not even be
> accurate.[108]

So even though Francisco Ayala and a few others began to
believe in the mid-1990s that the number of alleles of a gene
called HLA-DRB1 could be up to thirty-two separate versions,
the sequence Ayala used in his analysis was guaranteed to give
an overestimate of population size. A later more "careful" study
pushed the number down to only seven possible variations and
now research has it back down to as few as three or four ancestral
versions of the regions surrounding the HLA-DRB1 gene when
all sequence comparisons are taken into consideration. What this
means is that Ayala's hypothesis is now known to be false and
the original hypothesis of two original parents is very plausible

because three or four alleles can be carried by just 2 individuals, especially if after those two first "parents" came a period of rapid population growth. Dr. Gauger readily admits: "There are limits to what can be proven about past events, based on population genetics models and current human genetic diversity. Truth be told, we have no idea when the first true humans appeared. The fossil records don't record things like the emergence of intellect and will, so inferences about fossils and dates are indirect at best. A little caution and humility is called for. Given the potential number of unknown variables, and the limitations of the models involved, no one should be making claims of certitude about what happened in humanity's distant past."[109]

Dr. Gauger's closing comments above are spoken of like a true historian who knows that the historic past is combination of puzzle pieces and inferences and that these inferences are anything but "absolute." With that being said, why would or should the historian be "bottlenecked" by naturalism? The answer seems to be no reason whatsoever. So back to our hypothesis at hand—

1. Are there good grounds to believe naturalism to be false?

2. Does the philosophy of naturalism permeate through how we do history?

First of all, we have continued to look at not only the naturalistic sciences but also the philosophy of these to see that much like its big brother "positivism," which is now universally rejected, naturalism is on a plummeting decline with very few facts from science or philosophy to support it. Origin science as a history likewise confirms not only that there are very few reasons that support naturalism for the universe's origin and the origin of life, but not even the origin and evolution of humans seems to support any type of naturalism. As Casey Luskin comments in his review of the historicity of the fossil record:

> If Human beings evolved from ape-like creatures, what were the transitional species between the ape-like homi-

nids and the truly human-like members of the Homo genus found in the fossil record? There aren't any good candidates...There are many gaps and virtually no plausible transitional fossils that are generally accepted, even by evolutionists, to be direct human ancestors....The fossil record appears to be anything but a gradual Darwinian evolutionary process. The Darwin belief that humans evolved from apelike species requires inferences that go beyond the evidence and is not supported by the fossil record.[110]

Finally to the second point—we must sadly answer with a resounding "yes." The vast majority of historians since the mid-nineteenth century through today have endorsed a level of naturalism when dealing with the ancient past though when cornered these historians have in my personal experiences admitted that they have often accepted naturalistic Darwinism as the primer of ancient history though they really could not explain to me "why" to the slightest degree. This is a perfect example of naturalism retarding our social sciences; if a PhD historian cannot explain what he or she has written on the ancient past, then they have no business writing about it in my opinion. In other words, if I know little to nothing about the Byzantine Empire and then began writing about it I would expect someone to inform me that if I do not even know if what I am espousing is accurate then I should not be writing about the subject at all. Sadly many of these historians have said that their departments, universities, or publishers have oftentimes insisted on at least a few pages of support to a naturalistic worldview leading up to the ancient appearances of the first civilizations in Mesopotamia and Sumer. For example, the late Norman F. Cantor (emeritus professor of history, sociology, and comparative literature at New York University) dedicated approximately five pages for all history before 3,000 BC in which he too infers a rehashed naturalistic viewpoint in his book *Antiquity*.

On a much more extensive viewpoint, historian Dr. J. M. Roberts (previously of Oxford University), provides us with thirty-four pages on history "before" Sumer in his work *A History of the World*. Dr. Roberts asserts the naturalistic philosophy of history on page 2 when he discusses naturalistic evolution:

> This may seem remote from the human story, but it is necessary to an understanding of its roots in a very distant past. Biological evolution long inched forward with incredible slowness within the possibilities offered by diverse habitats, at first to different organisms and later to different animals. About 40 million years ago a long climatic phase began to draw to a close which had favored great reptiles. But the new conditions suited other animal strains which were already about, among them some mammals whose tiny ancestors had appeared 200 million years or so earlier....The first apes and monkeys appeared 25 million or so years ago. From them evolved the evolutionary line called 'hominids.' Fossil remains suggest that 3–4 million years ago we can begin to distinguish among them some who can be considered among our ancestors....This once more shows the speeding-up of evolutionary change. An enormous new range of capacities and skills comes into being somewhere between 1,000,000 and 100,000 BC, and they made the first human societies possible.[111]

While I am in no way attacking the historian who uses naturalistic philosophy to begin their discourses, my point is to show that if there is no good reason to believe naturalism to be true, then why espouse it in such elementary ways as the above quote shows? History and the social sciences are permeated with these types of introductions, which only begs the question "why." Moreover, we could seriously be retarding the way we do history, science, and education as a whole. Dr. Roberts goes on to admit that there is no real evidence however for language or writing evolving over time but that it seemed to rapidly come into existence with Sumerian language approximately 5,000 BC and written language by 3,500 BC. Again, this type of forced philosophy of history endorsing naturalism seems to not only be unwarranted based on what we have already seen but seems to force inferences that have no data to back them up:

> Traditionally, what happened before writing is called 'prehistory', and historians have left it to other scholars. Nondocumentary evidence was all that could be used to find out about it. Yet in prehistory much was settled to ensure that one day humans would know how to write—as well as engineer, build, organize and many other things. Though so much has happened so recently in the last 5,000 years or so, it does not start happening without any preparation. In sheer weight of years most of the story of human beings lies in prehistoric times, and that is why we have begun there. In looking at the beginnings of civilized life, we have to start with what lies behind it.[112]

These vague allusions to "much was settled in prehistory" to insure humans would know how to write and so on seems like a completely false assertion based on a strict form of unguided naturalistic processes. What is driving these undirected processes in "prehistory" to ensure human preparation? Alas, it is simply inferred as "closed" and not open to debate to most "prominent" historians. However, there are a growing number of what is often referred to as "amateur" historians such as Susan Wise Bauer of William and Mary College in Virginia that are actually taking a more "open" view of philosophy of history, and I find their work not only based on evidence and less on presuppositions, but it is refreshing and just as accurate as any closed-view of philosophy of history that I have read. For example in Susan's book, *The History of the Ancient World: From the Earliest Accounts to the Fall of Rome*, she is accused by *Publisher's Weekly* of "some of her assertions—for instance, that the biblical book of Joshua is the clearest guide we possess to the establishment of an Israelite kingdom in Canaan—contradict general scholarly opinion or are simply wrong. However, Bauer's elegant prose and her command of much of the material makes this a wonderful starting point for the study of the ancient world."[113] Basically, because she does give some merit/credit to a book such as the Bible in developing her historicity of the Hebrew nation, she is wrong or contradicts general scholarly opinion. Who or what is this scholarly opinion? Is it the closed philosophy of naturalism once again that we have cited repeatedly? By using an open philosophy of history Bauer is not restricted from "excluding" religious documents or letters in developing her historic prose. I can assure you as one that has read and studied numerous ancient and modern histories that it is indeed a breath of fresh air to see one such as Ms. Bauer shake free the shackles of closed philosophical inquiry and simply take the evidence where it leads; moreover, even *Publisher's Weekly* and other critics have said that she allows her prose to connect to the reader and *New York Times* even said her open philosophical approach could see "friends being conversant with Sophocles and Rene Descartes." This can happen when one simply drops their presuppositional standard amounting to a ball and chain attached to one's ankle and simply allows history to be open and free.

So what about her critics? Should religious text be off limits to the "serious" academic scholar or should they be included? Should they be ruled out *a priori* as so many other things that are not of a "naturalistic" flavor? Or should they be tested just as any other document of the ancient past would be? As I have said—I give no credence to "authority" unless that authority can show me where I am wrong, and they are correct on a given subject; if they do this, then I will gladly remit of my faulty premises or ideas, but without evidence for why I am wrong and why they are correct I have no reason for submitting to a yoke of passivity.

CONCLUSION

What I have hopefully been able to plausibly argue for thus far is that there is simply no sufficient naturalistic philosophy that adequately or empirically describes a great number of things in what has traditionally been called the "origin sciences." Moreover, I have hopefully made the case that this "origin science" is just as much a branch of philosophy of history than it is philosophy of science and should therefore be looked at through the lens of the historians' philosophy just as much as that of the scientists'. Philosopher and theologian Robert Stewart has summed up in an article titled "The Insufficiency of Naturalism" (in the book *Come Let Us Reason*)[114] many of the same points I have thus far discussed concerning naturalism's complete lack of explanatory scope and power concerning coherence, correlation, comprehensiveness, consistency, and commitment to the data should be relatively uncontested by my peers. What I have said thus far is mostly agreed to by even the most ardent of naturalistic supporters of a closed philosophy of inquiry. As J. B. Haldane once wrote: "If my mental processes are determined wholly by the motions of atoms in my brain, I have no reason to suppose that my beliefs are true...And hence I have no reason for supposing my brain to be composed of atoms."[115] Here the incoherence is made quite visible since there would be no way to ever know if your mental thoughts or inquiries were accurate since your cognitive faculties were simply based on naturalistic processes. Similarly as has already been discussed, there are areas such as consciousness that naturalism simply cannot adequately explain. Prominent naturalist Richard Dawkins admits:

> There are aspects of human subjective consciousness that are deeply mysterious. Neither Steve Pinker nor I can explain human subjective consciousness—what philosophers call qualia. In *How the Mind Works* Steve elegantly sets out the problem of subjective consciousness, and asks

where it comes from and what's the explanation? Then he's honest enough to say, 'Beats the heck out of me.' That is an honest thing to say, and I echo it. We don't know. We don't understand it.[116]

Even famous naturalist Richard Dawkins admits that they have no clue how to explain consciousness, but he still assures us there must be a "naturalistic" explanation we simply have yet to discover. For these reasons and more, I not only question the use of naturalistic presuppositions but find myself distrusting historians whose historic methodology is based on naturalistic philosophy.

It is reasons like these that have made many naturalists abandon their long-held beliefs. For half a century, the late Anthony Flew was the world's most famous intellectual atheist due to his belief in naturalism. Then in 2004, he made a shocking announcement: God must exist. In a headline-making reversal, Flew now holds that the universe must be the work of an intelligent designer. In an interview for *Philosophia Christi*, he added, "It now seems to me that the findings of more than fifty years of DNA research have provided materials for a new and enormously powerful argument to design."[117] More and more scientists agree with Antony Flew: The world appears designed because it is designed. They argue that the design in the world is just as real as the design in a computer chip, a car, or a sports stadium. These scientists have also observed another surprising thing: The hard empirical evidence for Darwinism is in fact very, very limited. Darwin's mechanism of natural selection acting on random variations can account for small-scale changes in living forms: variations in species themselves. But neither Darwin's mechanism nor any other purely natural mechanism explains how insects and birds came to exist in the first place. The theory is supposed to explain such large-scale adaptations, but it does not and there has not ever been one single point of evidence other than pure speculation and guessing, so I at least, am utterly dumbfounded why after 150 years since the release of Darwin's book that this theory is still taken seriously to the degree, which it claims, and has repeatedly thwarted my efforts in my field of history due to the assertion that naturalism is fact and thus I (as a historian) must adhere to its philosophy.

Having worked at the University of Arkansas' microbiology laboratories for over three years during my first undergraduate work in history, I can testify that even with the most laboring manipulation, things do not tend to organize themselves spontaneously. I realize that the naturalist could make the "special plea" to millions of years increasing the probability, but even today, the most ardent of naturalists admit that they do not know how life could have arisen spontaneously through natural processes. This however has not prevented textbooks today to proclaim that spontaneous generation of life from inorganic materials is a "fact." I will quote you from a major university's biology textbook that I picked up at random what the naturalist states as fact to students:

> Origin of Life: Today we do not believe that life arises spontaneously from nonlife, and we say that life comes only from life. But if this is so, how did the first form of life come about? Since it was the very first living thing, it had to come from nonliving chemicals.[118]

I may not be an expert in philosophy, but I am pretty sure those premises do not line up.

1. Today life does not come from nonlife.

2. The first life was early.

3. Therefore the first life came from nonliving chemicals.

How they were able to get premise 3 in the majority of university biology textbooks is mind-boggling. This is a classic example of horrible logic and reasoning within a modern collegiate textbook. Even more troubling to me is how and why the philosophy

of the social sciences feel obligated to work under the presuppositional belief that naturalism is true. Take for example a historians'
approach to causal explanations and ask yourself if you believe
naturalistic explanations (like the one above) provides a better
framework or if they simply infer the answer they wish to find:

> A good causal explanation describes all the events that
> significantly altered the probability of the occurrence of
> the event being explained. Clearly, a brief explanation will
> mention just the major causes, and a more detailed expla-
> nation will describe the minor ones causes as well. But rel-
> ative to the level of detail, all should be included. One way
> in which historical explanation can be biased is by select-
> ing just those causes which the historian has an interest in
> highlighting, and ignoring others of equal significance.[119]

I see the above example of "the first life came from nonliving
chemicals" being woefully weak in providing any evidence for a
naturalistic causation of life, much less any alternative theories
to how life could arise. Is this too much to ask? I have asked
large groups of students and professors repeatedly to give me reasons "for" naturalism and mostly what I have received is that it
is a "fact" and that reasons "for" simply are not needed. Equally
troubling is how many of my philosophy of religion and history advisors and professors have attempted to redirect any of
my inferences to the best explanation when and if they lead to a
nonnaturalistic conclusion or implication. When we compare the
origins of life against McCullagh's criteria for establishing the
most credible historic theory, naturalism as a whole comes away
very weak in explanatory scope and power, there is an enormous
amount of ad hoc assertions that must be made, and therefore
even if it is somehow true, we definitely have good grounds for at
least including an open philosophy of history which would not
exclude nonnaturalistic theories and causes. Until one can provide warrants for believing naturalism to be true and a reasonable

presupposition for all of academia to be held under via a closed philosophical system, then I will continue to challenge colleagues and peers alike to not settle for the status quo and allow the social sciences like history to operate under an open philosophical system that does not presuppose naturalism *a priori*. Moreover, I hope that one can begin to see why origins is just as important to the historian than it is to the cosmologist or biologist; while many may ask "why is a historian talking science," I think the question could be reversed. Cosmogony and therefore origins belong just as much within the umbrella of philosophy of history as it does philosophy of science.

HISTORIC EVENT 3:

ORIGIN OF CIVILIZATION
BEFORE THE COMMON ERA

Many ancient cultures around the world appear to have originated at about the same time of roughly five to six thousand years ago. They appear with an already developed high level of technical development. Pyramids, for example are not unique to Egypt, but a pyramid belt is found around the world, including the Americas and Asia. Can a satisfying and logically consistent explanation of these facts be obtained? There is a lack of evidence pointing to such a step-by-step development. Instead, each culture appears full-blown and fully developed right from its beginning.

—Donald E. Chittick, *The Puzzle of Ancient Man*

Sustainable history and the dignity of man is a philosophy of history proposed by Nayef Al-Rodhan where history is defined as a durable progressive trajectory in which the quality of life on this planet or all other planets is premised on the guarantee of human dignity for all at all times under all circumstances.[120] This theory not only goes in a complete opposite direction popularized by Samuel Huntington's *Clash of Civilizations* but against the very notion of Darwinism's "survival of the fittest" approach and instead "views history as a linear progression propelled by good governance, which is, in turn, to be achieved through balancing the emotional, amoral, and egoistic elements of human nature with the human dignity needs of reason, security, human rights, accountability, transparency, justice, opportunity, innovation, and inclusiveness."[121] Not only does this beg the moral question of "why should we act on behalf of others" but also stands completely against the philosophy of naturalism. In other words as we covered earlier, if naturalism is true, then we are simply organisms here by mere chance that have evolved relatively late as primates who have gathered a sense of contingency and will eventually become extinct in the inevitable "heat death" of this part of the universe, so "why" should we act on behalf of others and on what basis does Nayef build his philosophy of history on? Now do not misunderstand me, I at least in part agree with Nayef's philosophy, but he is still attempting to hold on to a naturalistic under-girding of history that is based on naturalism via there being a socio-evolutionary reason for history to be viewed as "linear" with human dignity and security at its heart. Nayef believes in naturalism (specifically physicalism), so I cannot see how his philosophy of history can be anything but subjective since by his endorsement of physicalism there cannot be any objectivity to morals or purpose since they are by definition "man-made" inventions so when he seeks to show history as "premised on the guarantee of human dignity for all at all times under all circumstances," we have no objective basis in which to build what "human dignity" entails since one culture may say the holocaust was "good" and some will say it was "bad"; without objectivity, we are in naturalistic relativism and thus there is no reason to seriously endorse Nayef's philosophy of history it would seem.

However, if morals and purpose are objective in their nature (nonnaturalistic), then Nayef's philosophy of history would have great plausibility, explanatory scope, and power to it. This would necessitate however that naturalism is either false or at least "most likely" false, which would thus necessitate an open philosophy of history and the social sciences. With that being said, we have reviewed origins of the universe as well as origins of life and found naturalism to be not only problematic but very weak in plausibility. Many will at this point argue that these first two fields are very difficult for the historian to adequately grasp and therefore we should not throw out naturalism too early, so I will move on to the dawn of civilization and recorded history (per se) to see if naturalism can be considered an adequate and plausible philosophy when dealing with the less ancient past and hence the field of ancient history. Again, I believe that the social sciences themselves can tell us much more about the ancient past than can a preconceived notion of naturalism driving our philosophy of established historicity.

At this point in our review of the philosophy of history, we come to a point in which we transpose from what many call "prehistory" into "history" with the advent of civilization. We have already reviewed in detail why any and all presuppositions maintaining a "closed" philosophy of history from the realm of "prehistory" should once and for all be removed due to naturalism's insufficiency in accounting for a multiplicity of prehistoric events. We have also shown why origin sciences are just as much a history as a science per se since it deals with the unrepeatable past. So what about what we normally refer to as the ancient histories of primitive homo sapiens evolving not only from simple dwellings to civilizations such as Sumer, but also the naturalistic explanation of language formation as well as writing; does a naturalistic philosophy of history adequately account for these? Having undergraduate work in history as well as philosophy of religion, I have found the explanatory scope offered by religion may in fact be greater than that of the naturalism that permeates virtually all textbooks today whereas religion is sidelined as being simply based on myth and superstition. Areas that I feel should be reviewed based on where we are as of 2013 in our review of historiography is that of:

1. Language

2. Writing

3. Civilization

4. Religion

The first thing that even the most ardent naturalist will acknowledge is that from primitive times into the Neolithic age and from Neolithic to modern civilization, each of these successions literally burst onto the scene without much if any gradualistic signs present if naturalism were true. Language, writing, civilization, and religion all seem to be in a fairly advanced stage of development all the way up until the advent of what we call modern civilization that originated in the areas usually referred to as the Fertile Crescent. We really have no record to follow or way of gauging a naturalistic viewpoint of each of these phenomena slowly progressing over time into their modern forms. Ancient Sumerian language or cuneiform writing is not less sophisticated than today's modern languages. Moreover, languages that still implore a pictogram form such as Chinese or Japanese are no more "primitive" for doing so than the modern English I am using now. In circa 3500–3000 BC, the earliest civilizations in the river valleys of the Tigris-Euphrates, Nile, and Indus emerged from Neolithic villages, which we know literally nothing about. With this, many historians infer a gradual progression of human development including domestication of plants and animals. With this, we see great organization, which included canals and irrigation systems and more advanced building and governmental systems forming. While what I have just commented on is for the most part universally agreed on by historians, what is not agreed on is that prior to this time we have anything better than an inference or assertion usually based on naturalistic presuppositions. For example, it is not uncommon to see a random date of 100,000 to 50,000 BC used to signify "when" primitive man began using fire.[122] First of all this is a very large area of error—this should at least signal the reader that what they are reading is very subjective. Moreover, it is an assertion built upon the fact that naturalism is true. While there is nothing wrong with making an assertion, we should not read this as a credible hypothesis unless the evidence is there to support it, and as we have already seen as of 2013, naturalism is most likely false so we should not allow it as the inference to the best explanation within how we conceptualize our philosophy of history.

Compare noted expert on early dynastic periods of developments John Anthony West when he comments on the early developmental periods of ancient Egypt:

> What is remarkable is that there are no traces of evolution from simple to sophisticated, and the same is true of mathematics, medicine, astronomy and architecture and of Egypt's amazingly rich and convoluted religion-mythological system. The majority of Egyptologists will not consider the implications of Egypt's early sophistication. These implications are startling. How does a complex civilization spring full-blown into being? Look at a 1905 automobile and compare it to a modern one. There is no mistaking the process of 'development.' But in Egypt there are no parallels. Everything is right there at the start. The answer to the mystery [of how civilization seems to explode into history] is of course obvious but, because it is repellent to the prevailing cast of modern thinking, it is seldom considered.[123]

Other more mainstream figures have also confessed puzzlement at the suddenness with which Egyptian civilization appeared. Walter Emery of the University of London (professor of Egyptology) commented:

> At a period approximately 3400 years before Christ, a great change took place in Egypt, and the country passed rapidly from a state of Neolithic culture with a complex tribal character to one of well-organized monarchy. At the same time the art of writing appears, monumental architecture and the arts and crafts develop to an astonishing degree, and all the evidence points to the existence of a luxurious civilization. All this was achieved within a comparatively short period of time, for there appears to be little or no background to these fundamental developments in writing and architecture.[124]

When we turn to the historical development and origin of language and writing it only seems to get worse when one attempts to understand it through a strictly naturalistic process. Director and professor at the German Federal Institute of Physics and Technology, Dr. Werner Gitt has commented: "Man's natural language is the most comprehensive as well as the most differentiated means of expression. This special gift has been given to human beings only, allowing us to express all our feelings and our deepest beliefs, as well as to describe the interrelationships prevailing in nature, in life, and in the field of technology. Language is the calculus required for formulating all kinds of thoughts; it is also essential for conveying information."[125] So the social scientist must recognize that there is simply no plausible explanation to date for explaining natural causation surrounding the origins of human speech and that should make us ask yet again "why not?" While I could cite linguist after linguist who will go into the intricate details surrounding the inner workings of human speech and how long is the leap from animalistic communication to human speech, I believe enough has been said in our "cumulative" case of showing why philosophical naturalism is not only untenable but unrealistic in reference to linguistics.

When we turn from spoken to written languages, we quickly discover that we can only speak of true *writing* when pictograms/drawings represent the spoken words of a given language through their shapes and sequencing. The spoken word acquires a temporal dimension through writing; historical traditions usually require permanent records to be kept, and the same holds for science in most communities. Various civilizations seem to have invented their own writing technique—the Sumerians used pictograms about 3500 BC, Egyptian hieroglyphics originated 3000 BC, in the Middle East cuneiform writing was in use around 2500 BC, and Chinese ideograms date from 1500 BC. With this in mind, it is important to understand that there are predominantly three kinds of writing systems:

1. Word based: Every symbol represents a word or a morpheme (ex: Chinese).

2. Syllabic: Every symbol represents a syllable (ex: Korean).

3. Alphabetic: Every symbol generally represents a phoneme (ex: English, French).

One thing that should be obvious though is that a pictogram-oriented language (such as Chinese) is no more primitive than the English I am using now to write this with. Any explanation explaining how we progressed from "no" written language to a "language explosion" where written language is common place is just as mistaken as saying that Sumerian cuneiform is a primitive writing system (just as Chinese is today) since it still utilizes a pictogram system. A naturalistic process of slow development of grunts and scribbles to a full-blown language and writing system is not where the evidence points and is thus not the best inference to the evidence it would once again seem.

So the question is: Are we being given an accurate portrayal of history based on a presupposition in favor of naturalism? What I have continued to see over and over again leads me to say "no" if we are referring to dates prior to 4,000 BC; moreover, as we will see, this presuppositional belief in naturalism not only affects our philosophy of history prior to 3,500 BC but through modern times. If naturalism is true, then I would unanimously agree, but I have yet to see any well-grounded reasons for believing it to be true through two degrees as well as my current endeavors in my masters in ancient history. For example, consider how naturalistic historians must always use words such as *explosion, bang, revolution* when attempting to describe these events. We have already reviewed the historical origin sciences concerning the origin of space/time/matter collectively called the "big bang." We have also reviewed the explosion of life referred to as "biology's big bang"; and for the explosion associated with civilization appearing with language/writing/religion already established and in place approximately 3,500 BC most history books will refer to this as the "Neolithic Revolution" or explosion. Consider how your typical history book portrays this "explosion:"

> The Neolithic Explosion was the wide-scale transition of many human cultures from a lifestyle of hunting and gathering to one of agriculture and settlement which supported an increasingly large population. Archaeological data indicates that various forms of plants and animal domestication evolved in separate locations worldwide, starting around 12,000 years ago (10,000–5,000 BC). However, the Neolithic Revolution involved far more than the adoption of a limited set of food-producing techniques. During the next millennia it would transform the small and mobile groups of hunter-gatherers that had hitherto dominated human history into sedentary societies based in built-up villages and towns, which radically modified their natural environment by means of specialized food-crop cultivation that allowed extensive surplus food production. These developments provided the basis for high population density settlements, specialized and complex labor diversification, trading economies, the development of non-portable art, architecture, and culture, centralized administrations

and political structures, hierarchical ideologies, and depersonalized systems of knowledge (e.g., property regimes and writing). The first full-blown manifestation of the entire Neolithic complex is seen in the Middle Eastern Sumerian cities (ca. 3,500 BC), whose emergence also inaugurates the end of the prehistoric Neolithic period.[126]

Again we hear the word *revolution* to describe anything that shows no signs of naturalistic evolution; when the scientist or, in this case, the historian does not understand something they simply put "bang/explosion/revolution" after it and hope no one will ask too many questions. Is this good history? I remember when I simply asked a professor of history this very question, and they could not answer any of my questions concerning what evidences they were using to extrapolate these explosions; what was directing them, and why did they happen all at once instead of gradually? I was met with silence and an angry reply that it is an "established" fact so there is no point in questioning it. As a historian in training, I simply find this methodology not only illogical but woefully naive and self-refuting. The one thing I do agree with and have found well established historically in the above quote is the last sentence concerning "the first full-blown" civilization of Sumerian cities approximately 3,500 BC. Susan Wise Bauer is honest enough to admit that any dating before Hammurabi is problematic and anything before about 2500 BC is complete guesswork by the historian, and these stories of "Neolithic explosions" may or may not be accurate as they must assume an enormous amount of contrived assertions that goes well beyond the evidence. Dr. Bauer recognizes this in her own writings and studies in which the historian is limited to the hierarchal structure that supposes "science" occupies the top chair:

> Trained in a university system where science was revered as practically infallible, historians too often tried to position themselves as scientists: searching for cold hard facts and

dismissing any historical material which seemed to depart from the realities of Newton's universe. To concentrate on physical evidence to the exclusion of myth and story is to put all of our faith in the explanations for human behavior in that which can be touched, smelled, seen, and weighed: it shows a mechanical view of human nature, and a blind faith in the methods of science to explain the mysteries of human behavior.[127]

I have studied quite extensively on early Sumerian culture and the development of language and personally own several artifacts dating back to this period. When the historian looks at the early yet advanced Sumerian civilization and then see some patterns of tradable goods and similar patterns found in ancient Egypt a century or two later, they may rightly infer that trade routes were established from the Fertile Crescent to Egypt and that Egyptian culture was in part influenced by ancient Sumerian cultures. There is no "naturalistic" presuppositions built into this; there is simply a logical deduction of the evidences we have to draw forth a conclusion. Whether it is a pre-Enlightenment mind-set that I have seen in some biblical believers that the Sumerian civilization must "not" have existed at 3,500 BC because they believe this contradicts their interpretation of when the Flood occurred or when the naturalist asserts "explosions/bangs/revolutions" to force history to meet a presuppositional philosophy they hold, history has been lost. So I am dumbfounded that many of my peers and colleagues feel that I "must" infer a naturalistic mind-set though there is no evidence to do so.

Byzantine historian Kenneth Harl, who I greatly respect, has posited many of these inferences while I was listening to him lecture on ancient civilizations when he made a few loose comments on historians being able to detect domestication of animals and plants between 11,000 and 6,000 BC and then in approximately 4,500 BC Neolithic civilizations were drawn to the lower Mesopotamian areas where then civilization exploded onto the scene. While he will readily admit these are complete extrapolations of evidence that is not there, he too is locked into a philosophy of history that must presume naturalism is true. This type of reasoning in part is why I strongly encourage historians to work within fields of origin science (at least make themselves familiar with it as well as philosophy 101) so that they too can begin to see the overwhelming problems with a closed philosophy of history and how it negatively impacts and limits historic methodology.

While jumping into a complete exegetical critique of our records and understanding of ancient civilization would take us quite far off course and be well beyond the scope of this book, we can conclude that the "explosions" concerning the development and origin of language/writing and civilization itself are very unlikely to be attributed to naturalistic causation; in other words, this does not mean "God did it," but it does mean that the historian should be allowed to explore nonnaturalistic causes while incorporating the historic umbrella of the "origin sciences" to discover more about early civilization without the confines of a closed naturalistic philosophy in its way. For example, we now know that Sumerian writing was well developed and adapted by both Akkadian and Elamite civilizations. Also figures such as the famous myth of Gilgamesh was discovered to be more than just a myth but is now recognized as an actual king of the city of Uruk around the years of 2700–2650 BC. Though the epic of Gilgamesh has many fantastical stories about very supernatural events, we would be at a great loss if we threw the entire historicity of this king out as fiction because we feel it does not fit our current mode of historic thought it would seem, and more and more historians are slowly beginning to see this. Does Gilgamesh read as a primitive story? Absolutely not—almost anyone taking world literature will find this a required read. Also a complex and well-established religious system seems to have been well in place at the time of Gilgamesh, which dates centuries before the two oldest religions of Hinduism and Judaism it would appear, so what is the best explanation for this based on naturalism? Again, if the historian is confined to "force" a naturalistic philosophy into ancient history, history will continue to become more and more jumbled and contrived with more "explosions" having to be included to attempt to describe the inexplicable.

Gilgamesh for example is recorded on the Sumerian King List as the fifth king of Uruk; this list has been found in at least seven different sources and is now considered at least minimally accurate even by the most ardent skeptic. The Sumerian King List is an ancient list originally recorded in the Sumerian language, listing kings of Sumer from Sumerian and neighboring dynasties, as well as their supposed length of kingship and locations thereof. Though I readily admit that many of the genealogies on the list are fantastically long—as an "open philosophy" of history looking at this documents origin and accuracy would force me to "not" rule it out *a priori*; instead, I would research it as well as other lists recording the same information, corroborating support (or lack thereof), and I would have discovered that this list is not entirely obsolete. Most historians with a closed philosophy in place ruled the list out in its entirety at first and only later decided that it was accurate at least in part; had they taken an open-philosophy from the onset that I am advocating, they would have came to this conclusion much earlier than they did.

However, since we know that some of the kings recorded on the list (pictured to the left) actually did live, we should not rule it out *a priori*. The list is broken into antediluvian kings and postdiluvian kings before and after a great flood. It lists eight kings before this "great flood" who reigned for fantastically long lengths of time (several thousand years) and then after the flood the lifespan/reigns diminished greatly (to around a hundred years). While the list was dismissed early on, it has since been authenticated in part with many kings post the flood being substantiated as historic figures, as early as Gilgamesh to much later ones such as Sargon of Akkad. Therefore, as an origin science or open philosophy, I see no reason why not explore the king's list with an open mind; I will be the first to admit that the idea of someone living hundreds if not thousands of years seems quite unbelievable, but since existence itself is by any probability quite unbelievable, then I do not feel this should simply be ruled out ad hoc simply because it does not match a preconceived naturalistic philosophy. Many have speculated different interpretations to these great dates as well as different meanings, which I believe is a great sign of healthiness since any origin science/history is based on unrepeatable events and cannot simply be ruled out simply based on modern modes of understanding "the present is always the key to the past." Bill Arnold, professor of Semitic languages and dean at Columbia University, noted that the Sumerian King Lists, Weidner Chronicle, Babylonian Chronicles all shed light on events discussed in the Old Testament historical books.

> Beyond obvious synchronisms with biblical historical books, these materials also illustrate the contrast between historiography in the ancient Near East and ancient Israel. The lists included here are the raw materials for history-writing. The Israelites also had such raw materials, but they moved beyond them to produce genuine historiography, with characterization, interpretive presentation of past events, multiple causal factors, etc.[128]

What can be agreed on by practically all historians as well as other social scientists is that language and writing is amazingly complex and it along with early civilization seems to have erupted onto the scene in a "bang," just like the origin of the universe and the origin of life. Ancient Mesopotamia still has many secrets that may never be discovered, but what is no secret is that its civilization burst onto the scene along with a sophisticated language/literature, mathematics, philosophy, and art; and naturalism simply does not supply the explanatory scope needed for satisfying a rigid and in-depth philosophy of history. Moreover, many historians and anthropologists alike are rethinking the way they have originally viewed religions' origins. Not only are there a growing number of evidences that monotheism may have preceded animism and polytheism, but with more archaeological discoveries such as the Gobekli Tepe of southeastern Turkey, more are agreeing that religion and its associated practices have been with mankind since their earliest origins. On a hill known as Gobkli Tepe (pictured below) in southeastern Turkey archaeologists have discovered enclosures dating five thousand years older than Britain's famous Stonehenge, (10,000–8,000 BC). Researchers agree that this religion-specific site appears to be a place of animal sacrifice and ritual and religious scholar Ben Witherington III commented in a 2013 issue of the journal on *Biblical Archaeology Review* that these megalithic enclosures certainly qualifies as a "high place," which the Hebrew Bible so often associates with religious rituals and early encounters with God. For over a century, anthropological and sociological theory has held that religion was a late development that occurred well after the hunter-gatherer stage of mankind, after civilization had been well established. This theory, however, seems to be more and more challenged with the more we continue to learn about ancient humanity.

The developments at Gobekli Tepe have led to Dr. Witherington concluding:

> For students of the Bible, Gobekli Tepe shows that religious sites and sacrifices may have already been an important part of human life at the dawn of human civilization, even before the emergence of village life. The [biblical] story of Cain and Abel presents primitive people who offer sacrifices to their God (Genesis 4:1–6). Gobekli Tepe reinforces what is clear from Israelite, Babylonian, Hittite and Assyrian cultures: Ancient religion involved sacrifices, and thus priests and sanctuaries. Both the Bible and the archaeological evidence seem to confirm that human beings were inherently religious from the very dawn of human civilization. The remarkable finds still being unveiled at Gobekli Tepe may cause something of a revolution in our thinking about the origin of human civilization and the role religion played in it. It appears this has always been true of human beings, as far back as archaeological evidences can take us.[129]

While much more could be said concerning the role of ancient religion and ancient man, I have yet to see anything in my travels from the ruins of Turkey and Greece to the ruins of Skara Brae (Orkney Islands Scotland) to have any real confidence in the naturalistic explanation that the origins of religion are to be inferred as simply a later part of human psychological development that occurred well after the supposed Neolithic "explosion." The evidences we have at present do not support this hypothesis.

ORIGINS OF ANCIENT CIVILIZATION

Our journey has now taken us from the very beginnings of space/time/matter through the assertion of an antiquated form of Darwinian Naturalism that entails everything from cosmology and cosmogony to early civilizations can best be described through naturalistic philosophies. Within this paradigm, the points of criticism and question are wholly acknowledged for the most part by even the most ardent of naturalistic proponents as being woefully lacking in any empirical type of evidence as well as containing a very low level of explanatory power/scope or plausibility. Similarly, we have seen that a naturalistic assertion of early civilization is also highly improbable since it leaves more questions unanswered than it provides answers for. We have no evidence of early hominids gradually learning language through a system of grunts/groans nor do we have anything more than loose inferences showing that early man slowly developed working civilizations. What we do have is a remarkably complex language system seeming to come into existence with no real understanding of how or why. Likewise, we see the early civilizations of Mesopotamia rapidly forming slightly ahead of Egypt with a lot of key features already well in place—basic language, writing systems, law code, and creation myths of God(s) already loosely in place. While I will be the first to admit that under a strictly "closed philosophy" of naturalism, slow gradualistic change from simple to complex is the best inference to the data, it is definitely "not" the best inference of the available data when we allow an "open philosophy" of understanding and inquiry.

For the reasons I have outlined thus far (amongst countless others) we are beginning to see a louder cry against such "enforced" naturalistic philosophies, which has not only led some longtime naturalists like Oxford's Anthony Flew to reject naturalism and even Richard Dawkins to embrace agnosticism. However, this has really came to light since the turn of the millennium with over 800 PhD scientists publicly signing the "*Scientific Dissent from Darwinism*" statement, which confirms most of what I have stated thus far. Signers of the Scientific Dissent From Darwinism hold doctorates in biological sciences, physics, chemistry, mathematics, medicine, computer science, and related disciplines from such institutions as Oxford, Cambridge, Harvard, Dartmouth,

Rutgers, University of Chicago, Stanford, and University of California at Berkeley. Many are also professors or researchers at major universities and research institutions such as Cambridge, Princeton, MIT, UCLA, University of Pennsylvania, University of Georgia, Tulane, Moscow State University, Chitose Institute of Science and Technology in Japan, and Ben-Gurion University in Israel.[130]

Since everything I have so far documented is relatively uncontroversial, the majority of my peers at this point will most likely agree, but they may challenge as to what philosophy should take the place of naturalism. This is somewhat of a mute and obvious point; regardless of what philosophy is to replace it, one should not continue adhering to one that is by most likely hood false. That is why I continue to argue for a nonrestricted/nonconfined open philosophy of inquiry in the natural as well as social sciences; I would also like to use a readily accessible example of a competing social science view of origins that can easily be compared and contrasted to naturalism. While I am in no way trying to "assert" a religion or philosophical view as empirically true information, by using the Bible as a potentially historic source of information, it will allow us to do the following:

1. Look at one competing view against naturalism—since under a closed philosophy presupposing naturalism one is obviously forbidden from challenging it or offering alternatives

2. Practice origin science as a history falling into the philosophy of history umbrella when utilizing an "open philosophy" vantage point

3. Check to see if the Bible (a religious source) provides greater explanatory scope/power than naturalism

4. Lastly, to see if historians such as Susan Wise Bauer should be ruled out of context *a priori* for using the Bible as a viable source of history since most religious texts are

ruled out by default since by their definition they are usually "nonnaturalistic" in their scope

Inevitably, many critics as well as many peers will attempt to circumvent everything I have said thus far and now make an elementary school attempt to simply disqualify me for trying to "assert my own religious biases." Though this is to be expected anytime one's own philosophical "closed" view of reality and life are challenged, I have been around long enough to ignore such attacks if they are not grounded in (non ad hominem) established facts that refute the points I have made and offer stronger points for their own philosophy that I am unable to refute. I gladly welcome open and public debate on any of these topics as I am no stranger to the debate field. What we are seeing amongst even ardent naturalists like Thomas Nagel in his recent work *Mind and Cosmos: Why the Materialist Neo-Darwinian Conception of Nature Is Almost Certainly False* is that though he is an ardent atheist, he does believe that naturalism as I have so far outlined it is false. I highly respect Dr. Nagel's courage to follow the evidence where it leads and thus arrive at agreement with what I have outlined so far in regards to the falsity of naturalism to explain even in principle:

1. The emergence from a lifeless universe of the staggeringly complex life on earth in such a short time

2. The development of such an incredible diversity of highly complex life-forms from first life in such a short time.

3. The appearance of conscious beings from brute matter.

4. The existence of objective reason and value and the existence of creatures with the sort of faculties apt for grasping objective reality and value and being motivated by value.[131]

What Nagel's 2012 work shows is that basically he agrees with everything I have so far outlined, but he rejects the notion of theism based on two points.

1. We should not go outside of the universe and seek and explanation for something.

2. Secondly, Nagel readily admits that he does not want theism to be true, and he simply cannot bring himself to believe it. [132]

I believe Nagel dismisses theism too prematurely. In the case of theism, we have the factors of natural theology already mentioned but also have what I believe is historically valid evidences for divine intervention based on a nonnaturalistic open philosophy of history. Once we begin to review these evidences along with natural theology, it becomes less plausible to set aside such a deity in explaining things of interest to Nagel just because it involves nonnaturalistic intervention. I believe this opens up valid grounds to review the historic credibility of the Judeo-Christian scriptures for historical plausibility; if they fulfill the historic validity of a worldview more than does naturalism (as Nagel admits is very implausible and weak in explanatory scope/power) then it should be added back into the historians' toolbox of live options instead of ruled out prematurely.

ORIGINS OF THE HEBREW RELIGION

It is ironic that prior to the seventeenth and eighteenth century one could literally be killed for challenging the closed philosophy of the church and today one can be (academically) killed for challenging the closed philosophy of naturalism. While I am equally against a church-led "closed philosophy" just like I am a naturalistic "closed philosophy," it does highlight a unique problem touched on at the beginning of this book concerning how limited any closed philosophy is in all areas of academia. When nontheologian Werner Keller wrote his agnostic viewpoint fifty years ago in his book *The Bible as History*, he not only took an open philosophical view of history but quickly sold ten million copies and was praised by his "following the evidence where it lead without forcing a contrived theology or a naturalistic one"[133] by skeptics and nonskeptics alike. This too is the viewpoint that I wish to take when comparing the Bible philosophically and historically to that of naturalism. While I readily admitted from the onset that I am a Christian theist, I also readily admit I have no preconceived alliances to any denominational guild nor do I endorse what I have often referred to as "church-ianity" in other published works. Having degrees in the fields of history and philosophy of religion (both from secular schools), coupled with my current masters of arts in ancient history should help me to take a similar approach of a "nontheologian" like Werner Keller and explore the world of the Bible and see if Susan Wise Bauer's (and those who use the Bible as viable history) critics are correct in their criticism against using the Bible as not only viable history, but as a viable world view.

As we transition into the origin of the Hebrew religion, many will ask if religion and metaphysics is a necessary conclusion as we transition into the historicity, or lack thereof, for the Bible. Questions to take into consideration include: At what point did religion evolve into the minds of the early humanoid race? Though religion can be traced back as far as the history of mankind, most naturalists believe this mechanism also can be explained by naturalistic evolution. How does naturalism account for the origin of religion? Most naturalists simply hold to religion as being man-made, created to help society create a purpose for living and striving, a cause greater than themselves. Though there is much evidence against it, most naturalists hold to a view that religion began animistic in nature (worshipping physical entities such as plants, animals, the sun, etc.) and then evolved into polytheistic and/or pantheistic religions and ultimately late in the game groups such as the ancient Israelites brought a type of monotheism into existence. Moreover, most naturalists hold that religious texts such as the Hebrew Scriptures that make up today's Old Testament Bible were created far from the time of the events they record are highly inaccurate in most cases and are of minimal historic value. But the question (again) is: "Is this an accurate assessment/hypothesis supported by the evidences?"

As previously noted, Thomas Nagel admits naturalism cannot adequately account for many of the features we see today and thus is quite weak in explanatory power, scope, and plausibility as an all-encompassing worldview. The next question is whether or not the biblical literature can account for the same criteria with a greater range of explanatory power, scope, and plausibility than naturalism based on the criteria we have reviewed.

WHY THE BIBLE?

People often ask me, "Okay then...I get that philosophy and science better support what you are saying concerning nonnaturalistic causation and even a form of deism perhaps, but why Christian theism and the Bible?" I usually approach this in a twofold approach; first of all, I am not approaching the subject material as a theologian attempting to convince one to think the way that I think; secondly and more importantly, the Bible does qualify as one of the oldest nonnaturalistic explanations of existence, and it is the only account written as an actual "history" and therefore it can be tested for its own accuracy opposed to other ancient religious accounts that are written in poetic or ritualistic monologue as opposed to a historic account. Also of interest to the historian is the Bible's account of origin science/history. The Bible provides its own answers to the subject of origins; origins of the universe, humankind, language, civilization are all discussed in the biblical account, which allows it to be testable by the same measures I earlier tested the competing views of naturalism. Finally, if the Bible (holistically) is the oldest religion in which offshoots of Montanism, Islam, Mormonism and others have been derived from, then it is worth investigating why well over 50 percent of the world's population is still influenced by this account today. While the historian cannot conclude definitively that the account is holistically accurate, they will be able to determine if it meets the criteria of plausibility, less contrived, greater explanatory scope/power, and so on than the competing naturalistic views. If it does, this should at least warrant a consensus for an open philosophy of history (including origin sciences as a history) over that of the current closed one. So the first place to begin would be with the historiography of the Bible itself to attempt to determine whether the biblical nihilist, minimalist, maximalist, or inerrantist is the most accurate position concerning the historicity of the Bible.

The four basic categories that could be used in approaching the historic texts of the Bible could be broken down as follows:

- Biblical nihilist—one who believes the Bible contains no true credible historic content.

- Biblical minimalist—one who believes the Bible has very limited credible historic content.

- Biblical maximalist—one who believes the Bible has much credible historic content.

- Biblical inerrancy—one who believes the Bible has complete credible historic content and is inspired by the ultimate reality (God).

For our purposes as far as the philosophy of history is concerned, we will limit our scope to the first three of these to discover on the same grounds of historic methodology used for evaluating any historic source, which of these three categories the Bible falls into and whether it should be included as not only a maximally trust-worthy historic document as Susan Bauer and others contend but also if it can be considered as more plausible in the areas of origin science/history than the competing view of naturalism that we have broken down already. For the biblical nihilists' view-

point to be accurate, the Bible should be inaccurate and fantastical in what it reports and therefore fail on all grounds of historic
plausibility. To qualify in the biblical minimalist camp, it would
have to be partially accurate but mostly inaccurate; and finally to
qualify in the biblical maximalist camp, it would need to be mostly
accurate in what it records. If it is to be a stronger qualifier for
established philosophy of history, it would need to be superior to
the current closed philosophical system built on naturalism that
currently directs our philosophy of history. If it is, then it follows inescapably that not only our current mode of philosophy of
history should include an open philosophy that does not presuppose naturalism and does not rule out nonnaturalistic worldviews,
such as the Bible, for discussing origin as well as ancient histories,
but such histories should be included in the historians' toolbox of
ideas and hypotheses.

Julius Wellhausen (May 17, 1844–January 7, 1918) was a
German biblical scholar and could be described as a biblical nihilist. Wellhausen is noted by most historians for his contribution to
the scholarly understanding of the origin of the first five books of
the Bible (Torah). He is credited with being one of the origina-
tors of the documentary hypothesis; his work *Prolegomena zur
Geschichte Israels* (*Prolegomena to the History of Israel*) is a detailed
synthesis of existing views on the origins of the first six books of
the Old Testament. Wellhausen's contribution was to place the
development of these books into a historical and social context
based on his belief that naturalistic philosophy is true and must
presuppose our interpretation of the Bible as a whole. The result-
ing argument, called the documentary hypothesis, remained the
dominant model among biblical scholars until late in the twentieth century. His documentary hypothesis (which stated that the
first five books of the Bible were authored by at least four authors
and written quite late in history well after the events they record)
was based on what was seen in his day as the natural evolution of
religious practice.[134] This hypothesis though mostly abandoned

by serious scholarship is still supported on a popular level by Karen Armstrong and countless other naturalistic historians as well as the media in their attempt to explain the Bible in light of the evolution of religion and humankind. The question arises however, "Is this an accurate viewpoint for historically understanding the Bible?"

No section of the Old Testament literature has been more fiercely debated than that of Genesis 1–11 (which deals with the creation of the universe, consciousness, life, and civilization). Though there have always been debates concerning the accuracy or lack thereof on Genesis 1–11 in regard to science, history, and geography; for the most part it was considered a prime authority regarding the origins of the world and humankind until the end of the eighteenth century. In the 1820s, Old Testament interpreters were challenged by the findings of geologists who argued that the world was much older than was implied by the Old Testament figures. Many orthodox interpreters responded to the geologists that the Flood had simply destroyed or distorted the original layers of the earth and the geologists were therefore misled in their conclusions. As already mentioned, the next large challenge came in 1859 with Charles Darwin's publication of *Origin of Species*, which along with geological findings challenged Genesis' account of the origin of humankind and the notion of a "Fall" from a near perfect state; instead, Darwinian naturalism argued that humankind had gradually evolved from elementary life-forms, and there was thus never a "Fall" or Golden Age of humanity.[135]

So the question remains whether or not Wellhausen's nihilist viewpoint of the Old Testament is accurate or not since it is still highly influential today. We have already reviewed in depth why naturalism is a very weak hypothesis on nearly every level of explanatory power and scope for accounting for any origins but this does not of course mean that the Bible is to be ruled "accurate" by simple default. If we review the Old Testament in the same light we did the theory of naturalism, we can at least discover if it is a coherent worldview that meets the historic and origin criteria of Dr. McCullagh's list for testing historic (and in our instant origin science), hypotheses and their credibility.

1. The hypothesis, together with other true statements, must imply further statements describing present, observable data.

2. The hypothesis must have greater explanatory scope than rival hypotheses.

3. The hypothesis must have greater explanatory power than rival hypotheses.

4. The hypothesis must be more plausible than rival hypotheses.

5. The hypothesis must be less ad hoc than rival hypotheses.

6. The hypothesis must be disconfirmed by fewer accepted beliefs than rival hypotheses.

7. The hypothesis must so exceed its rivals in fulfilling conditions 2–6 that there is little chance of a rival hypothesis, after further investigation, exceeding it in meeting these conditions.[136]

Again, though the criteria for establishing historicity may differ slightly from historian to historian, they each are very closely related to Dr. McCullagh's above list which is of course not exhaustive as nothing within the confines of "origin science" or "history" is, but gives us a good guide to judge by. So the question is should the Bible be ruled out as a possible explanation of existence as I and many other historians have been told today? I believe if the Bible as a whole meets the above criteria greater than that of naturalism not only should it be allowed as a source of historicity (whether minimalist or maximalist), but it should be an even more ardent reason for adopting an open philosophy of history in the historic sciences but should also really call into question the methodology we have used for the last 150 years for assessing ancient history.

The first immediate question that comes to mind is how will we judge the very ancient source and form criticism used for the composition of Genesis 1–11 and then for the rest of the Bible without using a modern twenty-first-century lens to do so? While this will be a great challenge, I will attempt to analyze the Genesis 1–11 account in the same manner we reviewed naturalistic hypotheses concerning the origins of the world, life, humankind, analysis of the stories of the patriarchs and kings into the New Testament period and gauge these in the same manner that we did with naturalism. Therefore, we will be reviewing the Bible on the following six bullets to see if its philosophy of history better meets McCullagh's criteria than philosophical naturalism:

- Philosophical plausibility
- Origins—universe, life, humanity
- Direct and indirect primary sources
- Historical scrutiny of the story of Israel through the Davidic Kingdom
- Fall of Israel and exile
- New Testament period

By not daring to take on the hat of the "theologian," I will only be touching on these bullets at a very high level through the hat of the historian as well as by utilizing our new methodology of origin (historic) science, which should allow us to competently judge if the Bible is a credible source of history or as Wellhausen and many others today believe has absolutely no credibility at all. Please note—the point here is not to "prove the Bible true" per se, but instead, it is to show how an open philosophy of history should work when the belief in a closed philosophical view presupposing naturalism is removed to allow the historian to make the inference to the best explanation, not just the inference to the best "naturalistic" explanation as Wellhausen and others have done.

ORIGINS OF THE UNIVERSE

Genesis 1–11 is often described as myth; if we define myth as a story about the gods, Genesis 1–11 is not a myth. It is true that these chapters tell of the involvement of the God of Israel with the origin and earliest history of the world and humankind, but there is nothing comparable here to what we find in Sumerian, Akkadian, and Greek myths where many gods are present, often in conflict and disagreement, and struggling for ascendancy. If, however, we mean by myth a story set in the beginning of time—a time different from that of the storyteller but one in which the conditions of the storyteller's own time were established once and for all—then Genesis 1–11 can be described as a myth.[137] Concerning the origins of the universe we will compare the biblical account by the same criteria that we previously did against naturalism:

1. Whatever begins to exist has a cause
2. The universe began to exist.
3. Therefore the universe has a cause.

Having reviewed these premises already against naturalism, it is important to review them against a nonnaturalistic source such as the Genesis account.

The Bible begins in Genesis 1:1: "In the beginning God created the Heavens and the earth." In Hebrew, there is no word for *universe* so in the Hebrew language if one wishes to represent the totality of physical reality they would use "heavens and earth" ("Burah" in Hebrew). Notice there is no battling gods, dragons, or preexisting materials; in this, the Genesis account separates itself from all of ancient creation accounts in representing "creation ex nihilo" or creation out of nothing. While the vast majority of Old Testament critics support the concept of creation ex nihilo from the Hebrew script of Genesis today, it was not until Claus Westermann's exhaustive studies of ancient Hebrew that a consensus was formed that not only did the Genesis account speak of creation out of nothing but that it was in fact the only such ancient creation narrative to do so.

Dr. Claus Westermann was an Old Testament scholar. He was born on October 7, 1909, in Berlin. Prof. Westermann taught at the University of Heidelberg from 1958 to 1978, and he died on June 11, 2000. Westermann is considered by many as one of the premier Old Testament scholars of the twentieth century. Particularly notable in his work is his lengthy and comprehensive commentary on the Book of Genesis, especially Genesis 1–11. Concerning the opening lines of the Genesis account, there are several keys to ancient Hebrew that Westermann has dissected and which are mostly agreed upon by scholars:

There is no evidence of a subordinate clause—"bara-shee burah elohim" (in the beginning God created).

- The oldest translations we have render the translation as an independent clause (Septuagint and Masoretic Text as well as Dead Sea Scrolls all reference "in the beginning" as an absolute beginning point).

- The Hebrew connecting word *waw* (and) has been universally accepted as a direct connecting factor connecting Genesis 1:1 with 1:2 reemphasizing a complete creation ex nihilo: "In the beginning God created the Heavens and Earth 'and' the earth was without form and void."[138]

So we do have an account of "creation ex nihilo" only in the Genesis account of ancient cosmogony; an account that was used against it when cosmologist held to an eternal universe that has simply always existed. While this account is not used to necessitate the existence of God (which is outside the realm of history), it is more plausible and less ad hoc than that of naturalism.

1. Whatever begins to exist has a cause.

2. The universe began to exist.

3. Therefore the universe has a cause.

4. The cause must transcend creation of the universe (be outside of it).

5. The only causation outside of space/time/matter is a transcendent being or abstract object.

6. Abstract objects do not have causal relations or powers.

7. Therefore a transcendent being (God) brought the universe into being ex nihilo.

8. Only the Bible records of just such an event occurring.

9. Therefore, the Bible is accurate concerning the origin of the universe via creation ex nihilo.

Again—if the premises are true, then their conclusions logically follow. While this is just scratching the surface, we can logically conclude that Genesis 1:1 is a logical inference to the best explanation of the evidences over that of naturalism. There could be any number of other possible explanations but for our purposes Genesis 1:1 does best fit with the known evidences while naturalism goes against it. So at least in its opening lines the biblical account has shown no reason to be ruled out of the historians' toolbox.

As mentioned earlier, agnostic astronomer Robert Jastrow who held the same seat as Edwin Hubble seems dumbfounded by this same conclusion in his book *God and the Astronomers*:

Now we see how the astronomical evidence supports the biblical view of the origin of the world....the essential elements in the astronomical and biblical accounts of Genesis are the same: the chain of events leading to man commenced suddenly and sharply at a definite moment in time, in a flash of light and energy.

Consider the enormousness of the problem: Science has proved that the universe exploded into being at a certain moment. It asks: 'What cause produced this effect? Who or what put the matter or energy into the universe?' And science cannot answer these questions.[139]

TO DESIGN OR NOT TO DESIGN?

Obviously, if Genesis 1:1 is a logically plausible theory, then it only goes to reason that the apparent design we see in the universe, the cell, and life itself may actually contain design (not just apparent design). Similarly, the question of consciousness, information theory, and moral values would be quite coherent with the concept of a transcendent being that brought reality into existence and serves as a foundation point in which to set objective moral values upon whereas naturalistic theories simply cannot to date account for consciousness, information origins, or objectivity to moral values and can only speculate as to "apparent" design that is really not design at all even though it appears to be. Therefore we have a strong explanatory theory on design, specified complexity, information/consciousness theory as well as "why" and "how" morals can be objectively true.

Moreover, we also have a concession of points within creation concerning origins. The key to understanding creation in the Old Testament is the word *order* according to Philip Davies and John Rogerson of the university of Sheffield England.[140] To say that the world is created is to say that it is ordered: divided into various sectors to each of which belong appropriate life-forms. The origin of the universe, origin of life-forms (plant/animal life), humankind, a Flood, scattering of peoples/languages/diversity, and the beginnings of history (post prehistory), all are collectively itemized in the Genesis account. This may at first sight seem so obvious that it is hardly worth mentioning; however, in the light of other worldviews of antiquity, it is quite striking. There is no place in this scheme for the gods that we find in Sumerian and Akkadian stories. We find nothing concerning chaos monsters of the seas; the seas and their life-forms in Genesis 1 belong entirely to this world and have no supernatural powers. Thus, the rather obvious (at least to us) order implied in Genesis 1 is significant in what it omits; it portrays an order of things entirely subordinate to one God.

But this carefully constructed narrative has a further aim—to order time as well as life-forms and their respected sectors. The ordering of time into blocks of seven days, of which one is a day of rest, while so familiar to us, was unique in the ancient world so far as we know. Even if it was not unique, it was an important way of organizing time into manageable blocks, and it was a further way of asserting God's sovereignty over the created world. By observing a day of rest (later known as the Sabbath), the Israelites would both imitate God and remember that he was the author of time itself.[141]

Regardless of whether Moses wrote the first twelve chapters of Genesis or this was a compilation of an older tradition of oral communication, the fascinating piece to me as a historian is that all of these ancient tablets and stories are telling a very similar story which would be expected if there is some truths in them. Though there are many ancient writings that we still do not know how to translate, of the ones we do we see great consistency in reoccurring themes concerning:

- Creation by God(s)
- Separation from God(s)
- Antediluvian series of kings/persons who lived/ruled for long periods of time
- A great flood that separated pre/post flood world

- A scattering of people groups and languages
- History beginning in the Mesopotamian regions of the Middle East

What is quite telling about these stories is that they not only share so many common parallels but that they are mostly agreed to by even the most ardent naturalistic anthropologist or physical historian. These overlapping ancient histories can help us gauge shared commonalities between the Genesis account in the Bible with that of other ancient origin histories (the Eridu Genesis, Enki and Ninhursag, Enki and the Ordering of the World, Enki, Ninmakh and the creation of Humankind, Epic of Atra-khasis, Enuma Elish, Baal Cycle, Heliopolis Pyramid Text, Memphis Creation Story, Epic of Gilgamesh, and the list goes on). The question lies as to whether these are simply coincidental in nature or if they are telling the same ancient story that has changed over time. For example, we have already discussed the Sumerian King List that has been discovered and correlates quite similarly with that of the persons/dynasties of Adam through Noah from the Genesis account. Moreover, as of the mid twentieth century most archaeologist have confirmed that there is enough evidence for a great flood in the archaeological strata to warrant that a massive flood did occur in the areas of Mesopotamia in the ancient world. While some may debate feverously that this flood is global in scale, the sedimentary rock strata does confirm that the world was at one point underwater (there if much disagreement when this occurred and if it was all at the same time); the point being that even the most skeptical of persons will admit that a flood on a grand scale did indeed occur and this is why well over two hundred flood legends from around the world are shared by most cultures. A very similar flood legend shared by the majority of ancient cultures makes this the closest thing the historian has to a "universally recorded history," which makes it even harder to ignore.

The existence of the flood traditions all over the world seems to be consistent with the Genesis account as Nozomi Osanai and others have continued to bring to light. While a naturalist can argue that the flood legends from around the world exist simply because flooding has occurred in most parts of the earth at one time or another. However, the detailed nature of the widely spread statements has too many common elements to yet again be placed in the category of "coincidence." In fact, even people who live far from the sea or in mountainous areas have flood traditions, which are similar to the Genesis account. For instance, the Pawnee tribe in Nebraska has the following tradition: the creator Ti-ra-wa destroyed the first people, who were giants, by water because of his indignation about their corruption and after that he created a man and a woman like present people, who became the Pawnees' ancestors. In addition, the Miao tribe who resides in southwest China had a tradition, which is like the Genesis account even before they met Christian missionaries. According to their tradition, when god destroyed the whole world by the flood because of wickedness of man, Nuah the righteous man and his wife Matriarch, their three sons, Lo Han, Lo Shen, and Jah-hu survived by building a very broad ship and embarked on it with pairs of animals. Furthermore, their genealogy records as follows: "The Patriarch Jahphu got the center of nations. The son he begot was the Patriarch Go-men."[142] The following is the analysis of over two hundred flood traditions from all over the world and what percentage of commonality each share with one another:

- Is there a favored family? 88%
- Were they forewarned? 66%
- Is the flood due to wickedness of man? 66%
- Is catastrophe only a flood? 95%
- Was the flood global? 95%
- Is the survival due to a boat? 70%

- Were animals also saved? 67%

- Did animals play any part? 73%

- Did survivors land on a mountain? 57%

- Was the geography local? 82%

- Were birds sent out? 35%

- Was the rainbow mentioned? 7%

- Did survivors offer a sacrifice? 13%

- Were specifically eight persons saved? 9%[143]

Thus, 95 percent of the above totals concerning these traditions have common elements with the Genesis narrative concerning the Flood. Although it is impossible to study all of the flood traditions around the world here, it seems to be very historically certain that a flood of some type (global or local is irrelevant at this point) did happen and does offer further credence to the Genesis account and therefore it seems reasonable to think that the Genesis account is consistent with the secular historical records and the existence of the flood traditions around the world. Nonreligious motivated explorer and sociologist Graham Hancock has written extensively on the subject and believes that the case can be made for a global flood as being the one area of ancient history that is global in its historicity. Did over two hundred various cultures just dream up this same story by coincidence?

> Flood Legends turn up in Vedic India, in the pre-Columbian Americas, in ancient Egypt. They were told by the Sumerians, the Babylonians, the Greeks, the Arabs and the Jews. They were repeated in China and south-east Asia, in prehistoric northern Europe and across the Pacific. Almost universally, where truly ancient traditions have been preserved, even amongst mountain peoples and desert nomads, vivid descriptions have been passed down of global floods in which the majority of mankind perished.

To take these myths seriously, and especially to countenance the possibility that they might be telling the truth, would be a risky posture for any modern scholar to adopt, inviting ridicule and rebuke from colleagues. The academic consensus today, and for the century, has been that the myths are either pure fantasy or the fantastic elaboration of local and limited deluges—caused for example by rivers overflowing, or tidal waves. Not all mainstream academics toe this line. But amongst those who don't it seems to have been generally agreed that almost any explanation, however harebrained, is more acceptable than a simple literal interpretation of the myth of a global flood—i.e. that there actually was a global flood or floods. My guess is that such thinking will not much longer survive the steady accumulation of scientific evidence which suggests that a series of gigantic cataclysms, exactly like those described in the flood myths, changed the face of the earth completely between 17,000 years ago and 8000 years ago.[144]

Hancock sees himself as a journalist who asks questions based upon observation and as someone who provides a counterbalance to what he perceives as the "unquestioned" acceptance and support given to orthodox views by the education system, the media, and by society at large. I wholeheartedly agree with this "open philosophy" point of view and believe Hancock (whether right or wrong) is allowing for the evidences to speak as opposed to mere orthodoxy.

Similar to the plausibility surrounding the various Flood Legends, the vast majority of naturalists confirm that humankind did indeed share a common language, as the Bible states, in the ancient past as well as confirming that the first civilizations did spring up in Sumer, the Indus Valley, and then into Egypt (as the Bible describes). The point being is that the Genesis account does record a well-balanced holistic record for a plausible inference; Genesis 1–11 does meet the criteria for a nonnaturalistic account of the history of origins of the universe and of being from nonbeing.

When moving into the tenth chapter of the book of Genesis, we find an area that seems to be quite accessible to the historian concerning the genealogy of humankind. Even higher critics have often admitted that the tenth chapter of Genesis oftentimes referred to as the "table of nations" is a remarkably accurate historical document, which accounts for the genealogy of all nations from a post-flood narrative. There is no comparable catalog of ancient nations available from any other source. It is unparalleled in its antiquity and comprehensiveness. Dr. William F. Albright, who was known as the world's leading authority on the archaeology of the Near East (and himself did not believe in the infallibility of the Bible) said concerning the Table of Nations in Genesis 10: "It stands absolutely alone in ancient literature, without a remote parallel, even among the Greeks, where we find the closest approach to a distribution of peoples in genealogical framework...The Table of Nations remains an astonishingly accurate document."[145]

Here we find the one link between the historic nations of antiquity and the prehistoric times pre-Noah and the antediluvians recorded in Genesis. While many other than Dr. Albright have studied the Table of Nations, I stumbled across a research document by Bill Cooper of the United Kingdom called *After the Flood* where Cooper painstakingly provides genealogical sketches, documented manuscripts, and much more to trace the Sons of Noah to the Chinese, the Aryan race of India, the European cultures, etc., from this Table of Nations:

> The test I devised was a simple one. If the names of the individuals, families, peoples, and tribes listed in the Table of Nations were genuine, then those names should appear also in the records of other nations in the Middle East. While I would have been quite content if I could have vindicated 40% of these; today I can say that the names so

far vindicated in the Table of Nations make up over 99% of the list, and I shall make no further comment on that other than to say that no other ancient historical document of purely human authorship could be expected to yield such a level of corroboration as that![146]

While a historian could still say these are not 100 percent certain, they would likewise have to admit that as of today they have yet to be refuted for their historical and genealogical accuracies so far tested which I too find quite astonishing though I readily admit this would just get us as far back as the times "after" the supposed great flood, it does not address the times before the alleged flood addressed in the Sumerian King List narratives. Again, I am not endorsing a theological stance for how to interpret the generations themselves or how long they are suppose to be, but I do see a cumulative case that the Genesis account does coincide to a very high degree of historicity.

When we read Genesis 11:1–9 (concerning why there are different languages and the formation of the Jewish Nation), we see an explanation (thus providing explanatory scope) for why these nations were scattered into different groups after this great flood and eventually how languages changed in the event known as the Tower of Babel. There is considerable evidence now that the world did indeed have a single language at one time. Linguists also find this theory helpful in categorizing languages. Sanskrit was the classical language of India, and today is considered the primary bridge between Hebrew and other Semitic languages, and the Greek/Phoenician and Latin of Western civilization. Gothic, Celtic, and Persian/Farsi languages also are now known as the Indo-European family of languages. But the similarities are not confined to this family. Wayne Jackson stated that the ancient languages of Assyria and Egypt had much in common with those of the Maya and Inca peoples of the Americas. Language scholars were rapidly concluding that all languages had a common root in the 1970s. Even secular scholars now admit that all languages did come from one common root just as the Bible describes (though this of course does not necessitate the Tower of Babel story, it definitely does not seem to refute it either). From here we see the Genesis account unfolding with the calling of a particular nation and a particular man in Abram (later to be known as Abraham), to lead his people toward the land of Canaan and thus the story of the Bible unfolds with Abraham, Isaac, Jacob, and the twelve sons/tribes of the eventual land known today as Israel. So the next question would be of the historicity or lack thereof concerning the era normally referred to as that of the Patriarchs. It should be noted however that though the majority of evidences supporting a potential historicity of Genesis is circumstantial, this circumstantial evidence is much more highly qualifying as a historic hypothesis than that provided by naturalistic hypotheses. Therefore, it is important to note that two kinds of evidence will play their part in my further breakout of the biblical texts in searching for historicity: explicit/direct and implicit/indirect evidences. Both are valid, a fact not yet sufficiently recognized outside the various and highly specialized historic disciplines of ancient history, Egyptology, subbranches of archaeology, epigraphy, etc. Explicit or direct evidence is the obvious sort that researchers prefer, but implicit or indirect can be equally powerful when used correctly as the historian of ancient history is well acquainted. It must be noted however, at this point the philosophical and scientific origin cosmogonies, which are not merely circumstantial, at least allow for the possibility of the Genesis account while ruling out (or at least making very unlikely) a naturalistic one.

THE ERA OF THE PATRIARCHS

Archeological excavations of the biblical city of Ur (home
of the Patriarch Abraham) at Tell el-Mukayyar, Iraq.

When we get past Genesis 1–11 and begin reading the stories of Abram (Abraham), the acclaimed founder of Judaism,
Christianity, and Islam, many historians since the time of
Wellhausen have concluded that nothing can be known about
any part of Genesis but this is a gross exaggeration that stemmed
from Wellhausen's naturalistic presuppositions that guided his
philosophy of history as well as many others today. As professor emeritus of Egyptology and research fellow at the School of
Archaeology in Liverpool, England, K. A. Kitchen has repeatedly confirmed that the last two hundred years (especially the
last fifty when archaeology has become more of a scientific discipline) researchers have been able to reach back ever deeper in
time exploring long-abandoned ruins, tablets, monuments, and

so on to bring the past ever more to life to the modern historian. In Syria, Mari yielded twenty thousand tablets of the eighteenth century BC, which we are still in the course of publication; Ebla, Ugarit, and Emar have yielded more besides. To the north, the Hittite archives as published so far fill over one hundred volumes of cuneiform copies. (With that being mentioned, it should be noted that in the early twentieth century many historians questioned whether the Hittite civilization even existed, noting it as an invention of the Bible). From Mesopotamia—rank upon rank of Sumerian, Babylonian, and Assyrian tablets fill the shelves of the world's major museums. Egypt offers acres of tomb and temple walls and a myriad of objects inscribed in her hieroglyphic script. And West Semitic inscriptions continue to turn up in the whole of the Levant. These we know about, but a myriad other untouched mounds still conceal these and other material sources of data totally unknown to us and wholly unpredictable in detail. Sadly much has been destroyed beyond recall across the centuries; this we shall never recover and never learn its significance. But these are "authentic" primary sources, real sources which, once dug up, cannot be reversed or hidden away again. The one caveat is that they be rightly understood and interpreted, which is not impossible, most of the time. The question is if the biblical narratives are historically credible as a growing number of historians are beginning to believe or if those like Wellhausen believe, a naturalistic-closed interpretation is to be preferred.[147]

As I have attested previously, my point is not to attempt to "prove" the biblical record as exhaustively accurate but to simply show that it should not be ruled out *a priori* and that it is a much more credible mode of both origin history as well as human history "if" one is not presupposed to a naturalistic philosophy. If this is correct, then we should hope to see even more like Susan Bauer, Wayne Keller, and others not only being allowed to exhaust the modes of historic inquiry but be allowed to follow the Socrates adage of "taking the evidence wherever it leads" even if that means the Bible. With that being stated from the outset, I will now switch from "origin history" to proto-historic methodology still adhering to the seven points of testing historic theory to see if there is enough established historicity within the Bible (at a very macrolevel) to allow and encourage its usage and testing at a more microlevel above and beyond that of simple naturalistic tendencies, which are presupposed to a biblical nihilist stance or at the very most a biblical minimalist viewpoint of historic events.

The first thing that is readily admitted by the historian is that the further back into the past we go the less our knowledge and evidences are and the more inferences to the data must be made. So the question once again becomes: "What is the best inference based on the data we have?" When dealing with the period of the patriarchs of the Bible, the historian of course would prefer explicit/direct information as noted above, but inexplicit/indirect is the vast majority of what any ancient histories consist of. For example, when dealing with the patriarchs, we have such indirect and extrabiblical evidences as:

- Social Customs and Covenants
- People groups—Amorites, Hurrians, Hittites, etc.
- Personal Names
- Geography
- Political conditions
- Battles

While these six points are only a broad-based list of indirect sources that the historian may use to confirm the historicity of a particular subject matter, these six will in our very macrolevel approach allow us to confirm if the events surrounding the patriarchs are at least plausible in their explanatory scope or not.

We are told in Genesis 11:31 that Terah took his son Abram; his grandson Lot, son of Haran; and his daughter-in-law Sarai, the wife of his son Abram; and together they set out from Ur of the Chaldeans to go to Canaan. But when they came to Harran, they settled there. From here, the Genesis 12 narrative picks up and discusses this "call" for Abram to leave the city of Ur and set out as the Father of the Jewish Nation. Abraham left a city called Ur then went into Egypt due to a famine (in Genesis 15:19 different people groups are mentioned—the land of the Kenites, Kenizzites, Kadmonites, Hittites, Perizzites, Rephaites, Amorites, Canaanites, Girgashites, and Jebusites.) Abram has a child with a slave woman Hagar to which he had a son but did not give his inheritance, Abraham was tested to sacrifice his son, his son Isaac becomes the father Jacob who in turn has twelve sons which become the twelve tribes of Israel, and one of those sons (Joseph) became a person of importance in Egypt, and this is where the Patriarch narratives end. If these accounts have historic plausibility, then we should at least have indirect evidences supporting all of these accounts as well as accurate portrayals of personal names used (such as Abram/Abraham). This is where one establishes either historic plausibility or lack thereof within the Patriarchic narratives.

For example, we have many documentary cuneiform tablets of the Middle Bronze Age containing specific types of covenant protocol that is specifically unique to the second millennia BC so we should expect some correlation between these and that of the patriarchal period if they are truly of that period. Middle Bronze Akkadian tablets show five elements for covenants: witness or deity, oath, stipulation, ceremony, and curse for breaking it (in that order) whereas later covenants of the late Bronze Age contain seven elements. The Genesis accounts of oath and covenant found in Genesis 21, 26, and 31 all share the same element and same order of the older Middle Bronze Age, which at the very least shows that the covenantal practices of the patriarchal period does match well with this older period (2100–1700 BC) and not the later Bronze Age (1550–1200 BC) as Wellhausen and others have and continue to suggest.

One area of historic documentation that helps the historian to compare and contrast similar laws/customs and codes with that of the Bible and the time setting in which they are allegedly written is the Code of Hammurabi. The Code of Hammurabi (approximately 1760 BC), is a well-preserved Babylonian law code, and one of the oldest deciphered writings of significant length in the world. When compared to many of the patriarchal accounts given in Genesis, we find a great deal of commonality. For example, the Code of Hammurabi requires a man's first wife, not that of his female slaves, to be given primary treatment in inheritance. Moreover, the Abraham of Genesis had resigned himself to the situation that Eliezer of Damascus, "one born in my house (ex: the son of one of his slaves) is mine heir" (Gen. 15:2–3). This statement is consistent with the practice of adoption as outlined in the Code of Hammurabi and other more ancient codes. Therefore, in the mind of Abraham, adoption of a child born to one of his slaves presented an acceptable cultural solution to God's promise as it was stated in Genesis 6:2–3.

In addition, the insistence of Sarah, Rachel, and Leah for their husbands to bear them children by their handmaids is consistent with the cultural custom that is described in the Code of Hammurabi (paragraphs 144 and 146). As written in the Code, it is apparent that the practice was common prior to the time of Hammurabi; however, his code protected all parties involved in this arrangement. Paragraphs 159–161 of the Code address fair treatment of the "purchase price" for a bride in the event the prospective groom or father-in-law should change his mind about the marriage. Although there are some differences, the practice of a purchase price or dowry is consistent with what we find in Genesis 24:10, 53 where we find Abraham's servant went in search of Isaac's prospective wife with "all goodly things of his master's in his hand," and then giving Rebekah and Rebekah's mother and brother precious things. The practice of a "purchase price" being paid to the father of the bride is especially notable in the case where Jacob, when he did not have possession of a "purchase price," was forced to work for Laban for two consecutive seven-year periods to satisfy the "purchase price" for Rachel and Leah (Laban's daughters).

Another point of historic consistency for the historian would be the record of slaves prices recorded in the Genesis account and beyond. For example, we have a number of well-documented sources over a period of about two thousand years that show what slave prices were at various points in time. If these are accurate secular sources, then they should match the biblical account if the biblical account is of that period. For example, we have a 2,300 BC Akkadian tablet recording the price of a slave at ten silver, another one (Lipit-ishtar) showing the price at fifteen silver, and by 1750 we have the Code of Hammurabi listing the price of a slave at twenty silver, which is the exact amount shown in the Genesis narrative for the price of Abraham's great-grandson Joseph (Genesis 37) is twenty shekels of silver, which fits the dates given in the Bible accurately. We later see the slave price recorded by Moses at thirty shekels of silver, which is also confirmed within the Nuzi Tablets of the same period that states slave prices at thirty silver. Though these points are merely scratching the surface of other available data, there is enough to conclude that there is at least some historic plausibility to the social customs and covenants recorded in the book of Genesis accounts to the times in which they infer they were written.

Another key feature for the historian to inquire into would be that of personal names used for example are the names of Abram/Abraham, Ishmael, Sarai, Isaac, Jacob, Esau, Labon, etc., of the Middle Bronze Age and Semitic? Historians universally agree that they are and that these names while still used were much less popular by the Late Bronze Age. From the sources at our disposal (such as the eighteenth century Yakov-Her scarab, Egyptian execration texts, Dilbat, Mari, and Ebla tablets) we are able to confirm that these type of stylized names found in the Genesis account comprised about 16 percent of names in the Middle Bronze Age compared to only 4 percent in the Late Bronze and 2 percent by the Iron Age. While this of course does not conclusively put the names into the Middle Bronze Age it does fit well within it. Moreover, the above mentioned Mari letters (as one quick example) not only reveal that such Semitic names exist, but these letters also support the recorded war in Genesis 14 describing five kings who fought against four others. The names of these kings are now seen to fit with the prominent nations of the day such as the Amorite king Arioch in which the Mari documents refer to as Ariwwuk. All of the evidences available support a conclusion that the source material of Genesis may have come from firsthand accounts during the time of the Middle Bronze Age. Lastly, domestication practices are also in alignment with known facts of the Middle Bronze Age though there were (and still are) many historians in the past before numerous archaeological discoveries that believed that the domestication of the camel was not until the later Bronze Age and therefore a sign that the Patriarchal narrative may have been out of place. The vast majority of these alleged anachronisms seem to be without warrant today as I have been unable to find any of them still left unrefuted by findings since the mid 20th century.

Similarly in 1927 Leonard Woolley identified Ur Kaśdim with the Sumerian city of Ur, which many historians had doubted its existence in the past in regard to the Patriarchal narratives involving the home of Abraham as recorded in Genesis. The Mesopotamian city of Ur, also known as Tell al-Muqayyar, was an important Sumerian city state between about 2100–1750 BC. Located in southern Iraq, on a now-abandoned channel of the Euphrates River, the city dates from the Ubaid period approximately 3750 BC and is recorded in written history as a city state from the twenty-sixth century BC. When Leonard Woolley excavated in the 1920s and 1930s, the city was a tell, a great artificial hill over seven meters high composed of centuries of building and rebuilding mud brick structures, one stacked on top of another. The ruins cover an area of 1,200 meters northwest to southeast by 800 meters northeast to southwest and rise up to about 20 meters above the present plain level. Although there may still be a few who question the exact relationship between Abraham and Ur, it is historically accurate to a consistent degree when combined with the above mentioned criterion.

CONCLUSIONS FOR THE HISTORICITY OF GENESIS

Dr. Paolo Matthiae, Director of the Italian Archeological Mission in Syria, "hit an archeological jackpot" in 1975. He discovered "the greatest third-millennium BC archive ever unearthed." It included "more than 15,000 cuneiform tablets and fragments" and unveiled a Semitic empire that dominated the Middle East more than four thousand years ago. Its hub was Ebla, where educated scribes filled ancient libraries with written records of history, people, places, and commerce.[148]

These early tablets display an ease of expression, an elegance that indicates complete mastery of the cuneiform system by the scribes," said Dr. Giovanni Pettinato, former epigraphist of the Italian Mission, who worked closely with Dr. Matthiae. "One can only conclude that writing had been in use at Ebla for a long time before 2500 B.C.[149]

The Ebla tablets verified the worship of pagan gods such as Baal, Dagan, and Asherah known previously only from the Bible. They mention the name "Abraham" and "Ur of Chaldees" (the Biblical Abraham's birthplace) as well as other familiar cities and places:

The names of cities thought to have been founded much later, such as Beirut and Byblos, leap from the tablets. Damascus and

Gaza are mentioned, as well as two of the Biblical cities of the plain, Sodom and Gomorrah. ... Most intriguing of all are the personal names found on the Ebla tablets. They include Ab-ra-mu (Abraham), E-sa-um (Esau)....[150]

Over the years there have been many criticisms leveled against Genesis and the Old Testament as a whole concerning its historical reliability. These criticisms are usually based on a lack of evidence from outside sources to confirm the biblical record. Since it is a religious book, many scholars take the position that it is biased and cannot be trusted unless we have corroborating evidence from extrabiblical sources. In other words, it is guilty until proven innocent, and a lack of outside evidence places the biblical account in doubt.

This standard is far different from that applied to other ancient documents, even though many, if not most, have a religious element. They are considered to be accurate unless there is evidence to show that they are not, which should immediately beg the question "why?" Although it is not possible of course to verify every incident in the Bible of course, the discoveries in archaeology since the mid-1800s have demonstrated the reliability and plausibility of the biblical narrative, and it is simply hypocritical to simply rule out the historicity of any document based simply on an *a priori* prejudice against it. Therefore I must agree with Emeritus of Egyptology and archaeology K. A. Kitchen's assessment of Wellhausen's biblical nihilist approach, whose philosophy of history is still followed by many (if not most) historians today when he comments:

> We are compelled, once and for all, to throw out Wellhausen's bold claim that the patriarchs were merely a glorified mirage of/from the Hebrew monarchy period. For such a view there is not a particle of supporting factual evidence, and the whole of the foregoing indicative background material is solidly against it. It should be clear, finally, that the main features of the patriarchal narratives

either fit specifically into the first half of the second millennium or are consistent with such a dating; some features common to that epoch and to later periods clearly must be taken with the early-second-millennium horizon. In contrast, the old Wellhausen-type view is out by the horde of contrary facts unearthed since 1878 and 1886. We have here the Canaan of the early second millennium and not the Hebrew monarchy period, in any wise. The oft-stated claim of a 'consensus' that the patriarchs never existed is itself a case of self-delusion on the data presented here; we do not actually need firsthand namings of the patriarchs in ancient records; plenty of other historical characters are in the same case. The tombs of Early, Middle, and Late Bronze Canaan nymity (no texts) does not render them nonexistent. What is sauce for the goose is sauce for the gander.[151]

In conclusion it should be reiterated that I have only skimmed the surface of the Genesis narrative to see if a nihilist or minimalist viewpoint is warranted for evaluating the Patriarchal narratives. First of all, I am not a biblical historian or archaeologist so I am unqualified in assessing every nuance of biblical exegesis; however, as a historian who specializes in philosophy and ancient history, I can assess the Genesis account at a macrolevel to conclude if there is at least enough historical evidences to render it as a reliable historical account worthy of further investigation. What I have found is that not only is the Wellhausen viewpoint of biblical nihilism unwarranted, it is blatantly false. If we are to hold other ancient historicity to the same criteria that the biblical nihilist or even minimalist does, we find that literally no evidence can count for establishing historical thought concerning ancient and classical history, which is obviously fallacious. Moreover, we find the "origin science/history" found within the Genesis narratives' cosmogony to be without comparison philosophically or historically. It not only gives the only ancient account literally founded on creation ex nihilo but also given an origin story for information, language, humankind, and civilization itself; but its historical account of the Patriarchs fits well with what we know concerning the Middle Bronze Age period both sociologically as well as geographically. From a strict attempt to assess the incredibly elusive ancient past, there is nothing more the historian can hope for in attempting to establish credible historicity and the Genesis account seems by all means to accomplish this. While this by no means "proves the Genesis account" to be completely accurate, it does force us to omit the biblical nihilist position held by Welhausen and many scholars today; moreover, it forces us far beyond the position of the biblical minimalist putting us somewhere between itself and the maximalist position. The only real way I can see for not concluding this is if I have a philosophy of history based against it; but as we have already seen, there seems to be no plausible reason for maintaining this type of closed philosophical view of history.

THE ERA OF MOSES AND JOSHUA

PBS ran a "Pro-Wellhausen" documentary in 2008 called *The Bible's Buried Secrets*. Not only does it demote Abraham and his descendants to the realm of mythology, it also dismisses the Exodus and denies any written Old Testament record prior to the sixth century BC. As a historian, I truly am dumfounded when I see such misreporting of facts and evidences; I understand that artifacts and evidences will have a level of interpretation made on the part of the historian, but how one can completely have such a closed philosophy of history in place that forces them to ignore such blatant evidences in which I have only touched on a few is cause for alarm. How can one set of historians look at the evidences I have touched on for example and conclude that the biblical nihilist is still accurate historically while another set can agree with my hypotheses in its entirety? This truly is a case for concern in my opinion and what is normally found in these type documentaries is that PBS who normally takes a very naturalistic philosophy in all of their programming will choose a historian that may have very "radical" or "extreme" theory, and if this theory fits the group's philosophy who is putting it on, they will purport it as completely factual evidence, which the layman will simply assume is accurate. We have seen this in such areas as Dan Brown's *The Da Vinci Code*, in which I sadly heard many layman comment "I wonder if that is true?" But have you ever asked yourself why PBS or any of these areas do not take their theories to the debate field? If two groups have radically different views, then I believe an open debate is the best way to flush out implausible versus plausible theories. Let us not forget that before the discovery of the Dead Sea Scrolls in the 1940s many historians pushed for many of the Old Testament biblical narratives being written in the first century AD. So the question as a historian yet again is to determine whether the events concerning the Exodus and entry into Canaan are historically plausible more so than their negation; again this will be at a macrolevel simply so one can see how an open philosophy of history operates.

Again my point here is not to cover or establish any type of biblical narratives in any great detail (nor is it to move into the realms of theology); my point is to simply look at a very macrolevel approach in how normal questions should be addressed from a naturalistic "Wellhausen-like" approach and how a historian (following an open philosophy) can address these concerns that potentially include:

- A lack of Egyptian texts describing the events of the Exodus events.

- Absence of evidence for a strong Egyptian influence on early Israelite culture.

- No material evidence of the forty years of wandering.

Typical explanations that I feel are inadequate for addressing these concerns have included:

- Egyptians would not record embarrassing events.

- Israelites would not have adopted or retained Egyptian culture because they were slaves there and wanted to distance themselves from it.

- Remains of nomadic cultures are never preserved (example: the Bedouins).

While these explanations are at least in part most likely accurate, they simply leave us in the same situation as naturalistic history that simply asserts "the Bible is a nonnaturalistic based world view; naturalism is true; therefore the Bible is false history." In other words though I find the naturalistic enforcement begging the question at practically every corner, I find the above explanations lacking in explanatory scope to the skeptical questions being asked. In other words, if the Exodus/Moses accounts are historically plausible there should be indirect evidences for:

- Presence of Israelite slaves in Egypt before 1446 BC.

- Presence of the Israelites in Canaan after 1400BC.

- Semitic "Yahweh worshippers" wandering on the way between Egypt and Israel.

The first thing to be admitted is that while the facts are not definitive, they are interesting. One must remember that there are basically three groups to be briefly discussed here that overlap with one another.

- Asiatics

- Semitics

- Israelites

Asiatics, as their name implies, could be any group of Asian descent or geographical locations. Semites (based on Semitic language groups) could include any number of groups such as Akkadian, Aramaic, Hebrew, Arabic, Canaanite/Phoenician, Amorite, Eblaite, Ugaritic, Sutean, Chaldean, Mandaic, Ahlamu, Amharic, Tigre, and Tigrinya among others. And of course Israelite would be the Hebrew people groups recorded in the Bible who worshipped Yahweh. So Semites were Asiatics but not necessarily Israelites and so on. Asiatics could therefore be Israelites but not necessarily of course. So the question is, are there historic/archaeological evidences for Asiatics, Semites, or Israelites in Egypt before the alleged Exodus date of approximately 1446 BC? Is there any evidence of their presence Canaan after 1400 BC? Are there any material evidences for their supposed wanderings between Egypt and Canaan? These three questions will not give us definitive answers of course, but they are historically assessable to such a degree that documentaries such as the above mentioned PBS one is either grossly confused or they are actually recording distorted information based on their closed philosophy of history that necessitates religious text like the Bible are false historically regardless of the evidences. I simply see no other options because the historical information we have is fairly straightforward.

From an ancient historiography perspective, there are moderate amounts of evidence of Asiatics in the Nile Delta (Tel el Daba) including:

1. The style of architecture from Northern Canaan

2. Series of large distinctly Asiatic Statues

3. Various tombs containing Asiatic weapons

4. Numerous findings of Middle Bronze Age Canaanite pottery

5. Numerous ceremonial artifacts that are Asiatic in form

Egyptian textual evidences include the Beni Hasan mural (Middle Egypt, 1870 BC) which is a mural that shows a caravan of people from Syro-Palestine visiting the governor (pictured above). Called *Aamu* in the hieroglyphic inscriptions but commonly referred to as Asiatics by Egyptologists today, they were known to regularly cross the Sinai from Canaan into Egypt—but seldom visited this far south. Both the biblical Patriarchs and the Beni Hasan Asiatics traveled from the same region (Syro-Palestine) to the same region (Egypt) during the same period (twentieth–nineteenth centuries BC). While no one proposes these are the Israelites, it is the right people, the right places, and the right time to offer greater insights into the world of biblical characters. Similarly, the Speos Artemidos inscription has been described as a type of global address, an historical source of unmatched importance, setting out Hatshepsut's (1508–1458 BC), political agenda early in her reign. Her program as king focuses on elements important to every ruler; her people, her commercial interests, and her military. Hatshepsut's inscription functions as pious dedication, as an outline of her accomplishments and of future political aspirations. This was an important decree, the purpose of which was Hatshepsut's presentation as predestined savior of the country, restorer of law and order, and legitimate descendant of the sun-god Amen-Re.152 It does indirectly confirm that there were Asiatics living in the Delta in Avaris and not worshipping the sun god Ra during this period. The eighteenth dynasty document Papyri Leningrad 1116A, Leiden 348 and Harris records the building of public projects by slaves—some Asiatic and Semitic, which is quite similar to what is portrayed in Exodus 1:11: "So they put slave masters over them to oppress them with forced labor, and they built Pithom and Rameses as store cities for Pharaoh." Likewise, texts such as the tomb of Rekhmire, Louvre leather roll and papyrus Anastas III, shows Semitic slaves as builders and brick makers with a quota to fill under task masters in sixteenth to thirteenth century; the 1740 BC Brooklyn Papyrus 35.1446 lists seventy-seven slaves in Egypt; at least thirty of these names are Northwest Semitic, many are Hebrew: Shiprah, Menahem, Issachar, Asher, Aqob, etc. Lastly, the historian knows from Egyptian records that Semites held positions from lowly slave all the way to chancellor. Most slaves in Egypt during the New Kingdom were females, Asiatic, with a high percent having Semitic names—while this of course does not necessitate that the biblical account is true, it does mean that there were Semitics in Egypt serving mostly as slaves during the time frame as the Exodus account records and which PBS negated to mention.

While this is just a handful of finds that help shed light on the biblical narrative, my point is not to go into detail on each of these items as many archaeologist have already done nor is it to show that the Bible is theologically true but to show how historically speaking there is more than enough historic evidences to build a very compelling case for the historicity of the biblical narratives if our philosophy of history is not closed and therefore allows for it. More Israelite-specific finds have also been found that PBS must have also mistakenly overlooked, which include a distinctively Israelite four-room pillared house plan discovered and excavated at Avaris, Egypt. This type of structure (Horseshoe dwelling, which is a prototype of Israelite dwelling) is most common in Israel through the Iron Age times and specifically Israelite in nature. Not Canaanite, not Semitic, but specifically Israelite in the Nile Delta.

Moreover "if" the Exodus from Egypt was at 1446 BC then entry into Canaan should be around 1406 BC and this is the direction that the historical record seems to point—three quick examples include:

1. Canaanite records (Late Bronze Age) between 1400–1200 BC show a period of culture and power change; sedentary Canaanites conquered by new inhabitants. We can actually see a transformation in Canaan that begins taking place during this time that virtually no historian completely denies though some will argue the timing, but giving them a two-hundred-year gap virtually all are in agreement of the transformation that was taking place at this time in Canaan.

2. Amarna Letters of the fourteenth century BC refers to raids and conquest of several Canaanite cities by a group known as the "Habiru." Habiru is a term used for nomadic people from all over the Ancient Near East it seems. While Habiru "might" be a derivative of "Hebrew," it is inconclusive as most historians agree; either way, the Habiru activities do match those of the Hebrews recorded in the Exodus, and Joshua accounts and therefore provides a great deal of circumstantial evidences to the events of "groups of people" raiding and conquering cities/villages throughout the Canaanite landscape in the same period that the post-Exodus and Joshua time frame would have been occurring.

3. The Merenptah Stele (1209 BC) records an attack on areas in Canaan by Pharaoh Merenptah. This stele mentions Israel as part of the settled peoples of Canaan. Canaan

as a land comprised three cities of Ashkelon, Gezer, and Yano'am—Canaan is described as the "People of Israel," which implies that Israel was the dominant nation in Canaan by this time. The "People of Israel" are listed as one of nine main enemies of Egypt. Obviously if by 1209 BC we see the people of "Israel" described not only as the dominant peoples in Israel but also as one of the main enemies of Egypt, it appears unlikely that Israel would have just arrived there as a nation calling into question Israel being a small nomadic tribe or a late dating for Exodus events.

There are even a sizable amount of indirect evidences that would have occurred during the nomadic wanderings from Egypt to Canaan as well including several Egyptian monuments referring to "Ta shasu Yahweh" (Land of the nomads of Yahweh) with some as early as 1400 BC. Similarly, inscriptions place these nomads in Moab, Edom, and Southern Jordan, which is a hugely significant find, showing that the Egyptians had enough of an impression of this people group for them to call them out in 1400 BC as "Nomads of Yahweh."

Though I have purposely only dedicated a few pages and a few points of historic comparison to that of the first five books of the Bible, as a historian, there is ample evidence already to indicate there was a migration of Israelites from Egypt to Canaan about the middle of the fifteenth century BC, otherwise known as the Exodus. Even skeptical historian George Mendenhall acknowledges:

> Too many problems, and too few solutions, are created by the assumption that these biblical traditions are complete fictions. The Exodus narrative simply diverges too much from too many of the well-known conventions of ancient fiction writing. In other words, no one has yet explained why Israelite fiction writers would create a narrative about Israel's origins in this particularly unusual way, inventing

a character named Moses and fabricating a plotline such as the exodus.[153]

While the historian cannot conclude the parting of the Red Sea of course, the biblical plagues, or the presence of Yahweh, they can, given the indirect evidences provided by textual criticism and archaeology, conclude that there is historic plausibility found within the Genesis and Exodus stories. Enough evidence is provided to rule out the "guilty until proven innocent" (and sometimes guilty no matter what) motif of Wellhausen and PBS; whether it was a religious text of any culture, it greatly alarms me as a historian that the "limited" powers of modern "academia-media" can blatantly leave out and manipulate evidences in order for a closed-naturalistic philosophy to be promoted and kept in its current hierarchical place of academic thought as PBS and many others wish to promote even if it means a falsification of facts.

JOSHUA'S CONQUEST AND ENTRY INTO CANAAN

Jericho Excavation

According to the biblical narratives, before entering Canaan, God commanded the Israelites to drive the Canaanites out of the land and to settle it (Numbers 33:50–53). With Joshua as their leader, the Israelites begin the conquest of Canaan by destroying and burning Jericho on the west side of the Jordan River (Joshua 6:1–21). The next city the Israelites destroy by fire is Ai in the central hill country (Joshua 8:3–28). The third and final city the Israelites under Joshua burn and destroy is Hazor in the north (Joshua 11:10–14). During the Judges period, the Israelites slowly gain control over more of Canaan. Each were specified as being destroyed by fire—this should make it easy for archaeologists to find burn layers since they are one of the most easily attestable and datable sources within archaeological science and thus for the historian to be able to reconstruct a narrative in order to test the validity of the biblical one. Again, we will only be covering the most macrolevel of details that are mostly uncontested in order to see if the narratives portrayed in the Bible concerning the entry into Canaan and eventual setup of tribes into villages in a pre-monarchical setting is historically accurate as well as plausible.

There is really no doubt where Jericho is located—three main excavations have been made—the first by Austro-German Ernst Sellin and Carl Watzinger in 1907–1909 and 1911 and the second by British John Garstang in 1930–36 and the third by Kathleen Kenyon in 1950–58. All three agree to the following points:

1. The walls of Jericho were impressively fortified.

2. The outer stone retaining wall held a steep plastered glacis.

3. The topping this was an upper red-mud brick wall estimated 4.5 feet thick and 12 feet tall.

4. Jericho's wall fell outward and created a ramp into the city. (Not a typical siege in which walls fall inward)

5. Excavations indicate the city was destroyed by fire.

6. Immediately inside the walls, houses of mud brick were built into the walls. (Joshua 2:15 reports the same level of specificity)

7. Many jars of grain were left intact. (Joshua said not to take spoil.)

8. Cypriot Pottery—1400 BC quite common is found in excavations (Kathleen Kenyon's excavations did not reveal this pottery but has since been reconfirmed as well as the early excavations prior to Kenyon had confirmed).

9. Egyptian scarab seals of Hatshepsut (1508–1458 BC), Thutmose III (1481–1425 BC), and Amenhotep III were excavated by Garstang from Jericho's cemetery. These Pharaohs were alive from 1500–1406 BC.

When we compare the biblical narrative with what we know from secular archaeology we find several areas in which the biblical narrative appears to be historically accurate even in minute details:

- Jericho was a strong, fortified city with walls and a gate. (Joshua 2:7, 6:5)

- The attack occurred after spring harvest (Joshua 3:15, 5:10).

- Full grain stores found in excavation, indicating destruction soon after harvest.

- The walls collapsed outward (Joshua 6:20).

- The city was not looted. Numerous full jars of grain found intact. Israelites forbidden to plunder Jericho. (Joshua 6:17)

- The city was destroyed by fire (6:24). Excavations reveal a conclusive destruction layer about three feet thick.

- The conquest of Jericho dates to 1406 BC (1 Kings 6:1, Joshua 5:6). Evidence from pottery and scarabs at Jericho date destruction to the period.

When considering the second city, Ai, there are only three real possible suggestions with only one (Kirbet Maqatir) fitting the geographical requirements of occupation, the timing and destruction by fire, but this one is currently under excavations so we really have no concluding evidences on this city to date. The last and largest of the cities Hazor was destroyed by fire; Late Bronze Age II palace or temple has been excavated from this site with evidence of destruction by fire. Canaanite and Egyptian statues of gods have been found with their heads and limbs hacked off indicating a possible connection with early Judaic monotheistic values in which they were instructed to destroy idols. Amara letters state Labaya, leader of Schechem, gave the territory to the Habiru. Similarly Joshua (8) states that the Israelites took this area peacefully. Destruction evidence from key Canaanite cities (Jericho and Hazor) in Late Bronze I period coupled with contemporary extrabiblical references to nomadic invaders in Canaan and the presence there of the Israelites confirms the "main" elements of the biblical account of the conquest as recorded in the Joshua and Judges biblical narratives.

As is evident by the manner in which I covered only the most basic facts, historic methodology can make quick and calculated affirmations based on evidences. For example, I have built a cumulative case against naturalistic/closed philosophy of history/origins early on followed by a brief break down of the first seven books of the Bible and have shown that nothing we see thus far from its narrative seems to be incorrect. There are of course more microlevel details subject to further research, but as I have debated many times in the past, the biblical narrative is stronger in every way than that of naturalism on origins and historic plausibility. This does not mean the Bible is accurate necessarily, but it does mean it is more plausible than the naturalism that guides all current modes of academic thought and philosophy today, and this is my main contention. Of course this may have theological and philosophical implications, but it is the very philosophy of history and origins and the freedom to pursue this evidence wherever it leads that is the focus of my work as I have repeatedly stated (I feel it is necessary to overemphasize this point).

Critics of the Bible have long claimed that the Bible's statements in Joshua about the conquest of Canaan in the time before the monarchy of King David were pure fiction. In light of this new type of archeological evidence critics are being forced to reconsider their rejection of the Bible's record of Israel's conquest as stated by Joshua. In the book of Joshua (6:5), God told Joshua, "When you hear them sound a long blast on the trumpets, have all the people give a loud shout; then the wall of the city will collapse and the people will go up, every man straight in." Even this "miracle of history" seems to be confirmed by archaeology. Professor John Garstang found and recorded his amazing finding, "There remains no doubt: the walls fell outwards so completely that the attackers would be able to clamber up and over the ruins into the city."[154] The evidence from all other archaeological digs around ancient cities in the Middle East reveal that the walls of cities always fall inwards as invading armies push their way into the city. The significance of this is that virtually no walls of a city fall outwards during a siege; however, the Bible records that these walls did in fact fall outwards and that is exactly what we see based on archaeological evidences. Does this means "God exists" in and of itself? Of course not, but it does mean that the accuracy of this siege seems to be well documented in microlevel detail so that we can verify its accuracy by archaeological data today. Moreover, if many of the micro details are accurate, then it is plausible that the macro details may in fact be accurate as well (unless we have verifiable reasons that they are not), thus providing a good deal of "explanatory power" within its historical credibility.

Both the book of Joshua and Judges recount the story of Israel's settlement in the land of Canaan and their first couple of centuries in the land describing both the early Israelites entry into the land and eventually how a group of leaders, chieftains, or judges led isolated Israelite groups. The narratives describe the various leaders of some of these groups as well as the intertribal conflicts that divided them. There are some archaeological discoveries that seem to support a hypothesis of a rapid conquest by Joshua including excavations at some of the cities of Hazor, Lachish, Debir, and Eglon that indicate these cities experienced massive destruction and then resettlement just as the Joshua narrative describes. Similarly, the cities mentioned specifically as not being destroyed shows no archaeological signs of such destruction. However, what we see more evidence of is that the group of Israelis was a smaller federation of tribes that were not unified in any real sense of the word until the monarchy of Saul. Though there are references to "all Israel" and that "Joshua took all the land" (Joshua 11:23) and so on, we also see that at the time of Joshua's death there were many people groups that were still unconquered (Joshua 13):

> When Joshua had grown old, the Lord said to him, "You are now very old, and there are still very large areas of land to be taken over." This is the land that remains: all the regions of the Philistines and Geshurites, from the Shihor River on the east of Egypt to the territory of Ekron on the north, all of it counted as Canaanite though held by the five Philistine rulers in Gaza, Ashdod, Ashkelon, Gath and Ekron; the territory of the Avvites on the south; all the land of the Canaanites, from Arah of the Sidonians as far as Aphek and the border of the Amorites; the area of Byblos; and all Lebanon to the east, from Baal Gad below Mount Hermon to Lebo Hamath.

So what can we conclude concerning the historicity of the Joshua/Judges account? Are the nihilists or maximalists correct?

In between these two extremes are biblical scholars and historians who evaluate the actual biblical texts to the best of their abilities in order to understand what the texts themselves communicate. Using both the methods of historical investigation as well as the tools of biblical study, they have attempted to understand the biblical texts on their own terms apart from the dogmas and ideologies of either side.[155]

This is therefore more of an issue of historiography; in other words just because a historic account of the ancient past does not match perfectly with the same historic method we use in the twenty-first century does not make it "non-history." In other words, in the same way we cannot judge a non-Western culture by Western culture values, we also cannot fully apply twenty-first century historic methodology to analyzing whether ancient history is "real" history or not. We know that the Joshua account is plausible, the nation of Israel did formulate into some type of confederation prior to the Davidic Kingdoms, that the cities described as occupied/destroyed/burnt do show signs of archaeological accuracy so the only real question of historic debate would be the holistic sweeping attack by Joshua on a mass versus a small scale. This is still (and should be) debated on the evidence, but as far as "history" goes we of course cannot prove that it was "God" that pushed the walls down, nor that "God" made time stop for a day, but neither should these narratives disqualify the Joshua account as anything but historic in nature and scope.

In conclusion, what may we fairly say concerning the period of Joshua and Judges at a macrohistorical level? Historic scholar K. A. Kitchen assures us that at a macrolevel the accounts of Joshua and Judges meets McCullagh's criteria for historic justification in light of it being less ad hoc, matches well with present observable data, and has good explanatory scope/power:

> A whole series of features ties the contents and styling of
> Joshua and Judges to known usage in the 2nd millennium,
> besides other realia not thus chronologically fixed. All of

this favors the authenticity of the Joshua-Judges narratives, regardless of the final date of Joshua and Judges as books. Likewise does the physical archaeology, once the common but erroneous dogmas about those books are discarded, as they have to be on a straight reading. We have almost all the mentioned places in the Joshua narratives, and list of kings, attested as inhabited in Late Bronze II; Jericho's top levels are long gone, Ai is a question mark. The gradual expansion east to west is mirrored in the central Canaan surveys in pottery patterns. The sudden presence of many more people in Iron IA after Late Bronze II favors new folk having come in—but neither by outright conquest nor by invisible infiltration, nor just a few tax dodgers. In short, along with many other details, there is no valid reason for denying the basic picture of an entry into Canaan, initial raids and slow settlement, with many incidental features that belong to the period, and transmitted in tradition into the books that we have now. None of the aforementioned features could be simply invented without precedent in the seventh century or later.[156]

With this being said, may the Susan Bauers of the world continue to confidently (until given historically plausible justification not to) use the Joshua narrative as an accurate source for how the Israelite people groups entered into the land of Canaan.

THE ERA OF THE KINGS

In the late nineteenth century, critical scholar Julius Wellhausen (again) claimed the biblical chronology of the kings of Israel was a literary invention for religious purposes, which had been edited and revised several times from a variety of different sources, rather than a genuine historical record.[157] Based on Wellhausen's naturalistic interpretation, for the next seventy years, critical scholars continued to treat the chronology as historically worthless and irreconcilable.[158] So is it possible that Wellhausen and the various critical scholars are wrong? One thing we can agree on is that one side is wrong (unless you believe in relativism of course). Both might be wrong but definitely both cannot be right. Wellhausen's entire critique of the Bible was based on the philosophical extrapolation that "naturalism is true"; however, if naturalism is not true, then Wellhausen is most likely false and that is exactly what the majority of historical evidences points to today. In 1951, biblical scholar Edwin Thiele published *The Mysterious Numbers of the Hebrew Kings*, a harmonization of the biblical record of the kings of Israel. By the time of the second edition, it was recognized that Thiele's work was a significant breakthrough in establishing the historical validity of the biblical chronology.[159]

Though criticisms have been made of Thiele's chronology, its value and general validity have been acknowledged widely. It remains the typical starting point for study of the chronology of the kings of Israel and Judah with few modifications and has been applied successfully in other fields of Ancient Near East study, such as the chronologies of Assyria and Babylon.[160] The reliability of the chronologies in 1–2 Kings has been supported by archaeological evidence; Grabbe notes that the chronology in these books "agrees with what can be gleaned from extrabiblical sources" and that "even if we had no external sources we could have reasonable confidence in the biblical sequence."[161] So we have both historic and archaeologically verifiable evidences that at least indirectly (as well as some directly) support the narrative of the Patriarchs through the Exodus period to that of the Israelite movement into Canaan; so the next question would seem to logically lead us to the Davidic monarchy in which the "wandering nomads" of Egypt that moved into Canaan reportedly progressed from a tribal/governor type system of government (Judges) into a unified monarchy.

THE DAVIDIC KINGDOM

One thing that any historian will acknowledge is that the further we get from the ancient past to the present, the greater our historic evidences become. Therefore we should see a continuation of indirect evidences from the Joshua/Judges period into the Davidic monarchy as well as possibly some direct evidences if the story does in fact have historical merit and that is exactly what we seem to find. Again, speaking not as a theologian, but as a historian following an open philosophy of history I can evaluate the biblical account without ruling it out in advance. When we come to the time of Israel being a loose confederation of "Judges" or governors to an actual unified monarchy, we would expect to see some areas of corroboration supporting this thesis around the time of 1,000 BC.

From 1230–1000 BC, we note a dramatic increase in settled villages versus nomadism; a shift from 29 to 254 small villages in the central hill country. During the Davidic monarchy (Iron Age II) we see the settlements increase to 520 and Jerusalem itself becomes a very important centralized city. Exciting developments in the last thirty years have given us actual "direct" evidences to this period. In 2005 excavation of the largest Iron Age II structure in Israel had begun and is still going on today. Phoenician and Jerusalem archaeologist Eilat Mazar has made the positive claim that this is in fact the Palace of King David. The walls are seven meters thick and both Kathleen Kenyon as well as Dr. Mazar have each dated this palace to the period of 1000–900 BC. Amihai Mazar, a professor of archeology at Hebrew University, and Mazar's cousin, called the find "something of a miracle." According to Mazar, "It's the most significant construction we have from First Temple days in Israel" and "It means that at that time, the 10th century, in Jerusalem there was a regime capable of carrying out such construction."[162] While the historian will not say this is "absolute" since historians rarely speak in terms of absolute facts, it is highly questionable if this is not a Davidic palace, then who built this structure in the 1000–900

BC in Jerusalem? The excavation continues today and for those who have not already made the closed philosophical distinction that "history must exclude such things as the Bible and other 'religious' books from our possible historic inferences," the find is definitely intriguing and does at least conclude that "some" force in Jerusalem between 1000–900 BC was capable of constructing the largest Iron Age II structure in all of Israel.

Khirbet Qeiyafa Ostracon

Equally interesting to the historian is the 2008 discovery of the Khirbet Qeiyafa Ostracon. The 5.9 × 6.5 inches ostracon pottery shard has five lines of text and was discovered during excavations at the site in 2008.[163] Although the writing on the ostracon is poorly preserved and difficult to read, distinguished professor and senior epigrapher Émile Puech of the École Biblique et Archéologique Française proposed that it be read:

1. Do not oppress, and serve God…despoiled him/her

2. The judge and the widow wept; he had the power

3. over the resident alien and the child, he eliminated them together

4. The men and the chiefs/officers have established a king

5. He marked 60 [?] servants among the communities/habitations/generations

Puech understood the ostracon as a locally written copy of a message from the capital informing a local official of the ascent of Saul to the throne. Similar to the type of open philosophy of history I have built my career on, Puech began his analysis with an extensive examination of each letter of the text and the way in which each is written—its proximity to adjacent letters, its direction as well as its position within the line along with alternative interpretations of the text itself before concluding it to be of the time of Saul—the first king of Israel. The text provides great insight into the organization of society in connection with the exercise of government and local justice. As Puech has concluded: "Though incomplete, it identifies concerns about the manner of rendering justice, which was not in conformity with that which is expected in the time of judges; finally, and most importantly the text informs us in line 4 about the establishment of a monarchy, an experience that is apparently new and thus not likely within an established monarchical line."[164] If Puech is correct, the Qeiyafa Ostracon is the only archaeological artifact yet discovered referring to Israel's first king Saul. And it is the earliest nonbiblical confirmation of the establishment of the Israelite monarchy.[165]

What about David himself? Was Wellhausen and many historians since his time correct in their assessment that the entire monarchy was simply dreamt up much later in order to fit into their religious purposes? Though there are a few die-hard biblical nihilist left today, they are fast becoming an endangered species simply because no matter how badly one wishes for the biblical stores to be complete fabrications, we are fast coming to the conclusions that at least in part, their historicity is arguably more solid than anything else we have from the ancient past. When the Mesha Stele was discovered AD 1868 and dated to 850 BC, not only did archaeologist have the longest written Iron Age inscription ever found in the region, but they had discovered the first inscription (line 31) to the "House of David" as well as confirmation by Mesha (king of Moab), that Israel and its king Omri had oppressed the Moabites. This offers a compelling parallel to 2 Kings 3 even though some scholars continue to debate the "House of David" inscription since technically the "D" (a Dalet) is missing. Though there is no logical fill in for anything other than "David" in this context, it did allow "Wellahausenian historians" to hypothesize that David did not exist and perhaps the Moabites too were also conspiring to invent the Davidic monarchy. However in 1993 (AD) the famous "Tel Dan Stele" was unearthed during an excavation in northern Israel.

Tel Dan Stele

The Tel Dan Stele is a stele (inscribed stone) that was discovered in 1993 during excavations in northern Israel under the direction of Avraham Biran. The stone was erected by an Aramaic king (likely Hazael of Aram-Damascus referred to in 1 Kings 19:15) in the mid-ninth century BC and consists of several fragments making up part of a triumphal inscription in Aramaic. The most notable feature of the inscription is the use of the expression "House of David" (*bytdwd*) in line 9, making it the earliest known extrabiblical mention of David and the dynasty he founded. Similar discoveries in the nineteenth century such as the now famous "Black Obelisk of Shalmaneser III" is a black limestone Neo-Assyrian bas-relief sculpture from northern Iraq, commemorating the deeds of King Shalmaneser III (reigned 858–824 BC), offers the most complete Assyrian obelisk yet discovered and is historically significant because it displays the earliest ancient depiction of an Israelite King (Jehu from 2 Kings 9–10). Its reference to Parsua is also the first known reference to the Persians. Tribute offerings are shown being brought from identifiable regions and peoples. Also of importance is the Kurhk Stele of Shalmaneser III that specifically mentions King Ahab of Israel and Ben-Hadad of Syria. The stele mainly deals with campaigns Shalmaneser made in western Mesopotamia and Syria, fighting extensively with the countries of Bit Adini and Carchemish. At the end of the Monolith comes the account of the Battle of Qarqar where an alliance of twelve kings fought against Shalmaneser at the Syrian city of Qarqar. This alliance, comprising eleven kings, was led by Irhuleni of Hamath and Hadadezer of Damascus, describing also a large force led by King Ahab of Israel.[166] The list of verifiable direct and indirect evidences is literally mind-boggling; we should not expect such corroborations in Ancient History. The lists simply go on and once we get to about 800 BC forward we find the accounts of the Babylonian conquest in 2 Kings, 2 Chronicles, and Jeremiah contain meticulous details, none of which are contradicted by archaeology or any textual sources. On the contrary, many are supported by external evidence, making these events some of the most well established in ancient history. While many more details have been found on the Temple of Amun, the Taylor Prism, Lachish reliefs, Nabopolasar, Babylonian Chronicles, Babylonian Ration Records, Cyrus Cylinder, etc., which adds further historic confirmation to the biblical narratives through their exile and reintroduction back into the lands of Israel, space does not allot me to go into each and every one of them.

Though each of these and more deserve much fuller attention than I have briefly touched on (secularist scholar K. A. Kitchen has dedicated almost seven hundred pages to the Hebrew Testament's confirmation via archaeology alone for example), for purposes of this book in breaking down our current modus operandi via philosophy of history, it should simply be noted that I have yet to see any reason whatsoever for accepting a Wellhausen nihilist approach of biblical criticism. Moreover, I have seen next to no reason for accepting a minimalist approach of the Bible; for the purposes of historic investigation the Era of Kings is literally a dream come true for many verifiable events and "direct" as well as indirect evidences from various sources putting together a powerful coherent cumulative case story that the Davidic Monarchy did in fact exist at least much in the manner that the Hebrew Testament confirms; we should not expect such corroboration in ancient history so I literally am dumbfounded both as a philosopher and as a historian when I hear my colleagues and peers state that we simply "cannot" trust the biblical account because it is written with a "religion" in mind. Evidence and facts is what I and all historians should be interested in, not the contrived and illogical regurgitation of an out of date Wellhausen-like philosophy of history. The list goes on and on, and I find myself at a loss not only by the sheer number of supporting nonbiblical evidences but by the specificity of corroborating facts. Whether one is an atheist, Muslim, Jew, Christian, or whatnot, the facts are the facts so why avoid their logical conclusions in the name of "history"? "The primeval protohistory embodies early popular tradition going very far back, and is set in an early format. Thus we have a consistent level of good, fact-based correlations right through from circa 2000 BC [with earlier roots] down to 400 BC. In terms of general reliability—the Old Testament comes out remarkably well, so long as its writings are treated fairly and evenhandedly, in line with independent data, open to all. There we stop."[167]

THE ERA OF EXILE THROUGH MACCABEES: THE INTER-TESTAMENT PERIOD

BETWEEN OLD AND NEW TESTAMENTS

With the Old Testament canon closing with the Book of Malachi approximately 397 BC, we see that this period between the Old and New Testament covering some four hundred years. The condition of the Jews as a nation and race at the beginning of this four-hundred-year period should be kept in mind. Two hundred years earlier Jerusalem had been overthrown and the Jewish people carried into the Babylonian exile (586 BC) as punishment for their unfaithfulness to God. At the end of this seventy-year punishment period, the Babylonian empire having been overthrown and succeeded by that of Media-Persia (536 BC), Cyrus, the Persian emperor, issued a decree permitting the return of the Jews to Israel (Cyrus Cylinder) pictured below.

Under the leadership of Zerubbabel, some five thousand Jews returned. Some twenty years after their return, after many set-backs, the building of the temple was completed in 516 BC. Then after another fifty-eight years had passed, in 458 BC, Ezra the scribe returned to Jerusalem with a small group of Israelites and restored the law and the ritual. Still another thirteen years later, in 445BC, Nehemiah had come to Jerusalem to rebuild the walls and become governor. Now, once again, there was a Jewish state in Judea though of course under Persian rule.[168] Such then is the picture of the Jewish people at the beginning of the four-hundred-year period between the Old and New Testaments that make up the Bible. The Jewish Remnant back in Judea for about one hundred and forty years (536 BC–397 BC) formed a small dependent Jewish state, Jerusalem and the temple were rebuilt, the law and the ritual restored, but the mass of the people remained dispersed throughout the Media-Persian Empire. This eventually led to the Greek conquest by Alexander the Great and the introduction of Greek culture throughout Israel. This also led to the formation of the Hasmoean Dynasty that is described in the Apocryphal books of Maccabees that introduced groups such as the Pharisees and Sadducees of Jesus's time and set up the eventual place of Roman rule, which endorsed King Herod. This is the point "in the fullness of time" that Jesus enters into human history according to Christian and Messianic Jewish traditions. We have Hasmoean coins as well as many other archaeological confirmations of this period, which are relatively uncontroversial. This also helps us to better understand the Qumran community located near the Dead Sea area in which the now famous Dead Sea Scrolls were discovered in 1946–56.

TEXTUAL CRITICISM AND THE DEAD SEA SCROLLS

One subtopic for most historians is that of textual and source criticism, which leads one to question when the earliest accounts of a written document are estimated to be, what is the oldest copy of this document to date, how much documentation is there, and how accurate do they parallel one another; similarly within form criticism is there a sign of embellishment for theological purposes that could have altered the account of historic recording. We have seen that we have a fairly consistent picture of the Old/Hebrew Testament with that of historic reliability and therefore no reason to dismiss it as anything but a historical document. So the question arises then is how reliable is the current Hebrew Testament we have today that we call the Old Testament? Again, while there is neither the time nor is it the point of this writing, I will touch briefly on the historic nature of the documentation we currently have compared to our most ancient sources and then move into the era of the New Testament and conclude with a snapshot of the historical Jesus.

As an ancient historian, I am used to having to make due with bits and pieces of texts as well as indirect evidences so I am doubly shocked when I began to realize how much materials we have for the biblical narratives, how well they coincide with extrabiblical sources, how many ancient documents we have available, and finally I am surprised at how many of my peers and colleagues assure me it is a nonhistoric book full of many false narratives; false narratives that they cannot specify to me in what way they are nonhistoric/false however. To touch on very briefly we know that in 1946/47 there were discovered a number of jars buried in the floors of caves lining the cliffs along the western shore of the Dead Sea in Israel containing about 230 manuscripts written in the languages of Hebrew, Aramaic, and Greek that included parts of every book of today's Old Testament except Esther. These were written on leather parchment and papyrus and also included numerous commentaries on the biblical text and through paleographic analysis and carbon-14 dating to have been dated from 408 BC to AD 68 (when the Dead Sea Community was destroyed).[169] In the case of the latter books of the Hebrew Testament, this means that we are only within a couple of generations of the original text, which make these documents incredibly valuable for historical analysis. Shockingly, some of these ancient manuscripts such as the Isaiah scroll (IQIsaA) dated from 335–125 BC were found complete and intact. What was more shocking was that this text in its entirety matched to today's translation of Isaiah (Masoretic Text) in more than 95 percent of it texts with the 5 percent variation consisting of spelling alterations but no change in textual agreement. This also proved to be the case for all of the other biblical scrolls found among the Dead Sea Scrolls (though many are fragmentary). So while this still allows for the possibility of corruption of texts of the oldest books of the Hebrew Testament, there really is no reason to assume there was any corruption to date; on the contrary if one thousand years of time means 95 percent exact agreement then it is at least plausible to assume that the one thousand years prior to this the text was relatively close to the same as well. Moreover, we continue to find the narratives told in the historical books to be incredibly accurate by indirect as well as direct evidences as we have already discussed. Therefore, as long as historians such as Susan Bauer and myself are allowed to follow an open philosophy of history that does not disqualify the Old Testament from fruitful discourse beforehand; it remains a factual statement that we have no reason to exclude it as an accurate historical portrayal concerning the ancient past.

CONCLUSIONS

There are a few voices today that seem to echo my same concerns on the validity of history as an origin science as well as the importance of an open philosophy of history, but by and large their voices are either muted or ignored. Vincent Taylor, a prominent form critic, shares many of my feelings and warns against too great a dogmatism with regard to the miraculous/nonnaturalistic:

It is far too late today to dismiss the question by saying that 'miracles are impossible;' that stage of the discussion is definitely past. Science takes a much humbler and truer view of natural law than was characteristic of former times; we now know that the 'laws of Nature' are convenient summaries of existing knowledge. Nature is not a 'closed system,' and miracles are not 'intrusions' into an 'established order.' In the last fifty years we have been staggered too often by discoveries which at one time were pronounced impossible. We have lived to hear of the breaking up of the atom, and to find scientists themselves speaking of the universe 'as more like a great thought than like a great machine.' This change of view does not, of course, accredit the miraculous; but it does mean that, given the right conditions, miracles are not impossible; no scientific or philosophic dogma stands in the way.[170]

So what are some conclusions that one can draw from a strict Wellhausen-nihilist view concerning the historicity of the Bible compared to today? Thomas McCall, PhD, Old Testament Studies and Semitic languages sees a large shift occurring since Wellhausen where the nihilist are all but extinct and the minimalist are showing signs of decreasing as well when confronted with modern-day archaeology. While the majority still maintain a minimalist view, which accepts only the minimal amount of biblical material as authentic history; and the minority a maximalist view, which accepts most, if not all, of the Bible as accurate in its historical references, there is beginning to be signs of a shift. Gradually over the years, the minimalists have grudgingly had to accept more and more of the Bible as accurate since every new archaeological find has tended to substantiate the biblical account. The great discoveries of the Herodian structures in Jerusalem and Caesarea, for instance, and the Dead Sea Scrolls at Qumran have demonstrated even to the greatest skeptic the authenticity of many of the New Testament descriptions of the Second Temple era. In more recent times, excavations in Jerusalem and Megiddo (to name just a couple) have uncovered strong evidence concerning the First Temple period, and discoveries in Syria and Egypt have confirmed many of the conditions described in the patriarchal era of Abraham, Isaac, and Jacob. In the last few years, stunning evidence has come to light that establishes the historicity of King David and his royal dynasty. The "House of David" stone that was discovered in Dan proves to all but a few die-hard minimalists that there really was a King David who founded a long-lasting dynasty in Jerusalem. Again, my point is not to enforce a maximalist view by any means, but it is that this option should be considered a possibility if that is where the evidence points.[171]

In my opinion, framing the whole discussion a dichotomy between "minimalists" and "maximalists" is not very helpful. There are not two camps, schools, or positions. If anything, the two terms represent a spectrum of possible views, with "minimalists" being at one end and "maximalists" at the other — and everyone else somewhere in the middle. I am not saying anything revolutionary here; most if not all scholars in the debate do not like the labels and have said as much in various publications. So I think it is time for everyone to put the labels to rest and focus instead on interacting with the views of scholars in an open philosophical view of history including the Bible. By doing this there will be less "knee-jerk" reactions of: "Well the Bible must be false because it records many nonnaturalistic causations—namely 'God.'" I have heard these near exact sentiments amongst various professors through two degrees (including my present MA work) and hundreds of hours of conversations; however when I ask "why" does this disqualify it from historic methodological analysis I am usually given the simple circular reasoning that if naturalism is true the Bible cannot be mostly accurate and if the Bible is mostly inaccurate then naturalism is true. When the constraints of naturalism are removed, then the historian is free to follow the evidences in an unbiased manner that an open philosophy of history necessitates.

One must remember that archaeologist proceed to excavate one layer at a time when they excavate a given site. During this process, it is very possible that just five meters over they could discover an entire library that sheds light on a given subject; alas, we may never find some discoveries that are only a breath away. However, what has been discovered in biblical lands and the Near East strongly supports the narratives found in the Bible. From creation accounts of the Babylonians, Sumerians, Greeks, Hindus, Chinese, and others to the Ebla tablets containing sixteen thousand cuneiform tablets, we see a very unique retelling of creation ex nihilo by the Genesis narrative, which is unique among them all. Moreover, from what we know of cosmology as well as cosmogony from the twentieth century to today, we find creation ex nihilo to be the most accurate nonnaturalistic hypothesis. This coupled with the fact that from a macrolevel (though any historian will admit the microlevel details may still be in question), the historic story portrayed in the Bible offers a very interesting historic portrayal of a specific people group from "prehistory" and their story to the turn of time, BC – AD that is supported by all the major criteria the historian looks at when assessing philosophy of history and historic methodology. It is supported by both indirect as well as direct historic information including textual as well as archaeological data, source material from the Dead Sea Scrolls verifying a very consistent account of not only the Greek Septuagint but of today's Hebrew Testament. When it comes to the New Testament (as we will review next) even the most ardent skeptical historian admits the New Testament holistically offers the most complete account of source materials and shortness of time span between actual events than any other ancient history we have today.

1. Theism (from the biblical standpoint) does have greater explanatory scope in its account of being, space, time,

matter, information, and morality than does a strict form of naturalism.

2. Theism does have greater explanatory power in regard to these same criteria.

3. Theism (assuming an open philosophy that does not rule it out in advance) is much more plausible than naturalism.

4. Theism assumes many less assertions than does naturalism—namely the only real assertion is the existence of God compared to many more assertions made by naturalism that seem unwarranted.

5. Theism is in accord with accepted beliefs concerning being only comes from being, what appears to be intelligent design in the universe as well as the origins of life and mankind whereas naturalism is not.

6. Theism and moreover the biblical explanation of the universe, life, and humankind philosophically and historically outstrips naturalism in meeting conditions 1–5.

HISTORIC EVENT 4:

THE COMMON ERA
OF THE HISTORICAL JESUS

As long as historiography does not begin dogmatically with a narrow concept of reality according to which 'dead men do not rise,' it is not clear why historiography should not in principle be able to speak about Jesus' resurrection as the explanation that is best established of such events as the disciples' experiences of the appearances and the discovery of the empty tomb.

—Wolfhart Pannenberg, *Jesus, God and Man*

Is the New Testament (NT) anything more than just a set of religious and theological texts full of myths and miracles that were pieced together long after the events they describe with little historic value? Can the historian attain a reasonable idea of the world of first century Palestine in which Jesus of Nazareth came onto the scene? What are the types of historical sources available to us concerning the New Testament period, and are they reliable? These are the types of questions that both the naturalistic as well as the nonnaturalistic historian can agree need to be answered if we are to assess the NT and its historicity or lack thereof.

How does the naturalist normally account for the historicity of Jesus and the New Testament? As mentioned earlier, most naturalists simply hold to religion as being man-made, created to help society create a purpose for living and striving, a cause greater than themselves so to speak. When it comes to the New Testament, most naturalists account for the narratives on the miraculous to be either invented or simply mistakes made by simpleminded people who did not understand the natural world around them. Moreover, religious texts such as the New Testament were created far from the time of the events they record are highly inaccurate and have too many textual errors to be of any significant historic value. Most naturalists do however hold that the Historical Jesus did indeed exist, died on a cross at the hands of Pontius Pilate, and believed himself to be a messenger from God. They do not however believe there is any real historic credibility to the Resurrection accounts or the postmortem appearances of Jesus. So one last time the question arises: "Are the naturalistic accounts mentioned above the best interpretation of the evidence?"

One area that I have always heard praise for is in the amount of New Testament documents available; I however did not realize quite how historically expansive this collection was in quantity as well as quality. The kinds of witnesses to the New Testament are similar in scope to that of any other historical literature but are incredibly abundant as even a naturalistic historian such as Bart Ehrman will acknowledge. The most important documents for recovering the most original wording of the New Testament would be the Greek manuscripts since they are the oldest and most common language of the time. To date we have 5,745 Greek manuscripts divided into four classes according to the materials from which they are made or their particular style of writing.

1. Papyri (118)—Manuscripts written in the second to sixth centuries AD on paper made from the papyrus plant into scrolls and written on with ink.

2. Unicals (317)—Manuscripts written in the fourth to tenth centuries AD in large elegant capital letters that are disconnected from one another, although words were not separated and no punctuation was used. These are written on parchment (goat or sheepskins) or vellum with ink.

3. Minuscules (2877)—Manuscripts written in the ninth to sixteenth centuries AD in small cursive script in which the letters are connected to one another.

4. Lectionaries (2433)—Manuscripts composed as early as the first century in which the books of the New Testament are arranged for daily study and meditation and not according to the canonical order.

The earliest of these are written on papyrus and though they are fragmentary, do date back to about AD 125. This earliest fragment of John 18 is Papyrus 52; it is partially unique because the Gospel of John is universally agreed to be the last of the Gospels written around AD 90–100, so this AD 125 date gets us back very close to the originals. Though there are fifteen of these early papyrus manuscripts, it is not until closer to AD 150 that we get a much more intact set of Greek manuscripts in the Chester Beatty Papryi, which contains fragments of all of the books of the New Testament including the oldest copy of Luke.

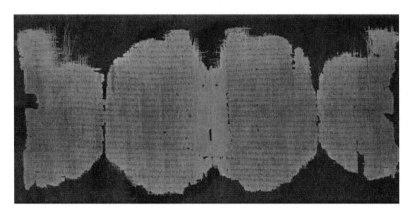

On November 17, 1931, the *London Times* announced the discovery of twelve manuscripts, said to be from a Coptic grave-yard in Egypt stowed away in jars. The documents were sub-sequently bought by Chester Beatty. This sensational find is of greater importance for New Testament studies than the Dead Sea scrolls. Among the manuscripts that were found is the earli-est surviving collection of the Apostle Paul's letters known as P46 (pictured above), which stands for the forty-sixth published NT manuscript on papyri. This collection has been dated by the style of the handwriting as early as the mid-second century (AD 150) and is now housed in the Chester Beatty Library, Dublin. Only about eighty-five years may separate this from the original let-ters of Paul. This makes the textual witness to the original New Testament unique when compared to other ancient books since it is not unusual for a thousand years or more to separate the lost originals of ancient manuscripts from the first surviving copy. The less the time, the less opportunity for embellishments to creep into the writings. One of the surviving pages form P46 contains a part of Paul's letter to the Corinthian Church (1 Corinthians 15:1–6), in which Paul outlines the important message that he announced to them. In this passage, Paul uses technical language to indicate that he was passing on an oral tradition in a fixed form from that even the most ardent of NT critics acknowledges as authentic and dates back to within three to five years of Jesus's crucifixion (approximately AD 36). In this creed, Paul summarizes that Christ died for our sins, rose again, and appeared to over five hundred people as well as the Apostles, to which Paul adds many were still alive at the time of his writing to the Corinthians and could therefore verify the truth of what he wrote. First Corinthians 15:1–6 has been dated by even the most skeptical of historians to within three to five years of the events themselves (that Christ died, was buried, was raised, and seen by many) and therefore has a firm historical foundation that these four areas of information (that the Gospels espouse upon) were already well in circulation right after the crucifixion itself and was therefore not a later invention. For these combined reasons as well as the rapid spreading of Christianity, most historians believe the complete Bible (at least for the most part) was well in circulation by AD 190. However it is not until AD 325 that we today have our oldest copy of the Old and New Testaments in the Codex Vaticanus and Codex Sinaiticus dated to AD 325.

Alongside these various Greek manuscripts, we have translations from the original Greek into Old Latin, Coptic, Old Syriac, Armenian, Ethiopic, Persian, Gothic, Georgian, Old Slavonic, and Arabic. Obviously the most important of these versions are those that are the earliest (Latin, Coptic, Syriac); these date from the third to the sixteenth centuries AD but the texts from which they were translated may go back into the second century. We have approximately ten thousand manuscripts fitting into this Latin category. The Coptic manuscripts number about a thousand and date from the third to fifth centuries and the Syriac date to the third century and number well over one thousand. If we add the other early versions of fourth century Gothic, fifth to sixth century Armenian, Georgian and Ethiopic as well as the eighth to ninth century Arabic and Old Slavonic we have approximately twenty thousand total manuscripts for the New Testament. However, one area that as a historian has greatly helped in my studies is that of what are often referred to as the "Church Fathers" or Patristic literature. This material dates as early as the first century AD and as late as the thirteenth century and the number of citations exceed one million. While many of the Church Fathers such as Papias bishop of Hierapolis around AD 130 and Polycarp bishop of Smyrna as well as Clement of Rome all were students of the Apostles first hand according to their writings and the dating of their materials; this does indeed help the historian see the transition from the first into the second century with Clement writing in AD 96 and through form criticism we see that there is not any significant changes in meaning or purpose. Papias, bishop of Hierapolis around AD 130, Polycarp, bishop of Smyrna, and others were students who walked with John first hand. We then have Irenaeus who was a student of Polycarp, and his writings also match what we are told in the Gospels, and so it goes down through history.[172]

The point of importance here for the historian is that as we enter into the era of the New Testament, the facts become quite clear and in all honesty overwhelming that when it comes to the New Testament itself, no other ancient writing is even close to being as well attested or documented as the New Testament writings. As mentioned above, we have to date at total of 5,745 Greek manuscripts of the New Testament; when we add the Latin, Ethiopic, Slavic, Armenian, and others, the total exceeds twenty thousand. Moreover, when we look at the manuscript evidence of other writings such as Cesar's Gallic Wars we have a total of 251 manuscripts to support it; Herodotus' History has 109, Tacitus Annals has 31. These are not even close to the reliability we have in the New Testament from a textual standpoint. But it does not stop there; Cesar's Gallic Wars were written in 100 BC, but the earliest copy we have is dated AD 900, Herodotus' History was written 400 BC and our earliest copy is dated AD 1000, Tacitus Annals was written in AD 100 and our earliest copy is dated AD 850.[173]

Does this mean they are accurate and without error? Of course not, but how a historian can say you cannot trust the Bible historically but you can Herodotus (the "founder" of history) is indeed dumbfounding and a sign that naturalism continues to guide the way the historian is told to analyze history and rule out certain sources and criteria *a priori*.

The next question that comes into play is on accuracy. The more I began questioning the number of textual evidences, the more I began to see that virtually all historians that I spoke to and interviewed agreed that the NT had the largest quantity of manuscripts with the shortest date between event and composition within the confines of ancient history. This however did not mean much if the accuracy of the text was greatly flawed. Textual critic Bart Ehrman has estimated there to be some four hundred thousand errors amongst these early manuscripts. However, one key fact that is quite astonishing is that from the earliest manuscript to the latest (a period of 1,400 years) the New Testament increased only by 2 percent (or about 2,500 words). Moreover these earliest text and the latest text agree on all major points, so what many of these errors end up being is simply spellings and rewordings no different than variants of today's Bible (New International Version, New American Standard, King James, etc). What I found was displayed on a radio interview with professor Ehrman when asked if the NT was so corrupted what then did he think the original noncorrupt one was like; after a pause, he said pretty much like what we have today. Over and over we see that other than many spelling variations that there is a virtual consensus that the New Testament manuscripts agree in over

99 percent of the text, which is by far the highest percentage of any other ancient work. This can be broken down in the following manner:

- The vast majority of variants (approximately 75 percent) are simply differences in spelling, which was never standardized.

- The next 24 percent of variants are meaningful but not viable—this could include word order of "Jesus Christ" instead of "Christ Jesus" or substituting "Christ" for "God" or "Lord" for "Christ," etc. We find the name "Jesus" added to Mark 6:34, 7:27, and 8:1 in the majority of later manuscripts for example, but this does not alter the meaning of the text.

- The last 1 percent (less than) are both meaningful and viable differences—this might be a sentence left out completely or a name mixed up, so these (though there are not many) are significant.[174]

So although the manuscripts agree in over 99 percent, there are a small number that have a sentence left out and some scholars believe passages such as the woman at the well may have been a later invention since it is not in their earliest manuscripts. However, two things should be pointed out, first of all as a historical analysis this changes the historicity of the text in no real way. Secondly, just because a manuscript has a specific notation from AD 175 but one from AD 150 does not, this does not necessarily mean that the AD 175 one is not the more accurate source drawing on an older source. In matters of historical agreement amongst manuscripts an 80 percent is considered adequate and usually then you have only a handful of manuscripts to compare against one another. For some easily assessable examples take the example of Livy's History of Rome—we are missing 107 of its 142 volumes or Tacitus' Histories; even the very best-preserved copies have significant gaps in the text that exist. Yet it is taken for granted that these histories are accurate by classical historians, and no one complains about their unreliability or that a great deal of their texts has been reconstructed by both ancient and modern editors. Moreover, it is the historic accuracy even more than the textual consistency that first shook me during my studies. Even the most ardent skeptic will acknowledge Luke's reliability as a historian. From one of the greatest archaeologists to have ever lived, Sir William Ramsay first doubted the reliability of Luke's account until he was forced to completely reverse his beliefs as more and more archaeological evidence began to be uncovered. "Luke is a historian of the first rank; not merely are his statements of facts trustworthy, this author should be placed along with the very greatest of historians."[175]

The noted Roman historian, Colin Hemer, has cataloged numerous archaeological and historical confirmations of Luke's accuracy in his book *The Book of Acts in the Setting of Hellenistic History*.[176] In this there are hundreds of pages of archaeological confirmations of the Book of Acts accuracy such as:

- Specialized details, which would not have been widely known except to a contemporary researcher such as Luke who traveled widely. These details include exact titles of officials, identification of army units, and information about major routes.

- Details archaeologists know are accurate but cannot verify as to the precise period. Some of these are unlikely to have been known except to a writer who had visited the districts.

- Correlation of dates of known kings and governors with the chronology of the narrative.

- Offhand geographical references that bespeak familiarity with common knowledge.

- Peculiarities in the selection of detail, as in theology, that are explainable in the context of what is now known of first-century church life.

- Cultural or idiomatic items now known to be peculiar to the first-century atmosphere.

And the list goes on. Roman historian A. N. Sherwin-White agrees: "For Acts the confirmation of historicity is overwhelming...Any attempt to reject its basic historicity must now appear absurd. Roman historians have long taken it for granted."[177] Similarly, EM Blaiklock, professor of classics in Auckland University concluded that: "Luke is a consummate historian, to be ranked in his own right with the great writers of the Greeks."[178] Noted philosopher of mind J. P. Moreland presents a logical question concerning ancient historiography: "Were ancient historians able to distinguish fact from fiction? Is there any evidence that they desired to do so? The works of Greek, Roman, and Jewish historians all probably influenced the New Testament writers; and they discussed the importance of giving an accurate account of what happened. Herodotus emphasizes the role of eyewitnesses in historical reporting. The historian must however evaluate and verify their reports using common sense. Reports of superhuman and miraculous occurrence should be regarded with suspicion. Polybius held very exacting standards. He advocated examination of sources, objectivity, and castigated superstition. He also advocated the questioning of reliable eyewitnesses."[179] If Dr. Moreland is accurate then the heavily influenced Hellenistic areas of the first century church should have at least been familiar with the basics of historic methodology it would seem and is dominantly evident in the writing of the New Testament. The main objection that historians like Bart Ehrman, Wellhausen, Bultmann, and many today give as a denial of historicity of the Bible is that it records nonnaturalistic events mixed with historic ones so therefore none can be trusted as historically reliable. But as we have already discussed in great depth there are a great many reasons for doubting naturalistic philosophy, and if naturalism is indeed false, then our philosophy of history most certainly should not be limited to it.

Analyst and researcher James R. Moore seems to share my sentiments when he states: "today scientists will admit that no one knows enough about 'natural law' to say that any event is necessarily a violation of it. They agree that an individual's non-statistical sample of time and space is hardly sufficient ground on which to base immutable generalizations concerning the nature of the entire universe. Today what we commonly term 'natural law' is in fact only our inductive and statistical descriptions of natural phenomena."[180] Noted historian John Montgomery denotes that the antisupernatural position is both "philosophically and scientifically irresponsible."[181] Montgomery continues, "As a historian, in facing an alleged 'miracle,' is really facing nothing new. All historical events are unique, and the test of their factual character can be only the accepted documentary approach that we have followed here. No historian has a right to a closed system of natural causation, for, as the Cornell logician Max Black has shown in a recent essay, the very concept of cause is a 'peculiar, unsystematic, and erratic notion.'"[182]

So why do so many seem to regard something as historically reliable as the Bible as "nonhistorical?" I was finally told point-blank by a colleague that if any historical account records "fantastical events" such as "God" or "Jesus rising from the dead," then these records simply disqualify themselves as being historic no matter the evidences. At last I finally received a clear and coherent answer, not one that I found logically based, but it was honest. However, if naturalism is false, then there is no reason to assume that nonnaturalistic causation should disqualify something from being historically credible. Literary critics still normally follow Aristotle's dictum that the benefit of the doubt is to be given to the document itself, not arrogated by the critic to himself.

Therefore, one must listen to the claims of the document under analysis and not assume fraud or error unless the author disqualified him or herself by contradiction or known factual inaccuracies. So this leads the historian to the main disqualifying feature cited toward the New Testament—namely that of the person Jesus of Nazareth.

THE HISTORICAL JESUS IN CONTEXT

The "Historical Jesus" has been of great interest ever since the seventeenth and eighteenth centuries when the philosophy of rationalism began dominating the intellectual scene. How can one decipher between what is myth and what is historic when discussing the person of Jesus of Nazareth? While book after book has been written on the Historical Jesus, I have attempted only to use a balanced/agnostic-minded research pattern during my research in order to provide the most simplistic historical analysis of Jesus in order to conclude my macrolevel critique of the historicity of the Bible as a whole; but one must remember that as already stated, history does not deal with absolutes and must be agnostic-based in most areas of research neither presupposing naturalism anymore than theism. For example, I specialized in military history for a brief time under Dr. Donald Engels at the University of Arkansas, during this time I found it difficult to accept that we could know very much about the "Historical Alexander the Great," especially that he was undefeated in battle while carving out one of the largest empires in history. This was partially due to the fact that the earliest histories we have for Alexander are more than three hundred years after his death, and they paint various different pictures of Alexander. (Plutarch and Arrian both wrote the most famous biographies of Alexander who died 323 BC although they both were late first century AD writers.)[183] For example, one writes of Alexander in a very positive light while the other portrays him in the negative; obviously both of these cannot be accurate; moreover, I found it quite difficult to accept that Alexander was undefeated in battle considering how wide was his areas of conquest. Nonetheless, after ardent studies on the resources available, I had no choice but to conclude as Dr. Engels and most of academia did, that based on the evidence we have, Alexander was indeed undefeated in battle. The historian understands, however, that this is no absolute fact and may change upon the discovery of additional evidence.

With this analogy in mind, I have used the same historic verification on the Historical Jesus that I did on the Historical Alexander and as I have outlined earlier so that we may focus on history alone and not theology in our assessment of the Historic Jesus. By limiting our assessment to historic verification, we will not be able to conclude any type of absolute identity for the historic Jesus, but we will be able to at least peel back some of the layers to see what we can conclude about him with a high degree of probability. By taking this strictly historic approach, I will be using an even number of Christian, non-Christian, and agnostic historian's research; I will be removing any theological assumptions from all sources I quote so that we can get a more unbiased understanding of the facts that we have to attempt to put together a picture of the historic Jesus that the majority of New Testament Critics will agree are accurate based on the data. With this in mind, we will not look at any writings of today's New Testament as infallible or inerrant but instead we will look at them in their original manuscript forms. One area that New Testament criticism has concluded since the twentieth century is the overwhelming conclusion (despite Wellhausen and nineteenth and early twentieth century scholarship) that Jesus of Nazareth did indeed exist as a person in the first century. Very few New Testament critics today hold to the position that Jesus of Nazareth did not exist. The most skeptical critics by and large agree with fellow skeptic Rudolf Bultmann's conclusion in *The*

Study of the Synoptic Gospel that: "By no means are we at the mercy of those who doubt or deny that Jesus ever lived."[184]

SOURCE CRITICISMS

If we review the manuscripts of the New Testament not as infallible or inerrant but just as any other historic manuscript we quickly come to the conclusion as mentioned earlier that there are many manuscripts from the New Testament accounts of Jesus that eventually became what we know of today as the "New Testament Bible." Regardless of one's interpretation on the reliability of these texts, there are few historians today that say we should throw them out because to do so would be as the renowned John Warwick Montgomery concluded: "To be skeptical of the resultant text of the New Testament books is to allow all of classical antiquity to slip into obscurity, for no documents of the ancient period are as well attested bibliographically as the New Testament."[185] As most scholars today agree, there is no ancient literature as well attested in sheer numbers or as close to the lives of the original authors as the New Testament manuscripts. But there are still problems with this even if this is true in comparison to our Alexander the Great example mentioned earlier, this still does not mean it is necessarily accurate or authentic. As New Testament Critic and skeptic Bart Ehrman states: "For most people, the Bible is a non-problematic book. What people don't realize is that they're reading translations of texts, and we don't have the originals."[186] Dr. Ehrman is accurate in this historic analysis; we do not have the originals of the New Testament or any other original ancient biographies. Therefore, the historians' next step is to do their best attempt at bridging the earliest sources we do have for the Historical Jesus in this instance, to the written sources in which they were derived, then to the oral traditions in which the written sources came from, and finally back to the actual historic events themselves. While any detailed analysis of this process is far beyond our scope, it is important to note that most scholars trace the Gospel of Mark back to as early as the late fifties AD to as late as late sixties AD; this still gives us an approximate time range of approximately thirty years from Jesus's death (approximately AD 30) to the writing of the first Gospel.

Redaction criticism is basically the method in which any historic manuscript is examined for potential authors' edits or purposes for writing in a skewed or altered way. Mark's Gospel is the shortest and simplest of the Gospels that most historians agree is the oldest Gospel. Mark was thus used by Matthew and Luke as well as a common source usually known as "Q."[187] (The "Q" document could have been the earliest document that is no longer in existence as far as we know; through this source criticism we are attempting to find the earliest sources in which the copies we have are derived.) Form criticism is basically an attempt to analyze early oral traditions and creeds that eventually led to the first writings; if we can capture what these earliest oral traditions may have been, we have a better chance of isolating what the authentic words of Jesus may have been. The oral traditions are derived from the historical events themselves. To give a good example of an early creed that the most skeptical historians such as Bart Ehrman, to the more moderate Marcus Borg, to the more conservative Gary Habermas, all agree, we will look (again) at 1 Corinthians 15:3–6, which is much older than the Gospel writings themselves.

> For I delivered to you as of first importance what I also received, that Christ died for our sins in accordance with the scriptures, that he was buried, that he was raised on the third day in accordance with the scriptures, and that he appeared to Cephas, and then to the Twelve. After that, he appeared to more than five hundred of the brothers and sisters at the same time, most of whom are still living, though some have fallen asleep.

As touched on previously, this confession is an early Christian pre-Pauline creed, which is recognized by virtually all critical scholars across a very wide spectrum. There are several indications that reveal this conclusion in the same format that form/source criticism is used by the historian. First of all, Paul's words *deliverer* and *received* are technical terms for passing on tradition. Moreover, we have Paul's statement that this material was not his own but received from another source. Also, a number of words in this creed are non-Pauline, which indicates another origin of the source material. Most scholars also agree that there are indications that there may be a Semitic source, such as the use of the Aramaic "Cephas" for Peter, again pointing to an earlier source before Paul's Greek translation. Other indications of Hebrew include the triple usage of "and that" along with the two references to the "Scriptures being fulfilled." So how early is this creed? While even the most skeptical NT critic acknowledges the legitimate form criticism of this specific creed, the earliest estimate is eighteen months after Jesus's death to the oldest at six years after. The historian in this instance for example will normally date Jesus's crucifixion to around AD 30, Paul's conversion would have occurred approximately AD 33, three years after his conversion he visited Jerusalem and met with Peter and James (Galatians 1:18). It is therefore reasoned by the form critic that the gospel of Christ's death/resurrection would have been a topic of discussion in which Paul specifically cites the presence of both Peter and James in the list of appearances (1 Corinthians 15:5,7); this reference in turn can point back to Paul receiving this during his initial visit to Jerusalem. The interest of this one example to the historian is that in searching for the "Historical Jesus" most will agree that this oral tradition found in 1 Corinthians 15 was present shortly after the death of Christ and can therefore be concluded as authentic. As German historian Hans von Campenhausen states concerning this creed: "This account meets all the demands of historical reliability that could possibly be made of such a text. The passage therefore preserves uniquely early and verifiable testimony. It meets every reasonable demand of historical reliability."[188] More could be said, but the explanatory scope of early creeds and the form criticism involved in the formation of literature is a good indicator to the reliability of a given text such as this one. What we can conclude is that the foundation of the Gospel message is verifiably preserved shortly after the death of Jesus so that the core message of the Gospel accounts were not a "later invention" but was formed shortly after the events they portray.

NON-CHRISTIAN SOURCES ON
THE HISTORICAL JESUS

I am often asked if there are any "nonbiblical" sources for Jesus; first of all, it must be pointed out that the plethora of manuscripts we have for Jesus today did not start as a "Bible" but were later put into what we call "The New Testament" today. So it must first of all be pointed out that to dismiss any of this manuscript evidence is in effect to dismiss the most primary sources we have on the Historical Jesus. With that said, we do have corroborating support from strictly non-Christian sources that do help us better confirm the manuscripts in which the New Testament was formed from; for the scope of this book, I will only mention the following six non-Christian sources on the Historical Jesus that I have previously written about in a published article, "Christianity in the 22nd Century:"[189]

Josephus (AD 37, sometime after 100) was a Pharisee of the priestly line and a Jewish historian working under Roman authority; he was a Jew and not a follower of Christ, but in his *Antiquities of the Jews*, SVIII, 33), had this brief description of a man called Jesus: "*Now there was about this time Jesus, a wise man, if it be lawful to call him a man, for he was a doer of wonderful works, a teacher of such men as receive the truth with pleasure. He drew over to him both many of the Jews, and many of the Gentiles. He was the Christ, and when Pilate, at the suggestion of the principal men among us, had condemned him to the cross, those that loved him at the first did not forsake him; for he appeared to them alive again the third day; as the divine prophets had foretold these and ten thousand other wonderful things concerning him. And the tribe of Christian so named from him are not extinct at this day."* This from a non-Christian historian. (Josephus also refers to the martyrdom of James the brother of Jesus, which was not included in the texts of the New Testament as well as John the Baptist, Herod, and others.)

Tacitus (AD 56–117)—First-century historian. Tacitus is considered one of the most accurate historians of the ancient world, wrote: *"Consequently, to get rid of the report, Nero fastened the guilt and inflicted the most exquisite tortures on a class hated for their abominations, called Christians by the populace. Christus, from whom the name had its origin, suffered the extreme penalty during the reign of Tiberius at the hands of one of our procurators, Pontius Pilatus, and a most mischievous superstition, thus checked for the moment, again broke out not only in Judea, the first source of the evil, but even in Rome, where all things hideous and shameful from every part of the world find their center and become popular."* (Tacitus, A, 15.44) The "mischievous superstition" to which Tacitus refers is most likely the resurrection of Jesus. The same is true for one of the references of Suetonius which follows.

Suetonius was chief secretary to Emperor Hadrian (who reigned AD 117–138); he confirms the report recorded in the Book of Acts 18:2 that Claudius commanded all Jews to leave Rome in AD 49 (Life of Claudius, 25.4). Speaking of the aftermath of the great fire at Rome, Suetonius reports, *"Punishment was inflicted on the Christians, a body of people addicted to a novel and mischievous superstition."* (Life of Nero, 16) Many historians believe this "superstition" referred to is that of the resurrection story.

Thallus wrote around AD 52 and was quoted in reference to the darkness that followed the crucifixion of Christ: *"On the whole world there pressed a most fearful darkness, and the rocks were rent by an earthquake, and many places in Judea and other districts were thrown down. This darkness Thallus, in the third book of his History, calls, as appears to me without reason, an eclipse of the sun."* (Chronograph, 18.1) This is described also in Luke 23:44–45.

Lucian, second-century Greek writer, wrote: *"The Christians, you know, worship a man to this day—the distinguished personage who introduced their novel rites, and was crucified on that account... You see, these misguided creatures start with the general conviction that they are immortal for all time, which explains the contempt of death and voluntary self-devotion which are so common among them; and then it was impressed on them by their original lawgiver that they are all brothers, from the moment that they are converted, and deny the gods of Greece, and worship the crucified sage, and live after his laws. All this they take quite on faith, with the result that they despise all worldly goods alike, regarding them merely as common property."* (Lucian of Samosata, DP, 11–13)

Emperor Trajan—The emperor gave the following guidelines for punishing Christians: *"No search should be made for these people, when they are denounced and found guilty they must be punished, with the restriction; however, that when the party denies himself to be Christian, and shall give proof that he is not (that is, by adoring our gods), he shall be pardoned on the ground of repentance even though he may have formerly incurred suspicion."* (Pliny the Younger, L, 10:97)

When we only use 100 percent non-Christian/nonbiblical sources of history such as Pliny, Trajan, Lucian, Suetonius, Tacitus, and Josephus just to name a few, we come up with the following facts about Jesus of Nazareth from outside sources:

1. Jesus lived during the time of Tiberius Caesar.

2. He lived a virtuous life.

3. He was a wonder-worker.

4. He had a brother named James.

5. He was acclaimed to be the Messiah.

6. He was crucified under Pontius Pilate.

7. He was crucified on the eve of the Jewish Passover.

8. Darkness and an earthquake occurred when he died.

9. His disciples believed he rose from the dead.

10. His disciples were willing to die for their belief.

11. Christianity spread rapidly as far as Rome.

12. His disciples denied the Roman gods and appeared to worship Jesus.[190]

While in no way exhausting, we can at least see that in light of these references, this is yet another confirmation of the Historic Jesus and how we are to better understand him today in formulating facts about him that most historians would agree have an incredible high probability of historic accuracy.

THE QUESTS FOR THE HISTORICAL JESUS

We must note of course that although most NT critics do agree that Jesus existed and in the validity of the early NT creeds such as 1 Corinthians, they do not universally agree on if he was a first century magician like Morton Smith believes or a Cynic-like teacher as Burton Mack holds to, a Jewish social prophet promoting social revolution as Richard Horsley holds to, etc. So from a historic standpoint we must attempt to further peel back the layers to see if we can all agree that Jesus did exist and that he did work for social reform for example and so on. We must remember that as a historian holding to the steps for establishing historicity outlined by Dr. McCullagh, we will start with the highest probabilities such as "Jesus did exist" and then work our way down to what the next highest probability may be, such as Jesus was a social reformer perhaps and continue to move down the list so that we can gain a better picture of the historical Jesus in the same way that we would for the historical Alexander the Great and so on.

Thankfully, a large amount of research for the Historical Jesus has been going on for over a century now thanks to the first application of historical criticism of the Bible during the Enlightenment of the seventeenth and eighteenth centuries when rationalism dominated the intellectual scene. It was not however until the nineteenth century that we see the "First Quest" for the historical Jesus taking root in an attempt to explain Jesus from a rationalistic perspective. The common thread during this quest was to describe Jesus as a mere man; Ernst Renan and Adolf von Harnack wrote much during this time concluding that Jesus was an ethical teacher proclaiming the love of God and brotherhood of all mankind. It was also during this time that the raising of Lazarus was described by HEF Paulus as Jesus rescuing his friend from a mistaken state of comatose, the walking on the water as Jesus simply walking near the shoreline so it appeared that he was walking on the water, and the famous "swoon theory" in which Jesus was crucified but did not really die from it and recovered later so his disciples thought he had risen. By the end of this first quest scholars such as Albert Schweitzer in his book *The Quest for the Historical Jesus*[191] had begun to recognize that these somewhat far-fetched rationalistic explanations could in no way replace the explanatory scope of the original writings; moreover, the Jesus that emerged seemed to be completely detached from his first-century Palestinian context.

It would not be until the 1950s that the "Second" Quest for the Historical Jesus would emerge with a very similar rationalistic view of the first with an *a priori* rejection of miracles. James Robinson's book *A New Quest of the Historical Jesus* summarizes this movement's core beliefs as follows: "Jesus came from Nazareth; he was baptized by John; he preached and told parables about the kingdom of God; he viewed this kingdom as coming in the near future and possibly as already present in some sense; he performed, or was believed to have performed, exorcisms and healings; he gathered a group of disciples around him; he associated with outcasts and sinners; he challenged the Jewish leaders of his day; he was arrested and charged with blasphemy and sedition; and he was crucified by the Romans."[192] The Second Quest normally denied that Jesus physically rose from the dead however. With only meager publications coming from this second quest we see it mostly coming to an end in the mid 1970s and would be replaced by two new movements in the 1980s; one known collectively as the "Jesus Seminar" and the other as "The Third Quest" for the historical Jesus. What is interesting to note from these first two quests is that while they were strictly based on "rationalistic naturalism" and resisted the thought of miracles or resurrection, the Jesus Seminar and the Third Quest are not as quick to dismiss the thought of miracles or the notion of historic facts. Marcus Borg and John Dominic Crossan for example of the Jesus Seminar do not dispute Jesus' resurrection. They do however dispute what it meant or if it was physical; they also are skeptical that it can be substantiated historically. They also tend to focus more on Greco-Roman influences and noncanonical and hypothetical sources such as the Gospel of Thomas, Peter, the alleged "Q" document, and are more "noneschatological" in nature. The Jesus Seminar has been heavily criticized by main-stream academia for both a pattern of disconnecting Jesus from his Jewish context and his early followers as well as for circular reasoning involving a presupposition of Jesus as an itinerant Cynic sage and then rejecting solid evidence contrary to this portrait (their minds were already decided in most instances they admitted).[193]

The Third Quest on the other hand focused on the "Jewishness" of Jesus more than the Jesus Seminar's Greco-Roman influences and is predominantly more eschatological in their portrayal of Jesus than the Jesus Seminar. The Third Quest has also changed gears due mostly to source criticism in arguing for a priority of the canonical Gospels as biographical sources; much of the Synoptic Gospel materials are authentic (though they view the Gospel of John with caution). Not all within the Third Quest agree with their fellow member and professor for twenty years at Cambridge, McGill, and Oxford Universities N. T. (Nicholas Thomas) Wright. Dr. Wright sought to construct a portrait of Jesus within first-century Judaism that could explain the rise of early Christianity and the view that many held concerning Jesus as savior of the world. Dr. Wright has went as far as to state that it is historically certain that Jesus portrayed himself as the embodiment of Yahweh himself, retuning to Zion to bring his people out of exile. This identification helps to explain also how the early church (though monotheistic) came to worship Jesus as divine. Wright's massive/multivolume works on the origins of Christianity and the Historical Jesus has brought the Historical Jesus into a new light and is regarded as the premier work of early twenty-first century historical Jesus research. Concerning the Third Quest for the Historical Jesus, Wright writes in his book *The Challenge of Jesus*:

> I am neither a secular historian who happens to believe in Jesus nor a Christian who happens to indulge a fancy for history. Rather, I am someone who believes that being a Christian necessarily entails doing business with history and that history done for all it's worth will challenge spurious versions of Christianity, including many that think of themselves as orthodox, while sustaining and regenerating a deep and true orthodoxy, surprising and challenging though this will always remain.[194]

The five main portraits of Jesus that developed during this third quest is Jesus as: Cynic-sage, spirit person, social revolutionary, eschatological prophet, and Messiah. It is quite ironic that the first "Quest for the Historical Jesus," which used historic research that was so permeated by rationalism that it ruled out much authentic historicity in the process. We see however by the time of its "Third Quest" a reversal of such rationalistic views being replaced by a much more unbiased set of conclusions that regardless of "miracles or not," the Jesus of the Synoptic Gospels was much more historic with the first century Palestinian Jesus than we ever had historically considered.

Of particular interest is that there are a growing number of areas that thanks to continued archaeological discoveries (such as the pictured Pontius Pilate Stele (pictured above) discovered in 1961) that even the most ardent skeptics (such as Dominic Crossan or Bart Ehrman) consider as being firmly established historically: the baptism of Jesus, his crucifixion by Pontius Pilate, and that the original disciples and various groups of people experienced appearances of Jesus alive from the dead (just as the Gospels state). But the obvious next question the historian must somehow grapple with is: "What about the Resurrection?"

THE RESURRECTION

Oxford historian N. T. Wright has come to the conclusion based on decades of historic research that if one does not presuppose that philosophical naturalism is true, history would lead us to the conclusion that the Resurrection of Jesus is a historic account:

> The rise of early Christianity, and the shape it took in two central and vital respects, thus presses upon the historian the question for an explanation. The early Christian retained the Jewish belief in resurrection, but both modified it and made it more sharp and precise. They retained the Jewish belief in a coming Messiah but redrew it drastically around Jesus Himself. Why? The answer early Christians themselves give for these changes, of course, is that Jesus of Nazareth was bodily raised from the dead on the third day after His crucifixion.[195]

Such statements from such a highly respected historian as N. T. Wright of the Third Quest for the Historical Jesus are not only hurting his reputation with some of his nontheistic peers but are also marking a huge shift in what we saw from the First Quest for the Historical Jesus based on rationalism over a century ago. Moreover, it is a historian's duty to conclude what N. T. Wright stated some years ago when pressed to give an account for the rise of early Christianity: "That is why, as an historian, I cannot explain the rise of early Christianity unless Jesus rose again, leaving an empty tomb behind him;"[196] or did N. T. Wright cross the "historical line" in drawing such a conclusion?

While I agreed that I will neither conclude a miracle as a historian nor will I rule them out *a priori*, I will simply investigate on what grounds N. T. Wright would make such an assertion and moreover I will attempt to pull together what both skeptical as well as nonskeptical historians agree to (for the most part), concerning the origins of the Christian faith in light of the Historical

Jesus. There are four historical facts, which must be explained by any adequate historical hypothesis: Jesus's burial, the discovery of his empty tomb, his postmortem appearances, and the very origin of the disciples' belief in his resurrection itself. What I have discovered is that there seems to be four key facts that almost every historian from the skeptical Bart Ehrman/John Crossan camps of the Jesus Seminar to the Third Quest, collectively agree to concerning the death of Jesus.[197]

Fact 1: After his crucifixion, Jesus was buried by Joseph of Arimathea in a tomb.

This is highly significant because it means that the location of Jesus's tomb was known to Jew and Christian alike in Jerusalem. Evidence supporting this fact that most historians agree to:

1. Jesus's burial is attested in the very old information handed on by Paul in his first letter to the church in Corinth, Greece.

2. The burial account is part of very old source material used by Mark in his gospel.

3. As a member of the Jewish high court that condemned Jesus, Joseph of Arimathea is unlikely to be a Christian invention.

4. The burial story lacks any signs of legendary development.

5. No other competing burial story exists.

Fact 2: On the Sunday after the crucifixion, Jesus's tomb was found empty by a group of his women followers.

Evidence supporting this fact:

1. The old information transmitted by Paul implies the empty tomb (ex. "He was buried" or "He was raised")

2. The empty tomb story is also part of Mark's very old source material.

3. The story is simple and lacks signs of legendary embellishment.

4. The tomb was probably discovered empty by women. This is significant because in Jewish society, the testimony of women was regarded as unreliable. In patriarchal Jewish society, the testimony of women was not highly regarded. In fact, the Jewish historian Josephus says that women were not even permitted to serve as witnesses in a Jewish court of law. Now in light of this fact, how remarkable it is that it is women who are the discoverers of Jesus's empty tomb. Any later legendary account would certainly have made male disciples like Peter and John discover the empty tomb. The fact that it is women, rather than men, who are the discoverers of the empty tomb, is best explained by the fact that they were the chief witnesses to the fact of the empty tomb, and the Gospel writers faithfully recorded what, for them, was an awkward and possibly embarrassing fact.

5. The earliest known Jewish response to the proclamation of Jesus's resurrection presupposes the empty tomb.

Fact 3: On multiple occasions and under various circumstances, different individuals and groups of people experienced appearances of Jesus alive from the dead.

Evidence supporting this fact:

1. The list of eyewitnesses to Jesus's resurrection appearances that is quoted by Paul imply that such appearances occurred. (Ex: Cephas, the Twelve, more than five hundred brethren, James, all the apostles, Paul. (1 Cor. 15:5–8)

2. The appearance narratives in the gospels provide multiple, independent attestation of the appearances. Gerd Ludemann: "It may be taken as historically certain that Peter and the disciples had experiences after Jesus' death in which Jesus appeared to them as the risen Christ."[198]

Fact 4: The original disciples suddenly and sincerely came to believe that Jesus was raised from the dead despite their having every predisposition to the contrary.

The situation the disciples faced following Jesus' crucifixion:

1. Their leader was dead.

2. Jesus's execution exposed him as a heretic.

3. Jewish belief about the afterlife precluded anyone's rising from the dead before the general resurrection at the end of the world.

4. Nevertheless, the disciples suddenly came to believe so strongly that God had raised Jesus from the dead that they were willing to die for the truth of that belief.[199]

Of these four facts only the empty tomb seems to be disputed by some historians; but again, if these same historians accept the early Pauline creed of 1 Corinthians 15, "He was buried and he was raised," it would seem to necessitate an empty tomb. Moreover, the first account formulated by the Sanhedrin would be that the "Disciples had stolen the body"; if this was false, the Sanhedrin or the Romans would have simply shown the body still in the tomb it would seem, so it seems logical to infer an empty tomb for this reason. It is interesting to note that Bart Ehrman in 2001 reversed his stance (and written work) on these topics in which he partially rejected at the time to a position post 2001 in which he now concludes these are factual statements concerning the historicity of the death of Jesus. Though he will not conclude a miracle such as N. T. Wright, this change from his published work shows not only that Dr. Ehrman is willing to follow the evidence but also attests to the strong historicity of these above mentioned facts. While more could be said on this subject, we will leave it at that and begin to pull in the threads on what we should be able to conclude concerning the Historical Jesus.

So what can we conclude in such a short and concise summation on the Historical Jesus? If we utilize the criteria for establishing historicity that we have used as a gauge throughout this book, we should at least be able to establish certain key factors that would be agreed to by the vast majority of New Testament historians as well as by the majority of members of the "Quest for the Historical Jesus" (1, 2, and 3). These factors too would need to satisfactorily meet Dr. McCullagh's seven points when compared to any competing views of Jesus. So I am of the opinion that though the points we have covered are anything but "exhaustive," we can draw a set of highly probable historical affirmations or conclusions on the Historical Jesus which must include:

1. Jesus of Nazareth did exist. Nonbiblical sources such as Josephus, Tacitus, Thallus, and others tell us the following—Jesus lived during the time of Tiberius Caesar. He lived a virtuous life. He was a wonder-worker. He had a brother named James. He was acclaimed to be the Messiah. He was crucified under Pontius Pilate. He was crucified on the eve of the Jewish Passover. Darkness and an earthquake occurred when he died. His disciples believed he rose from the dead. His disciples were willing to die for their belief. Christianity spread rapidly as far as Rome. His disciples denied the Roman gods and worshipped Jesus.

2. Most historians do agree that the source and form criticism of the New Testament can trace the tradition of 1 Corinthians 15, which expounds the death and supposed resurrection of Jesus to within 1.5–6 years of Jesus's death. No historian disputes that the New Testament has more manuscript evidence than any other ancient source or that it was the closest to the events themselves (though still approximately thirty years after) though they do disagree on the accuracy of the manuscripts. Most historians confirm

that early church historians did record a very similar attestation to these N. T. manuscripts; for example, Tertullian stated that by AD 150 the church in Rome had compiled a list of the New Testament books matching our list of today. We have 32,000 quotes from before AD 325, from Irenaeus (AD 182–188), Justin Martyr (before AD 150), Polycarp (AD 107), Ignatius (100), Clement (AD 96) and many other second and third century fathers (Ignatius and Polycarp were reported as followers of the Apostle John who died approximately AD 100 and would have had access to John's firsthand knowledge concerning the historical Jesus). All but eleven verses of the New Testament can be reconstructed through their writings and commentary alone.

3. First and Second Quest for the Historical Jesus—Jesus came from Nazareth. He was baptized by John; he preached and told parables about the kingdom of God; he viewed this kingdom as coming in the near future and possibly as already present in some sense; he performed, or was believed to have performed, exorcisms and healings; he gathered a group of disciples around him; he associated with outcasts and sinners; he challenged the Jewish leaders of his day; he was arrested and charged with blasphemy and sedition; and he was crucified by the Romans.

4. Third Quest—Jesus was at least in part viewed as a type of cynic-sage, spirit person, social revolutionary, eschatological prophet, and Messiah. The Jewishness of Jesus must not be overlooked; the Synoptic Gospels do fall into the genre of historical narrative (with theological implications) and therefore cannot be discredited a priori.

5. Jesus's Death—Four historical facts which must be explained by any adequate historical hypothesis: Jesus's burial, the discovery of his empty tomb, his postmortem appearances, and the very origin of the disciples' belief in

his resurrection itself. The vast majority of New Testament critics agree on these four established facts though they do not agree on their conclusions; even the most skeptical do acknowledge that the early followers of Jesus at least "thought" he had risen from the dead (whether by hallucination as Gerd Ludemann believes, a spiritual [nonphysical] resurrection as Marcus Borg believes or a physical resurrection as N. T. Wright has came to believe), the vast majority of scholars do concede that from the early disciples to James the Brother of Jesus (who did not believe in Jesus as the Messiah while he lived, but after he supposedly rose from the dead became an ardent follower of Jesus who was martyred for this belief that he did not hold while Jesus was alive), all did at least "think" Jesus had risen from the dead and thus led to the rise and rapid spread of Christian theism.

Though these conclusions are purposefully all too brief in its coverage of the Historical Jesus, we can agree that the six points I mentioned above are virtually agreed by all N. T. Critics and historians concerning the Historical Jesus, and they also are recorded as such in the New Testament itself, which demonstrates its own incredibly high degree of historicity. Whether Jesus really was the "Son of God" or "God Incarnate" and whether he really "walked on water" or "performed actual miracles" is a philosophical and theological discussion that it beyond our scope at this junction for the Historical Jesus. What we can conclude to a high probability is that the picture of the Historical Jesus outlined above without philosophical or theological assumptions is better established than any person of the same era or before; so to doubt the historicity of the above mentioned six points that virtually all historians (believers or not) agree to is to doubt the entire methodological system we base "history" on in the first place. Moreover, the above six points do seem to fit the criteria outlined by Dr. McCullagh for establishing the historicity of the Historical Jesus much more conclusively than any other naturalistic hypothesis considering it:

1. Has great explanatory scope.

2. Has great explanatory power.

3. It is plausible.

4. It is not ad hoc or contrived.

5. It is in accord with accepted beliefs.

6. It far outstrips any of its rival theories (such as any naturalistic hypotheses) in meeting conditions 1–5.

So while the debate on miracles, a possible conspiracy that happened at the immediate time of Jesus's death in which all historic materials could have been corrupted immediately thereafter, etc., will continue to be debated and theorized; I see virtually no historian from any of the past or present quests for the Historical Jesus disputing these six "historic" conclusions. Therefore, we can establish them as "nonabsolute" historic facts for the life and times of the fascinating and mysterious individual known as the Historical Jesus. So what we have seen is that from Genesis through the New Testament and the Historical Jesus, the amount of established historicity is literally mind-boggling. While the historian cannot confirm or disconfirm the miraculous, from an open philosophy of history it is literally without question that theism and moreover the Bible itself, far outweighs that of philosophical naturalism. A closed philosophy based on naturalism basically says not to challenge "naturalism" as I have reviewed from the onset and closely behind that is not to use religious text such as the Bible for attempting to construe an open philosophy of history. What I have seen in various travels through the world as well as have attempted to outline thus far is how this "closed philosophy" needs to be challenged and is overtly wrong as well as out of date much like Wellhausen's hypotheses are today. So again the question must be asked to academia: Why continue to endorse naturalism and/or Wellhausen philosophy if they are most likely incorrect? Why force students to pretend the emperor has clothes when the fact is he may not?

MIRACLES?

I have found that in most situations it is not for a lack of evidences or historic qualifications that the Historical Jesus has continued to be viewed through a "Wellhausenian lens," but it is due to the nonnaturalistic association with "miracles." Though anything within "origins" or "non-naturalism" can qualify as a "miracle" per se, it is important to briefly breakdown possible "nonnaturalistic" versus "purely naturalistic" venues that can be used as an "inference" to the best explanation of the data by both sides. Are "miracles" possible? By miracle, I am referring to something that is nonnaturalistic in its causation. A person flying unaided by any type of airplane for example would qualify as a "miraculous" event unless we could explain why this happened naturalistically. The only way a miracles is not possible or not credible is if there is nothing beyond space/time/matter (nature). If there is a transcendent cause beyond space/time/matter, then the miraculous could be a credible philosophical inference to the best explanation if no natural cause can explain it. Though there have been many who doubt the possibility of miracles even by this simple definition, it was probably Scottish philosopher David Hume who made the largest impact with his commentary *Of Miracles* where he argues that we are never justified in concluding that a miracle has occurred. Hume's principle of analogy appeals to antecedent probability: "We ought to give the preference to such as are founded on the greatest number of past observations. But though, in proceeding by this rule, we readily reject any fact which is unusual and incredible in an ordinary degree."[200]

Although countless replies have been made to Hume and many historians now do not see that holding to a naturalistic worldview is a necessity, there are still many, like skeptical historian Bart Ehrman, who still argue based on Hume's principle of analogy. Pieter Craffert, who takes a social-scientific approach, likewise comments: "The principle of analogy which is one of the basic principles of all social scientific study, is not restricted to the skeptical historian, but applies to all historiography as well as everyday life. There is no other option but to apply to present practical standards of everyday life to determine whether the decision of the historian to reject the claims of some events narrated in ancient sources, is valid."[201]

One can see that based on this quote from Craffert that a type of naturalism/positivism still permeates much of history today, which again I feel is completely unwarranted. Examples or origins from the universe, life, human contingency, civilization, and so on could be interpreted as a credible testimony on the behalf of a miraculous event and therefore rejected (although these events obviously took place), so the closed principle of analogy can easily be taken too far. Another problem is its incredible restrictiveness as philosopher Norman Geisler writes:

> If it were true that no present exception can overthrow the supposed 'laws' of nature based on our uniform experience in the past, then there could be no true progress in our scientific understanding of the world... This is precisely what happened when certain outer-spatial 'exceptions' to Newton's law of gravitation were found and Einstein's theory of relativity was considered broader and more adequate. Without established exceptions, no progress can be made in science. In short, Hume's objections to miracles seem to be unscientific.[202]

Does the principle of analogy allow for the possibility of a transcendent being (a. k. a. God) to act within time or does it rule it out *a priori*? If it was known that God does not exist, then the a prior exclusion of miracles would be justified but as we have seen the arguments for a transcendent being are stronger today than perhaps ever before while naturalism/materialism is becoming weaker and less plausible. If a historian does not follow the principle of analogy and allows for the "possibility" of a metaphysical reality and thus an "open philosophy" of history, I do not see that this discredits them in the slightest. As Oxford historian N. T. Wright concluded: "The natural/supernatural distinction itself and the near-equation of 'supernatural' with 'superstition' are scarecrows that Enlightenment thought has erected in its fields to frighten away anyone following the historical argument where it leads. It is high time the birds learned to take notice."[203] Mike Licona likewise confers: "The historian would be epistemically justified in embracing a theistic worldview while making historical considerations. After all, why should an atheist or agnostic worldview be awarded a default position, especially when good data exists for a theistic reality?"[204] Similarly in the 2006 theme issue of *History and Theory*, David Gary Shaw opened with the following words:

> Another claim… is that history is against religion, as its other and opposite, but that this is not as it should be. The opposition is an artifact of modernity. Indeed, throughout these papers the theme develops that modernity is the obstacle or prejudice that stands not just between historians and the people of the past, but also between historians and many religious people today… We appear to be at a moment when we need new intellectual and professional approaches to deal with religion. Accounting for our own position is tricky, but always worthwhile, if only to try to appreciate our prejudices and assumptions in advance of doing our scholarship. This Theme Issue shows historians and others concerned with the study of religion to be at a sort of confessional watershed, a moment of collective acknowledgment that the interaction between religion

and history is not at the position that most historians have though, especially when we fall back only upon our own learned memories, graduate training, prejudices, or our grand narratives of historical development. The Issue's papers pulse with a sense that religion has turned out in a variety of ways to be more important and a more clearly permanent factor in history than our paradigms had supposed. The consequences of this include a need to reassess the historian's attitudes toward religious phenomena and religion's trajectory within the mass of forces we call historical... The methods that historians used may need revision or defense if they are to cope productively with believers past and present, even if we can disregard what historians themselves believe.[205]

This sums up perfectly why an open philosophy of history is beginning to make progress with more and more professional historians showing signs that the epistemological ice age of antisupernaturalism appears to be coming to an end. Scholars are beginning to rightly claim their rights to investigate miracle claims in and of their own merit, and they are finding themselves ever less alone in doing so.

CONCLUSIONS

In 1989, syndicated talk show host Larry King interviewed Shirley MacLaine on the New Age Movement. When a Christian caller contested her view with an appeal to the New Testament, MacLaine brushed them off with the objection that the Bible has been changed and translated so many times over the last two thousand years that it's impossible to have any confidence in its accuracy. King was quick to endorse her "facts." "*Everyone knows that,*" he grunted.

As we have reviewed, this type of adolescent review with no evidence to support it is simply an assertion made by both King and MacLaine. While this type of review may be more than adequate by the media, PBS, and even the layperson in our relativistic age, we have seen firsthand that the professional historian or philosopher of history must conclude the exact opposite of what King and MacLaine so articulately concluded in regard to biblical inaccuracy based on (I assume) a Wellhausen-like interpretation. Again, while I am not attempting to wear the hat of the "theologian" nor am I attempting to state that the Bible is inerrant or divinely inspired per se. What I am concluding as a philosopher of history is that the Bible as a whole must be ranked at a supreme level both philosophically as well as historically. The Bible includes many minute details on what we know concerning the world today and can be verified historically by many direct and indirect extrabiblical sources. When we get to the New Testament, this evidence becomes literally overwhelming. Not only do we have more intact texts than any other ancient documentation, but they are the closest to the time of the original autographs. It is quite ironic that the ancient text that would have the most textual evidences and shortest time frame from autographs would be the same, and it is more surprising why so many persons state as MacLaine as well as Wellhausen that the "New Testament is simply inaccurate, but other ancient writings are accurate."

As a philosopher of history, I simply cannot make sense of these types of statements especially when there are no evidences to support such ad hoc assertions. Minute details within the New Testament documents naming geography, rulers, governors, and systems that can and have been verified by both archaeology as well as extrabiblical sources coupled with the fact that we have a plethora of early sources as well as quotes from early church historians that match up with the texts themselves has caused me to conclude that such statements made by historians like John Montgomery in regard to being skeptical of the N. T. is equal to being completely skeptical of all other ancient writings is an accurate one. This, coupled with the fact that the N. T. does not read as a mythical invention, as does the much later Gnostic Gospels, increases the chances that the information recorded within it is plausibly accurate. The only conclusion for dismissing the N. T. as a historian is the fact that biases want it to be inaccurate and/or the problem with miracles; however, after covering how an open philosophy of history cannot simply rule out nonnaturalistic causation (since naturalism is most likely false) I no longer believe that the "naturalistic crutch" is an adequate enough reason for the historian to dismiss the entirety of the New Testament or the Bible as a whole.

So the question remains that if this is the case, then what in the world would justify a historian to rule out our best account of ancient history *a priori*? The simple answer that I have seen time and time again is nothing more than a presuppositional belief for naturalism incarnated into their philosophy of history. I have openly debated both liberal as well as conservative scholars on these topics, and I have yet to see any compelling reason to completely rule out the biblical account if it is one of the best historic accounts both quantitatively and qualitatively simply because it does not align with naturalism. Professor emeritus of Egyptology and archaeology, Liverpool, England, K. A. Kitchen comes to similar conclusions when reviewing naturalistic evolution steering Wellhausenian philosophy of history:

> The 19th century just loved evolution, in the wake of Charles Darwin's spectacular theories of the natural world. And in historical terms, it gave Wellhausen the concept of arranging the development of Israel and her institutions on an ascending line from the most primitive level to the most sophisticated: from primitive tribes-folk having a 'natural,' free-and-easy, very simple religion, through a rudimentary monarchy. So Wellhausen worked in a near vacuum and could speculate freely. But that day has long, long since gone. We today do have vast historic resources that enable us to profile ancient history accurately in its

broad sweep. And straight bottom-to-top evolution is out. It never happened like that; no, not ever. What did happen was the emergence of a culture with its political format, followed by an undulating history of ups and downs, until the political format was lost and the culture-bearing population either scattered or absorbed into other peoples and traditions. For the ancient powers (Egypt, Mesopotamia, Anatolia), the facts have been available for most of the last century, but were never studied as a continuum phenomenon. This final scheme, pumped into generations of students is and always was pure, unadulterated fantasy. I am sorry, but that's how life is—and wasn't. It clashes horribly with real-life historical profiles for the cultures that we can test; that is how things are, and it wrecks the Wellhausen scheme of evolutionary-history completely.[206]

More and more philosophers of science are beginning to agree that there are no solid grounds for endorsing naturalism and moreover there are definitely no solid grounds for endorsing a closed philosophy of history that dismisses anything nonnaturalistic. Let us hope that this trend will continue into the twenty-first century and beyond.

FINAL CONCLUSIONS

I say this as someone who cannot imagine believing what
(a theist) believes. But even those who cannot accept the
theist alternative should admit that (Alvin) Plantinga's
criticisms of naturalism are directed at the deepest problem
with that view—how it can account for the appearance,
through the operation of the laws of physics and chemistry, of conscious beings like ourselves, capable of discover-
ing those laws and understanding the universe that they
govern. Defenders of naturalism have not ignored this
problem, but I believe that so far, even with the aid of evolutionary theory, they have not proposed a credible solution. Perhaps theism and materialistic naturalism are not
the only alternatives.

—Thomas Nagel, *NY Review of Books* (Oct. 2012)

Should we be suspicious of a book on Russian history if it
were written only by Marxist philosophers? Should we be suspicious if it were written only by non-Russian capitalists? The
answer to both of these questions should be a resounding "yes."
In the not so distant past history was predominantly written by
Caucasian, upper middle-class males; should this make us suspicious if we are reading a history of women's rights or Native
American Culture by this group of authors? Perhaps. Historians

are a product of their culture and with that will have their own personal and cultural biases. While this is to be at least partially expected, an inquirer looking for a book on Native American culture should expect to receive a well-balanced, thought-out, and articulated source when they go to a library, bookstore, or lecture hall. Historian C. Behan McCullagh believes that too many have been misled for far too long:

> Bias of any sort, be it cultural or personal, is deplorable. If cultural bias is difficult to overcome, personal bias is easier to detect and correct, once the need to provide a fair account of the past is clearly recognized and accepted. A commitment to rationality will help historians overcome personal bias, motivating them to check the adequacy of their preconceptions and descriptions of historical subjects, the scope and intelligibility of their interpretations, and the completeness of their genetic explanations. The search for adequate interpretations and explanations can be limited by a failure of imagination, a failure to see patterns in events, or to imagine possible causes at work, and that failure is the product of the historian's personal interests.[207]

Why is this not the case when one raises an objection to naturalism as a whole or suggests an open philosophy of inquiry? Dr. Alex Rosenberg, who describes himself as a "disenchanted naturalist," provides the following summary of atheism's answers to some of life's most persistent questions:

- Is there a God? *No.*
- What is the nature of reality? *What physics says it is.*
- What is the purpose of the universe? *There is none.*
- What is the meaning of life? *Ditto.*
- Why am I here? *Just dumb luck.*
- Is there a soul? *Are you kidding?*

- Is there free will? *Not a chance!*

- What is the difference between right/wrong, good/bad? *There is no moral difference between them.*

- Does the human past have any lessons for our future? *Fewer and fewer if it ever had any to begin with.*

- Does history have any meaning or purpose? *It's full of sound and fury but signifies nothing.*

- He concludes: *So much for the meaning of history, and everything else we care about.*[208]

Rosenberg admits that if you are going to be atheistic, "you will have to be comfortable with a certain amount of nihilism.... And just in case there's always Prozac."[209] One need not look far to see how Dr. Rosenberg's biases affect his writing and teaching at Duke University. Dr. Rosenberg eloquently spells out and reconfirms quite plainly what I have already summarized in this book. We are forced to sacrifice virtually everything we know about reality if we wish to accept that naturalism is true, including history itself though we are given no reasons whatsoever for such a conclusion. If this is the best the naturalist can offer for why we must not allow nonnaturalistic hypotheses (such as theism) into play, then I, for one, will continue to follow Plantinga's advice that naturalism, like positivism before it, should be consigned to the scrap heap of philosophical history and that an open philosophy of history should welcome theism (and even the Bible) back into the pool of live options for reality as we know it based not only on its better fulfillment of McCullagh's seven points but of plain common sense.

While I have been warned by several well-meaning individuals that I would be much better off focusing my efforts on a mode of history using current historic methodology even if there "may" be an undergirding of naturalistic philosophy driving it, I simply cannot leave it alone. The very reason I first began studying history was to attempt to discover the truth of humanity's past and purpose, and if I am to do this, it is implausible for me to take a naturalistic point of view as my frame of reference if it is indeed false. What we have therefore concluded in this book are the following:

1. There are no good reasons to believe naturalism to be true, and if there is no good reason to believe it to be true, then it should not guide the way in which we look at ancient history (closed philosophy).

2. There are good reasons to believe that naturalism is false, and if there are good reasons to believe it to be false, then it should most definitely not guide the way we look at ancient history (open philosophy).

3. What has traditionally been referred to as "origins science" would be better described as "origins history" and therefore a component of philosophy of history.

4. Lastly, we have seen that the Bible (for better or worse) does remain a viable and coherent record of the historicity of the universe and humanity and does make solid philosophical and existential sense by providing a reasonable answer to origin, meaning, ethics, and destiny of life.

If these four points are true (which I continue to challenge anyone to dispute or debate these points), then it follows that my conclusion must also be true. Moreover, if my conclusions are true, then it logically follows that academia should support the concept of an "open philosophy" of history, which would not only support the abandonment of naturalistic presuppositions but would also make a valid case for the adoption of what has normally been called "origin sciences" into the realm of philosophy of history.

While this obviously does have theological implications, my point of reference is that the history perpetuated in the Bible itself is of a superior caliber and should be welcomed by the philosopher as well as the historian. If naturalism is indeed false, so be it—I see no logical reason for basing my discipline upon a philosophy that is most likely false. I prefer to keep my education in the public/secular (per se) arena, but before I even consider pursuit of doctoral studies in history, it would have to be under an open philosophy of history. If I am told that I must follow a strict naturalistic philosophy of history, then I honestly can say I have no interests in pursuing doctoral studies, and I am not alone.

Having traveled broadly, I have come in contact with many scholars from a variety of disciplines. I have already mentioned the Discovery Institute, to whom many have questioned "Why in the world would I associate with such a group?" as though they had the plague or were members of the Klu Klux Klan. But after visiting extensively with many of the scholars at Discovery and hearing both sides of the argument, I am still amazed why if the evidence is overwhelmingly on the naturalists' side (and if my points concerning naturalism are false) then why not simply show why this is instead of reverting to censorship? In December 2005, US district court judge John E. Jones III permanently prohibited the Dover, Pennsylvania, school district not only from teaching intelligent design but also "from requiring teachers to denigrate or disparage"[210] Darwinian evolution (and presumably, the methodological naturalism that underlies it). By judicial fiat, naturalism is now state law at least in the Middle District of Pennsylvania. All criticism of it in the public schools is discouraged under penalty of law. Since when are evidences decided by the court system and censorship? Two such proclamations that such groups have fought in court are as follows:

> Analyze, review, and critique naturalistic explanations, including hypotheses and theories, as to their strengths

and weaknesses using scientific evidence and information-
Texas Textbook Proclamation 2001.

In all fields of science, analyze, evaluate, and critique
naturalistic explanations by using empirical evidence, logical reasoning, and experimental and observational testing, including examining all sides of scientific evidence
of those scientific explanations, so to encourage critical
thinking by the student.

Texas Essential Knowledge and Skills standard, submit-
ted for 2011 state approval and local adoption

Simply teaching students to "analyze, review, and critique
naturalistic philosophies" are taboo? But this obviously is not
limited to naturalism alone. We have seen gross distortions in
the annals of history in the name of twenty-first century relativism and political correctness growing at an alarming rate. I have
had the privilege of also meeting various Middle Eastern scholars
who share a very similar concern on being unable to follow an
uncoerced philosophy of history that simply follows the evidence
where it leads. One such parallel example to that of subverting
information to fit a naturalistic paradigm is that held by many
theocratic governments such as Pakistan. I had the privilege to
meet and work with Daniel Scot in Bartlesville, Oklahoma, in
September 2012. Daniel Scot was born and educated in Pakistan
where he was a university mathematics lecturer. He was the first
Christian that had blasphemy charges brought against him under
the 295c law in Pakistan. He went into hiding numerous times
around the country for security reasons. He eventually found it
necessary to flee Pakistan and has lived in Australia since 1987
and taught mathematics at Queensland University of Technology
and the University of Queensland. After five senior professors
asked him to convert to Islam and launched an investigation
into his religious beliefs, he became the first person successfully
charged under Pakistan's then-new blasphemy laws. Quoting the
Quran and the Hadiths (collected sayings of Muhammad); Scot

meticulously broke down the historic implausibility of Islam as a simple extrapolation of heavily Gnostic-influenced Christian thought with an Arabic twist in the late sixth century, which resulted in his condemnation by death sentence. Once the charges were publicized, a mob came after Scot with pistols and knives, and he was forced into hiding. When the mob threatened to burn down all the churches in the area to find him, he fled the country.

In his native Pakistan where Christians make up less than 3 percent of the population and blasphemy laws quickly lead to death sentences, such a ruling would be tame. But the next case unfolded in Australia where Scot has worked as a professor and pastor since 1987 and is now a naturalized citizen. Scot was cited for nineteen counts of vilifying Muslims, yet fifteen of nineteen of these statements were direct quotes from the Quran. The charges were brought in Melbourne, a city better known for lively coffee bars and generous beaches than for restricting free speech due to a law passed in Victoria State in 2001, the Racial and Religious Tolerance Act, criminalized not only race discrimination but any "vilifying conduct" against "a religious belief or activity." Scot calls these campaigns "intellectual terrorism." He blames Islamic groups that take advantage of open democracy in countries where Muslim populations are growing rapidly. They lobby in favor of the restrictions as a way to stifle legitimate debate over Islamic-inspired terrorism and the meaning of Quranic texts. "Teaching about Islam is not a popular subject, especially if you know the Quran," Scot told the January 26 gathering sponsored by the Kairos Journal where he received an annual award honoring his courage in light of academic persecution. This case made it all the way to Australia's Supreme Court before the court overturned it and found Scot not guilty of doing anything wrong since distorting history in the name of political correctness in the face of persecution is not mandatory as of 2013 in "most" Western countries.[211] Scot's story should serve as a perfect example of what can happen when a relativistic philosophy is allowed to rule; whether via naturalism or Sharia (Islamic rule), once a paradigm is in place, no one is allowed to question it even if it is false. This is why it is so important to question naturalism and the methodology associated with it now.

Similarly there have been approximately five hundred thousand to one million Armenians killed by Turkish forces in World War I, but due to Turkey not preferring such an accusation and threatening to cut off diplomatic relations with countries that will not join them in writing this out of the annals of history, many Western countries are choosing to rewrite and falsify history in order to appease Turkey and avoid being labeled "politically incorrect" or "racist." Whether it is the denial of the Jewish Holocaust in WWII, the Rwandan Genocide, Japan Genocide against the Chinese in WWII, many groups are seeking to rewrite history in order to "appease" those who do not like what the past is. The victors write the history books! May indeed be what happens to the philosophy of history as we know it if historians do not regain what I call tactful honor in the light of fear or persecution. I am a Christian theist and of European and Native American decent, and I would never dream of denying the fact that European Christians committed genocide of the Native American people groups—should I? Perhaps I should seek to deny this fact of history and make up my own imaginary one? I think not. This is going to be the real pressure for philosophy of history as we go further into the twenty-first century; will more and more historians take the side of London in agreeing to minimize their historic coverage of the Jewish Holocaust in lieu of Islamic pressure groups who deny the event, or will a few honorable historians stand in the way and say, "No, this is nonsense"? Will the history books in the next century be devoid of the 9-11 attacks in New York City (where I have spent the last two years) to appease the 60 percent of British and Turkish Muslims who deny the historicity of the event? Even as I write this, Egypt (like many other Islamic governmental countries), has passed laws increasing the illegality of questioning Islamic doctrine or in reading the Bible as a competing hypothesis. Not only do I find this dumbfounding since "if" Islam is true and accurate (such as naturalism holds), then why would anyone wish to silence competing views? If their account is a true one, then why not welcome all competing viewpoints and measure them each against all evidences available? As for me, I am not politically correct nor do I ever wish to be; I will continue to challenge and push back on "half-truths" that I am spoon-fed but am told not to challenge but to just accept in order to maintain job security, financial security, and the status quo. I will be persuaded by facts and evidence not blind or bold-faced assertions and threats. There will be many who say I am "wrong" in the points I have covered including academic freedoms to record the "truth" in the hopes of obtaining a pure and open philosophy of history; these same people will most likely provide no refutations for what I have written and will instead side with the ever-changing "victors" to alter the philosophy of history to the side that at that time is winning. Let us all hope that objective truth in history will be the victors and that fear and intimidation will not change this fact anymore than it will the truth that 2+2=4.[212]

Historiographer Jeremy Black comments on philosophy of history and religion as follows:

> An overlap between secular and the religious histories, and historians was frequent. History, alongside religion, formed the key way of explaining the world. The past was central to the processes of reference and relevance, and in a way that is alien to many modern cultures. History illuminated God's purpose and the interconnectedness of the cosmic and earthly, the divine and the human. In doings so, history fulfilled the role given to science today. This interconnectedness of the divine and the human was not only general, but also specific, with history serving to present the importance of particular sites, relics and individuals. It did so by recording origins and provenance, providing

an equivalent to dynastic histories. Religious texts were regarded as history and vice versa. Historiography deals with the evolving or changing interpretations of history, with the legacy of historical writing, and with today's perspectives on previous scholarship, and is the art of depicting historical controversy. In its narrower sense, historiography relates to the study of historical writing, mainly the philosophy and theories of history, and, in a wider sense, to how historical debate has developed. As such, historiography is not a subject or tendency restricted to the works of academics, nor to their views of the past.[213]

Perhaps Dr. Black is correct in his analysis; perhaps the day is dawning in which an open philosophy of history and religious text such as the Bible will be recognized not only as compatible but as necessarily compatible. If naturalism is indeed false, then the future of philosophy, history, and existentialism is wide open, mysterious, and exciting once again. May the future generations have the freedom and privileged opportunity to take the unadulterated evidence wherever it leads.

AFTERWORD

The incredibly counterproductive fads, fashions, and dogmas of American education—from kindergarten to the
colleges—have yet to take their full toll, in part because
all the standards of earlier times have not yet been completely eroded away. In short, too many American schools
are turning out students who are not only intellectually
incompetent but also morally confused, emotionally alien-
ated, and socially maladjusted.

—Thomas Sowell, *Inside American Education*

While I did not intend to end this work by possibly sounding like
a Christian apologist per se, I must admit as I reach the conclusion that if this is where the evidence leads, so be it. Though I am
certain many of my peers and reviewers will completely dismiss
my entire case that has been made thus far simply for my inclusion
of this afterword, I would contradict everything I have written on
concerning following an open philosophical knowing of history if
I now retracted or redirected where this evidence seems to point.
Some years ago while finishing my philosophy degree, I read a
work by philosopher Francis Schaeffer in which he proposed that
human culture (ethics/art/history) itself hinged on the ultimate
reality of Christian theism as portrayed in the Bible; therefore,
cultural degradation itself could be traced to an abandonment

of biblical Christian theism in light of cultural relativism. I at first assumed that Dr. Schaeffer, like so many others, was simply basing his own personal biases/beliefs on his own personal philosophy and therefore I did not place any real value in his work. I now, however, believe that I may have dismissed Schaeffer's point of view prematurely. After rereviewing Schaffer's work, it could be categorized that Schaeffer's main focus was that until recently within human history there has always been a presuppositional belief in "objective" absolute truth and that with our demise into a relativistic society we have lost this sense of reason and logic. Though Schaeffer wrote and spoke on this subject over fifty years ago, it appears his warnings were not only unheeded but were quite well founded and can be seen quite visibly today.

> This little formula, "A is A" and "If you have A it is not non-A," is the first move in classical logic. If you understand the extent to which this no longer holds sway today, you will understand our present situation. [However] No artificial barriers can keep out the flow of ideas. As the world has shrunk, and as it has largely become post-Christian, both sides have followed the same methodology and the same basic monolithic thought-form—namely, the lack of absolutes and antithesis, leading to pragmatic relativism. In our modern forms of specialized education there is a tendency to lose the whole in the parts, and in this sense we can say that our generation produces few truly educated people. True education means thinking by associating across the various disciplines, and not just being highly qualified in one field, as a technician might be.[214]

While I have stated from the onset of this book that this subject nor my research was based on or meant to be written as a theologian (which I am neither inclined nor qualified to write as), I cannot however pretend that it does not have theological implications. If these implications are even possibly true, then I do believe they should be taken seriously, explored further, and shared with others. If we follow an open philosophical mind-set, then we should have nothing to fear, but we may in turn find a lot to discover up to and including the objectivity of truth itself. It is somewhat perplexing yet gratifying that with each century that goes by we see scientific discoveries overturned or replaced with new theories and hypotheses along with the various concepts and interpretations of humanism and pluralism come and go; the Bible and the concept of Christian theism remains a very plausible and unchanging worldview with incredibly great explanatory power and scope.

> God has set the revelation of the Bible in history; He did not give it in the form of a theological textbook. Having set the revelation as history, what sense then would it make for God to give us a revelation in which the *history* was wrong? God has also set man in the *universe*, which the Scriptures themselves say speaks of this God. What sense then would it make for God to give His revelation in a book that was wrong concerning the universe? It is plain, therefore, that from the viewpoint of the Scriptures themselves there is a unity over the whole field of knowledge. God has spoken, in a linguistic propositional form, truth concerning man, history and the universe.[215]

With this quote, Francis Schaeffer (shockingly) summarizes the exact same conclusions that I have reached in the compilation of this book. Regardless of what one does with this information, it cannot be denied that the Bible is anything but a holistic worldview that supplies a history of origins on virtually all areas of "being" that a naturalistic closed philosophy simply cannot.

I truly mean this in a nonoffensive way, but people are growing more and more nonintellectual it would seem. I do not know how many students have given me responses such as: "My professor told me so therefore it is true." Or even people of a certain religious affiliation saying to me while I lived in New York:

"My pastor/imam told me so it must be true." I usually encourage them to try and think on their own, but I am dumbfounded how many of these people have simply lost this ability. In a culture and time in which the media and scientocracy has replaced the Bible as "infallible," I truly wonder if Schaeffer's points of reference are more accurate than I at first believed them to be.

I suppose I should not be surprised. In a day in which governmental education policies, such as "no student left behind," forces teachers to give students passing grades regardless of whether or not they are ready for advancement or when the vast majority of Americans wish an evenly balanced portrayal of controversial areas such as presentation of both the strengths and weaknesses to Darwinian naturalism instead of only one side is answered by the government involving itself to enforce a one point of reference closed view that will only allow it (naturalism) to be taught as fact has resulted in our national average of standardized testing being much lower than that of even the most simple private Christian schools in "all" subjects including science[216] or when a country like France threatens measures up to and including expulsion from their country for raising such issues as I have in this book which could label me as a "creationist" and therefore a candidate for expulsion on the same grounds as an Islamic terrorist.[217] In a time in which all forms of abortion are considered acceptable, where groups such as the ACLU will force such statements to be abolished from school campuses such as "do not murder" or "do unto others as you would have them do unto you" simply because they could be taken from the Bible—should I be surprised that education, morality/ethics, and the ability to think and reason logically are in such an abysmal state? Perhaps I should not be that surprised after all.

The twenty-first century will be a telling point for the world. Either we will stand behind objective truth or sink into the abyss of relativism in the name of political correctness. May the future of historic methodology allow for the unraveling and discovery of objective truth (that does exist) if we are only allowed to uncover it one piece at a time.

GLOSSARY OF TERMS

a priori—Known to be true independently of or in advance of experience of the subject matter; requiring no evidence for its validation or support.

ad hoc—Lacking generality or justification: an ad hoc decision; an ad hoc committee.

agnosticism—A person who claims, with respect to any particular question, that the answer cannot be known with certainty.

atheism—The doctrine or belief that there is no God.

deism—The belief in the existence of a God on the evidence of reason and nature only with rejection of supernatural revelation (distinguished from theism). Belief in a God who created the world but has since remained indifferent to it.

epistemology—A branch of philosophy that investigates the origin, nature, methods, and limits of human knowledge.

history—The branch of knowledge dealing with past events.

logic—The system or principles of reasoning applicable to any branch of knowledge or study.

materialism—The philosophical theory that regards matter and its motions as constituting the universe, and all phenomena, including those of mind, as due to material agencies.

metaphysics—The branch of philosophy that treats of first principles, includes ontology and cosmology, and is intimately connected with epistemology (literally meaning "beyond" normal physics).

naturalism—The view of the world that takes account only of natural elements and forces, excluding the supernatural or spiritual. The belief that all phenomena are covered by laws of science and that all teleological explanations are therefore without value.

ontology—The branch of metaphysics that studies the nature of existence or being as such.

origin science—The branch of "science" dealing with past unrepeatable events.

philosophy—The rational investigation of the truths and principles of being, knowledge, or conduct.

physicalism—The doctrine that all phenomena can be described in terms of space and time and that all meaningful statements are either analytic, as in logic and mathematics, or can be reduced to empirically verifiable assertions

positivism—A philosophical system founded by Auguste Comte, concerned with positive facts and phenomena, and excluding speculation upon ultimate causes or origins (ex. Talk of "God" is utterly meaningless).

scientism—The belief that the assumptions, methods of research, etc., of the physical and biological sciences are equally appropriate and essential to all other disciplines, including the humanities and the social sciences.

theism—The belief in one God as the creator and ruler of the universe, without rejection of revelation (distinguished from deism).

END NOTES

1 Discovery Institute's Science Education Policy, at http://www.discovery.org/a/3164

2 David DeWolf, John West, and Casey Luskin, "Intelligent Design Will Survive Kitzmiller v. Dover," Montana Law Review, 68:7 (Winter, 2007).

3 Jay D. Wexler, "Kitzmiller and the 'Is It Science?' Question," *First Amendment Law Review*, 5:90, 93 (2006).

4 Douglas D. Axe, "Estimating the Prevalence of Protein Sequences Adopting Functional Enzyme Folds," Journal of Molecular Biology, Vol. 341: 1295-1315 (2004); Douglas A. Axe, "Extreme Functional Sensitivity to Conservative Amino Acid Changes on Enzyme Exteriors," *Journal of Molecular Biology*, Vol. 301: 585-595 (2000).

5 Michael Behe and David Snoke, "Simulating Evolution by Gene Duplication of Protein Features That Require Multiple Amino Acid Residues," *Protein Science*, 13: 2651-2664 (2004).

6 Michael Behe and David Snoke, "Simulating Evolution by Gene Duplication of Protein Features That Require

Multiple Amino Acid Residues," *Protein Science*, 13: 2651-2664 (2004).

7   Douglas D. Axe, "The Limits of Complex Adaptation: An Analysis Based on a Simple Model of Structured Bacterial Populations," *BIO-Complexity*, Vol. 2010(4):1-10.

8   Ann Gauger and Douglas Axe, "The Evolutionary Accessibility of New Enzyme Functions: A Case Study from the Biotin Pathway," *BIO-Complexity*, 2011 (1): 1-17.

9   George M. Whitesides, "Revolutions In Chemistry: Priestley Medalist George M. Whitesides' Address," *Chemical and Engineering News*, 85: 12-17 (March 26, 2007).

10   Kevin J. Peterson, Michael R. Dietrich and Mark A. McPeek, "MicroRNAs and metazoan macroevolution: insights into canalization, complexity, and the Cambrian explosion," *BioEssays*, 31 (7):736-747 (2009).

11   Ernst Mayr, *What Makes Biology Unique?*, p. 198 (Cambridge University Press, 2004).

12   Noam Chomsky, *Language and Mind*, 3rd ed. (Cambridge: Cambridge University Press, 2006), 59.

13   Stephen Hawking and Roger Penrose, *The Nature of Space and Time* (Princeton, NJ: Princeton University Press, 1996), 20.

14   Charles Townes quoted in Bonnie Azab Powell, "'Explore as much as we can': Nobel Prize winner Charles Townes on evolution, intelligent design, and the meaning of life," *UC Berkeley News Center* (June 17, 2005), accessed March 14, 2012, http://www.berkeley.edu/news/media/releases/2005/06/17_townes.shtml.

15   Timothy P. White, "Letter to the University of Idaho Faculty, Staff and Students" (October 4, 2005), http://www.president.uidaho.edu/default.aspx?pid=85947

16   Jonathan Wells, *The Politically Incorrect Guide to Darwinism and Intelligent Design*, pgs. 189-190 (Regnery, 2006).

17   Robert Crowther, "Academic Freedom Expelled from Baylor University" (September 5, 2007) at http://www.evolutionnews.org/2007/09/academic_freedom_expelled_from004189.html ; Brad Briggs and Grace Maaluf, "BU had role in Dembski return," The Lariat (November 16, 2007), at http://www.baylor.edu/lariat/news.php?action=story&story=48260 ; Casey Luskin, "Credibility Gap: Baylor Denies Robert Marks' Situation Has Anything to do with ID," October 1, 2007 at http://www.evolutionnews.org/2007/10/credibility_gap_baylor_denies004290.html

18   "Leading Biochemistry Textbook Author: Pro-ID undergraduates 'should never have [been] admitted,'" at http://www.evolutionnews.org/2006/11/author_of_leading_biochemistry.html

19   "Jerry Coyne: '...adherence to ID... should be absolute grounds for not hiring a science professor.'," at http://www.evolutionnews.org/2011/03/jerry_coyne045001.html

20   Council of Europe, The dangers of creationism in education, September 17, 2007, http://assembly.coe.int/main.asp?Link=/documents/workingdocs/doc07/edoc11375.htm

21   Hawking and Mlodinow, *The Grand Design*, 2010, p 5

22   Craig, 2012. Under "Hawking and Mlodinow: Philosophical Undertakers"

23   Mike Licona, *The Resurrection of Jesus,* 2010

24   Gary Habermas and Mike Licona, *The Case for the Resurrection of Jesus,* 2004 p 82)

25   John G. West, ed. *The Magician's Twin: C.S. Lewis on Science, Scientism, and Society.* 2012

26   Ibid

27   Ibid

28   Thomas Nagel. *The Last Word,* 1997, p 130

29   Kelly James Clark. *Philosophers Who Believe,* 1993, p 11

30   Peter S. Williams, "The Definitional Critique of Intelligent Design Theory," http://www.arn.org/docs/williams/pw_definitionalcritique.htm

31   Ibid

32   Tyler Burge and Alfredo Paternoster, *Linguaggio E Mente,* 2005 (Quoted by Williams)

33   Peter S. Williams, http://www.arn.org/docs/williams/pw_definitionalcritique.htm

34   Craig debates Atkins, www.youtube.com

35   C. S. Lewis, *Miracles,* 1947, p 21

36   Ibid

37   John Edward Philips, *Writing African History,* 2005

38   Paul Froese, Forced Secularization in Soviet Russia, Vol. 43, No. 1 (Mar., 2004), pp. 35-50

39   http://www.merriam-webster.com/dictionary/science

40   James E. Stroud, *Christianity in the 22nd Century,* 2010

41   Peter S. Williams, http://www.arn.org/docs/williams/pw_definitionalcritique.htm

42   Bradley Monton, *Seeking God in Science,* 2009, p 58 (Quoted by Peter Williams)

43   Peter S. Williams, http://www.arn.org/docs/williams/pw_definitionalcritique.htm

44   JH. Zammito, *Discipline, Philosophy, and History,* 2012 (Quoted by Mike Licona in *The Resurrection of Jesus,* 2010, p 103)

45   Mike Licona, *The Resurrection of Jesus,* 2010, p 118

46   Richard J. Evans, *In Defense of History,* 1999, p 73

47   R. G. Collingwood, *An Autobiography,* 1939 (Quoted by William Lane Craig in *Reasonable Faith,* 2008, p 226)

48   R. K. Harrison, *Introduction to the Old Testament,* 1969

49   Norman L. Geisler and Ronald M. Brooks, *When Skeptics Ask,* 1990

50   Aviezer Tucker, *Our Knowledge of the Past,* 2004, p 258

51   C. Behan McCullagh, *Justifying Historical Descriptions,* 1984, p 19

52   Kaiser, Walter C Kaiser and Lyman Rand Tucker (quoting Richardson) *Toward Rediscovering the Old Testament,* 1987, p. 67

53   William L. Craig, "The Challenge of History: An Interview with William Lane Craig (Australian Presbyterian), 2012

54   Ravi K. Zacharias, *Beyond Opinion,* 2007

55   *The Magician's Twin C. S. Lewis on Science, Scientism, and Society,* 2012. (Dr. Richards was one of many contributors)

56   Peter W. Atkins, *On Being,* 2011

57   Debate between Dr. Krauss and Dr. Craig titled: *Is There Evidence For God?,* http://www.reasonablefaith.org/the-craig-krauss-debate-at-north-carolina-state-university

58   Alexander Vilenkin, Video-Presentation titled: *Did the Universe Have a Beginning?* http://www.youtube.com/watch?v=NXCQelhKJ7A

59   Robert Jastrow, *God and the Astronomers*, 1978, p 105

60   Ibid

61   William L. Craig, Article under: *Theistic Critiques Of Atheism* http://www.reasonablefaith.org/theistic-critiques-of-atheism (A paraphrase of Craig's arguments concerning the cosmological and teleological arguments)

62   George Gamow, *One, Two, Three— Infinity: Facts and Speculations of Science*, 1988

63   *The Cambridge Companion to Atheism.* Edited by Michael Martin (article by William Lane Craig). New York: Cambridge University Press, 2007. 69-85.

64   *"A Scientist Caught Between Two Faiths: Interview With Robert Jastrow," Christianity Today, August 6, 1982*

65   *The Cambridge Companion to Atheism.* Edited by Michael Martin (article by William Lane Craig). New York: Cambridge University Press, 2007. 69-85.

66   Paul CW Davies, *The Physics of Time Asymmetry*, 1974

67   William L. Craig, Article under: *Theistic Critiques Of Atheism* http://www.reasonablefaith.org/theistic-critiques-of-atheism (A paraphrase of Craig's arguments concerning the cosmological and teleological arguments)

68   Subodh K. Pandit, *Come Search with Me*, 2008

69   Hugh Ross, *The Creator and the Cosmos*, 1993

70   John D Barrow and Frank J. Tipler. *The Anthropic Cosmological Principle*, 1986

71   Brad Lemley, "November 2000." *Discover Magazine*

72   Lee Strobel, *The Case for a Creator*, 2004, ch 6

73 Dennis Overbye, *The New York Times*. Article: Zillions Of Universes? Or Did Ours Get Lucky? Oct, 2003

74 William L. Craig, Article under: *Theistic Critiques Of Atheism* http://www.reasonablefaith.org/theistic-critiques-of-atheism (A paraphrase of Craig's arguments concerning the cosmological and teleological arguments)

75 Robin Collins, "CSC–*The Fine-Tuning Design Argument*, September 01, 1998. http://www.discovery.org/a/91.

76 William L. Craig, Article under: *Theistic Critiques Of Atheism* http://www.reasonablefaith.org/theistic-critiques-of-atheism

77 Ibid

78 Norman L Geisler, (ed), *To Everyone an Answer*, 2004, p. 76 (Dr. Geivett was one of many contributors to the book)

79 Ibid (Quoting Paul Draper, p. 76)

80 Lindsay Judson, *Aristotle's Physics: A Collection of Essays*, 1991

81 Stephen C. Meyer, Abstract *Signature in the Cell*, 2009, http://www.signatureinthecell.com/about-the-book.php

82 Norman L Geisler, (ed), *To Everyone an Answer*, 2004, p 90 (Dr. Dembski was one of many contributors to the book)

83 William L. Craig, and James Porter Moreland. *The Blackwell Companion to Natural Theology*, 2009, p 340

84 Brett Miller, *Complexity and Specified Complexity*, 2012 http://www.evidentcreation.com/DE-Spec.html

85 William A Dembski, *The Design Inference*, 1998

86 Michael Ruse, "Evolutionary Theory and Christian Ethics," in *The Darwinian Paradigm* (London: Routledge, 1989), pp. 262-269.

87   Michael Ruse, *Darwinism Defended* (London: Addison-Wesley, 1982), p. 275.

88   Tim Ingold, *On the Distinction between Evolution and History*, http://www.socionauki.ru/journal/articles/130380/

89   James Porter Moreland and William L Craig (ed). *Philosophical Foundations for a Christian Worldview,* 2003, p 62

90   Ralph O. Muncaster, *A Skeptic's Search for God,* 2002

91   Subodh K. Pandit, *Come Search with Me,* 2008

92   William A. Dembski and Sean McDowell. *Understanding Intelligent Design,* 2008

93   William A. Dembski and Sean McDowell. *Understanding Intelligent Design,* 2008, p 21

94   Daniel Clement Dennett, *Darwin's Dangerous Idea,* 1996

95   Stephen C. Meyer, "Discovery Institute–Article Database–What's in a Name: A Disservice to the Truth, Dec 1999 http://www.discovery.org/a/12421

96   Jonathan Wells, *The Politically Incorrect Guide to Darwinism and Intelligent Design,* 2006, p 16

97   "Intelligent Faith 315." *Cambrian Series* http://www.intelligentfaith315.com/2012/02/series-icons-of-evolution-darwins-tree_13.html

98   Stephen Gould, *(Evolution's Erratic Pace, Volume 86, No. 5, Pg 14 (1977)*

99   Aristotle, *History of Animals, HH*http://classics.mit.edu/Aristotle/history_anim.html

100   James Porter Moreland and John Mark Reynolds. *Three Views on Creation and Evolution,* 1999, p 85

101   Eugenie Scott, http://www.evolutionnews.org/2009/06/eugenie_scott_claims_evolution022041.html

102   David Berlinski, "David Berlinski on Science, Scientists, and Darwinism." *Uncommon Descent,* http://www.uncommondescent.com/darwinism/david-berlinski-on-science-scientists-and-darwinism

103   Jonathan Wells, *Icons of Evolution,* 2002, p 221 (Wells quoting Henry Gee)

104   Ibid

105   Brian Thomas, *Acts and Facts Journal, 2012* http://www.icr.org/icr-magazines

106   Ibid

107   Ann Gauger, Douglas Axe, and Casey Luskin. *Science and Human Origins,* 2012

108   Ann Gauger, "Adam and Eve Redux." *Christian Research Journal* 35.01 (2012): 26-29

109   Ibid

110   Ann Gauger, Douglas Axe, and Casey Luskin. *Science and Human Origins,* 2012

111   J.M. Roberts, *A Short History of the World,* 1997, p 2-3

112   Ibid

113   *PublishersWeekly.com.* Review: *The History of the Ancient World,* 20 Nov. 2006

114   Paul Copan, and William Lane. Craig (ed). *Come Let Us Reason,* 2012

115   J. B. S. Haldane, *Possible Worlds,* 2000, p 227, 286

116   Richard Dawkins, *Edge 53,* http://www.edge.org/documents/archive/edge53.html

117   Gary Habermas, "EPS Article Library." *Antony Flew's Deism Revisited.* Philsophia Christi, 2007

118   Slyvia Mader, *Biology–Origins of Life Pg 320.* 7th ed. N.p.: McGraw-Hill Higher Education, 2005

119   C. Behan McCullagh, *Bias in Historical Description,* 2000, p. 49

120   Nayef Al-Rodhan, "GSCP." *Geneva Centre for Security Policy,* http://www.gcsp.ch/Globalisation/Publications/Books/Faculty-Publications/Books-and-Edited-Volumes/Sustainable-History-and-the-Dignity-of-Man-A-Philosophy-of-History-and-Civilisational-Triumph

121   Ibid

122   DM. Bowman, *Fire in the Earth System.* Science Magazine, Oct. 2012. http://www.sciencemag.org/content/324/5926/481

123   John Anthony West, *Serpent in the Sky,* 1979, p 11

124   Graham Hancock, *Fingerprints of the Gods,* 1995, p 134 (Quoting Dr. Emery)

125   Werner Gitt, *In the Beginning Was Information,* 1997, 209

126   Appel-Bocquet, Jean-Pierre. *When the World's Population Took Off: The Springboard of the Neolithic Dem.* SCɛCE, Oct. 2012.

127   Susan Wise Bauer, *The History of the Ancient World,* 2007, p xxv-xxvii

128   Bill T. Arnold, and Bryan Beyer. *Readings from the Ancient Near East,* 2002

129   Ben Witherington, "Religion at the Dawn of Civilization." *Biblical Archaeology Review* 39, no. 1 (January/February 2013): 57-60.

130   http://www.dissentfromdarwin.org/

131   Thomas Nagel, *Mind and Cosmos, 2012*

132   Ibid

133   Werner Keller and Joachim Rehork. *The Bible as History*, 1981

134   Rabbi Nathan L Cardozo, "On Bible Criticism and Its Counterarguments." 1995. http://www.aishdas.org/toratemet/en_cardozo.html.

135   R. E. Clements, *A Century of Old Testament Study*. Guildford, Surrey: Lutterworth, 1983.

136   C. Behan McCullagh, *Justifying Historical Descriptions*, 1984

137   J. W. Rogerson and Philip R. Davies. *The Old Testament World*, 1989

138   Claus Westermann, *The Genesis Accounts of Creation*, 1964

139   Robert Jastrow, *God and the Astronomers*, 1978, p 79

140   J. W. Rogerson and Philip R. Davies. *The Old Testament World*, 1989

141   Ibid

142   Nozomi Osanai, Article: *Secular Sources for a Global Flood*, http://www.answersingenesis.org/articles/csgeg/comparison-secular-historical-records

143   Ibid

144   Graham Hancock, *Underworld*, 2002, p. 20-21

145   Bill Cooper, *After the Flood: The Early Post-flood History of Europe*, 1995, p. 15

146   Ibid, pg 10 (Introduction)

147   K. A. Kitchen, *On the Reliability of the Old Testament*, 2003

148   Howard LaFay, *Ebla: Splendor of an Unknown Empire*, National Geographic, December 1978, Pp. 735

149   Ibid

150   Ibid

151   K. A. Kitchen, *On the Reliability of the Old Testament*, 2003, p 371

152   F. L. Griffith, *Archaeological Survey of Egypt*. London: Regan Paul, 1905.

153   George E. Mendenhall and Gary A. Herion. *Ancient Israel's Faith and History*, 2001, p 44

154   John Garstang. *The Story of Jericho*, 1948

155   Dennis Bratcher, "History and Theology in Joshua and Judges." 2011. http://www.cresourcei.org/conquest.html

156   K. A. Kitchen, *On the Reliability of the Old Testament*, 2003, p 239

157   Julius Wellhausen, *Prolegomena to the History of Israel*, 1994

158   Edwin Richard Thiele, *The Mysterious Numbers of the Hebrew Kings*, 1965

159   Ibid

160   Rodger C. Young, *Inductive And Deductive Methods As Applied To OT Chronology* http://www.galaxie.com/article/11507

161   Lester L.Grabbe, Ahab Agonistes: The Rise and Fall of the Omri Dynasty, 2007

162   Abe Selig, "J'lem City Wall Dates Back to King Solomon" Jerusalem Post, 23 Feb. 2010

163   "University of Haifa." *Most Ancient Hebrew Biblical Inscription Deciphered.* http://newmedia-eng.haifa.ac.il/?p=2043

164   Puech Emile, "The BAS Library." *BAR 38:06* http://members.bib-arch.org/publication.asp?PubID=BSBA

165   Ibid

166   Brian Peckham, *From Babel to Babylon: Essays on Biblical History and Literature,* 2006

167   K. A. Kitchen, *On the Reliability of the Old Testament,* 2003, p 500

168   Raymond F. Surburg, *Introduction to the Intertestamental Period.* St. Louis: Concordia Pub. House, 1975.

169   Peter W. Flint and James C. VanderKam. *The Dead Sea Scrolls after Fifty Years,* 1998.

170   Vincent Taylor, *The Formation of the Gospel Tradition,* 1964, p. 11

171   McCall, Thomas S. *The Bible Jesus Read Is Exciting!: A Popular Introduction to the Old Testament, Featuring Scripture's "hidden Plot"* Garden City, NY: Doubleday, 1978.

172   Randall Price, *Searching for the Original Bible,* 2007

173   "Updating the Bibliographic Tests for New Testament Documents" 2012, http://bbhchurchconnection.wordpress.com/2012/09/17/updating-the-bibliographic-test-for-new-testament-documents

174   Randall Price, *Searching for the Original Bible,* 2007

175   William Mitchell Ramsay, *The Bearing of Recent Discovery on the Trustworthiness of the New Testament.* Grand Rapids: Baker Book House, 1953, p 222

176   Colin J. Hemer, and (editor) Conrad H. Gempf. *The Book of Acts in the Setting of Hellenistic History*, 1989

177   Josh McDowell, *Evidence for Christianity*, 2006, p 112

178   James Porter Moreland, *An Apologetic Critique of the Major Presuppositions of the New Quest of the Historical Jesus*, 1979, p 92

179   John Warwick Montgomery, *Christianity for the Tough-minded*, 1973, p 284

180   Ibid, Montgomery quoted James R. Moore

181   John Warwick Montgomery, *History, Law and Christianity*, 2002

182   Ibid

183   Donald W. Engels, *Alexander the Great and the Logistics of the Macedonian Army*, 1978

184   C. Behan McCullagh, *Justifying Historical Descriptions*, 1984 (Quoting Bultmann, p 60)

185   John Warwick Montgomery, *Christianity for the Tough-minded*, 1973, p 26

186   Bart D. Ehrman, *Misquoting Jesus: The Story behind Who Changed the Bible and Why*, 2005, p 14

187   Mark L. Strauss, *Four Portraits, One Jesus: An Introduction to Jesus and the Gospels*, 2007

188   Hans Von Campenhausen,. *The Events of Easter and the Empty Tomb*, 1968 (Quoted by: Habermas, Gary in *The Historical Jesus*, 1996, p 156)

189   James Stroud, *Christianity in the 22nd Century*, 2010

190   Norman L Geisler and Frank Turek, *I Don't Have Enough Faith to Be an Atheist*, 2004

191   Albert Schweitzer and (editor) John Bowden. *The Quest of the Historical Jesus*, 2001

192   James M. Robinson, *A New Quest of the Historical Jesus*, 1959 (Quoted by Witherington, Ben. *The Jesus Quest*, 1995, p 11.)

193   Jerrell G. White,. *First Century Palestine*, 1978

194   N. T. Wright, The Challenge of Jesus, 1999, p 16.

195   Paul Copan, William Lane. Craig, and NT Wright. *Passionate Conviction*, 2007, p 129.

196   NT. Wright, "The New Unimproved Jesus." *Christianity Today*, September 13, 1993, p 26.

197   William L Craig, *Philosophy of Religion: A Reader and Guide*, 2002

198   Gerd Lüdemann and Alf Özen. *What Really Happened to Jesus*, 1995, p 207

199   Craig, William L. "Rediscovering the Historical Jesus: The Evidence for Jesus." Faith and Mission. 1998. http://www.reasonablefaith.org/rediscovering-the-historical-jesus-the-evidence-for-jesus.

200   George Campbell and John Stuart Bute. *A Dissertation on Miracles Containing an Examination of the Principles Advanced by David Hume, Esq.; in An Essay on Miracles*, 1790

201   Pieter Craffert and Mike Licona. "Pieter Craffert on Jesus" http://earliestchristianity.wordpress.com/2012/01/12/pieter-craffert-on-jesus-resurrection-liconas-summary-and-evaluation

202   Norman L. Geisler, Quoted by: Geivett, R. Douglas and Gary R. Habermas. *In Defense of Miracles*, 1997, p 81

203   N. T. Wright, *The Resurrection of the Son of God*, 2003, p 707

204   Mike Licona, *The Resurrection of Jesus*, 2010, p 159

205   David Gary Shaw, "Volumes 36-40, 1997-2001." *History and Theory*, http://www.historyandtheory.org/archives/archives8.html

206   K. A. Kitchen, *On the Reliability of the Old Testament*, 2003, p 487

207   C. Behan McCullagh, *Bias in Historical Description*, 2000, p. 65

208   Alexander Rosenberg, *The Atheist's Guide to Reality*, 2011, p 3-4

209   Ibid

210   "Kitzmiller vs. Dover." Discovery Institute, 4 May 2007

211   Mindy Belz, "Kangaroo Court." *WORLD NEWS*. N.p., 10 Feb. 2007, http://www.worldmag.com/2007/02/kangaroo_court

212   Meg Bortin, *Muslims Still in Denial about 911*. NY TIMES, 22 June 2006; Head, Jonathan. "Turkey p.m.Says French Bill on Genocide Denial 'racist'" *BBC News*. BBC, 24 Jan. 2012

213   Jeremy Black, *Historiography: Contesting the past; Claiming the Future*, 2011, ch 1 p 15

214   Francis A. Schaeffer, *The God Who Is There*, pgs 11-12

215   Ibid, pg 100

216   Elissa Kido, "For Real Education Reform," The Christian Science Monitor. November 15, 2010.

217   Editor, Tom Heneghan, Religion. "France Steps up
Struggle against Religious Radicals." Reuters. December
12, 2012. http://www.reuters.com/article/2012/12/12/
us-france-religion-extremists-idUSBRE8BB0VA20121212.

WORKS CONSULTED

Albright, William Foxwell. *Archaeology and the Religion of Israel; the Ayer Lectures of the Colgate-Rochester Divinity School, 1941.* Baltimore: Johns Hopkins Press, 1956.

Albright, William Foxwell. *Archaeology, Historical Analogy & Early Biblical Tradition.* Baton Rouge: Louisiana State University Press, 1966.

Al-Rodhan, Nayef R. F., and Lisa Watanabe. *A Proposal for Inclusive Peace and Security.* Geneva: Editions Slatkine, 2007.

Al-Rodhan, Nayef R. F. *Sustainable History and the Dignity of Man: A Philosophy of History and Civilisational Triumph.* Zurich: Lit, 2009.

Ann, Gauger. "CRI Journal Articles I." CRI Journal Articles I. July/August 2012. Accessed December 27, 2012. http://www.iclnet.org/pub/resources/text/cri/cri-jrnl/crijnl.html.

Archibald, David. "Online Research in Philosophy." J. David Archibald, Edward Hitchcock's Pre-Darwinian (1840) "Tree of Life" Accessed December 27, 2012. http://philpapers.org/rec/ARCEHP.

Arnold, Bill T., and Bryan Beyer. *Readings from the Ancient Near East: Primary Sources for Old Testament Study.* Grand Rapids, MI: Baker Academic, 2002.

Aron, Raymond. *Introduction to the Philosophy of History: An Essay on the Limits of Historical Objectivity.* Boston: Beacon Press, 1961.

Atkins, P. W. *On Being: A Scientist's Exploration of the Great Questions of Existence.* Oxford: Oxford University Press, 2011.

Atkinson, R. F. *Knowledge and Explanation in History: An Introduction to the Philosophy of History.* Ithaca, NY: Cornell University Press, 1978.

Axe, Douglas A. "Estimating the Prevalence of Protein Sequences Adopting Functional Enzyme Folds." Journal of Molecular Biology, Vol. 341: 1295-. 2004. Accessed December 28, 2012. doi:http://www.toriah.org/articles/axe-2004.pdf.

Axe, Douglas D., and Ann Gauger. "The Evolutionary Accessibility of New Enzyme Functions: A Case Study from the Biotin Pathway." BIO-Complexity, 2011 (1): 1–17. 2011. Accessed December 28, 2012. http://bio-complexity.org/ojs/index.php/main/article/view/BIO-C.2011.1.

Barker, Graeme. *The Agricultural Revolution in Prehistory: Why Did Foragers Become Farmers?* Oxford: Oxford University Press, 2006.

Barrow, John D., and Frank J. Tipler. *The Anthropic Cosmological Principle.* Oxford [Oxfordshire: Oxford University Press, 1986.

Bauer, S. Wise. *The History of the Ancient World: From the Earliest Accounts to the Fall of Rome.* New York: W.W. Norton, 2007.

Beckwith, Francis, and Gregory Koukl. *Relativism: Feet Firmly Planted in Mid-air.* Grand Rapids, MI: Baker Books, 1998.

Behe, Michael, and David Snoke. "Simulating Evolution by Gene Duplication of Protein Features That Require Multiple Amino Acid Residues." National Center for Biotechnology Information. 2004. Accessed December 28, 2012. http://www.ncbi.nlm.nih.gov/pubmed/15340163.

Berlinski, David. "David Berlinski on Science, Scientists, and Darwinism." Uncommon Descent. Accessed December 28, 2012. http://www.uncommondescent.com/darwinism/david-berlinski-on-science-scientists-and-darwinism.

Bible History Online–El Amarna Letters (Biblical Archaeology). Accessed December 28, 2012. http://www.bible-history.com/archaeology/israel/el-amarna-letters.html.

Black, Jeremy. *Historiography: Contesting the Past.* London: Social Affairs Unit, 2011.

Blomberg, Craig, and Jennifer Foutz. Markley. *A Handbook of New Testament Exegesis.* Grand Rapids, MI: Baker Academic, 2010.

Blomberg, Craig. *Making Sense of the New Testament.* Grand Rapids, MI: Baker Academic, 2004.

Bortin, Meg. "Muslims Still in Denial about 911." NY TIMES. June 22, 2006. doi:http://www.nytimes.com/2006/06/22/world/europe/22cnd-pew.html?_r=0.

Bottéro, Jean. *Religion in Ancient Mesopotamia.* Chicago: University of Chicago Press, 2001.

Bowman, DM. "When the World's Population Took Off: The Springboard of the Neolithic Demographics." SceCE. Accessed December 28, 2012. http://www.sciencemag.org/content/324/5926/481.

Bratcher, Dennis. "History and Theology in Joshua and Judges." 2011. http://www.cresourcei.org/conquest.html.

Brodd, Jeffrey. *World Religions: A Voyage of Discovery*. Winona, MN: Saint Mary's Press, 2003.

Budge, E. A. Wallis. *The Gods of the Egyptians: Or, Studies in Egyptian Mythology*. New York: Dover Publications, 1969.

Burge, Tyler, and Alfredo Paternoster. *Linguaggio E Mente*. Genova: De Ferrari, 2005.

"Cambrian Series." Evolutionary Trees. Accessed December 28, 2012. http://www.intelligentfaith315.com/2012/02/series-icons-of-evolution-darwins-tree_13.html.

Campbell, George. *A Dissertation on Miracles: Containing an Examination of the Principles*. Edinburgh: Printed for A. Kincaid and J. Bell, 1762.

Campenhausen, Hans Von. *The Events of Easter and the Empty Tomb*. Philadelphia: Fortress Press, 1968.

Campenhausen, Hans Von. *The Events of Easter and the Empty Tomb*. Philadelphia: Fortress Press, 1968.

Cardozo, Rabbi Nathan L. "On Bible Criticism and Its Counterarguments." 1995. http://www.aishdas.org/torate-met/en_cardozo.html.

Carr, Edward Hallett. *What Is History?* New York: Vintage, 1961.

Charlesworth, James H. *The Messiah: Developments in Earliest Judaism and Christianity*. Minneapolis: Fortress Press, 1992.

Chittick, Donald E. *The Puzzle of Ancient Man*. Newberg, OR: Creation Compass, 1997.

Chomsky, Noam. *Language and Mind*. New York: Harcourt Brace Jovanovich, 1972.

"Christianity Today Journal." http://www.christianitytoday.com/.

Clark, Kelly James. *Philosophers Who Believe: The Spiritual Journeys of 11 Leading Thinkers*. Downers Grove, IL: InterVarsity Press, 1993.

Clements, R. E. *A Century of Old Testament Study*. Guildford, Surrey: Lutterworth, 1983.

Collingwood, R. G., and William H. Dray. *The Principles of History: And Other Writings in Philosophy of History*. Oxford: Oxford University Press, 1999.

Collins, Robin. "CSC–The Fine-Tuning Design Argument:." CSC–The Fine-Tuning Design Argument:. September 01, 1998. Accessed January 22, 2013. http://www.discovery. org/a/91.

"A Comparison of Ancient Works with the New Testament." Baker Book House Church Connection. Accessed December 28, 2012. http://bbhchurchconnection.wordpress. com/2012/09/17/updating-the-bibliographic-test-for-new-testament-documents.

Cooper, Bill. *After the Flood: The Early Post-flood History of Europe*. Chichester: New Wine Press, 1995.

Copan, Paul, and William Lane. Craig (ed). *Come Let Us Reason: New Essays in Christian Apologetics*. Nashville, TN: B & H Academic, 2012.

Copan, Paul, and William Lane. Craig. *Passionate Conviction: Contemporary Discourses on Christian Apologetics*. Nashville, TN: B & H Academic, 2007.

Corradini, Antonella, Sergio Galvan, and E. J. Lowe. *Analytic Philosophy without Naturalism*. London: Routledge, 2006.

"Council of Europe Parliamentary Assembly." September 17, 2007. Accessed December 28, 2012. http://assembly. coe.int/main.asp?Link=/documents/workingdocs/doc07/edoc11375.htm.

Coyne, Jerry. "Jerry Coyne: "...adherence to ID... Should Be Absolute Grounds for Not Hiring a Science Professor."–Evolution News & Views." Evolution News & Views. Spring

2011. Accessed December 28, 2012. http://www.evolution-news.org/2011/03/jerry_coyne045001.html.

Craig, William L. "The Challenge of History: An Interview with William Lane Craig (Australian Presbyterian)." Accessed December 28, 2012. http://www.reasonablefaith.org/the-challenge-of-history-an-interview-with-william-lane-craig.

Craig, William L. "Defending Biblical Christianity." Article Database. Accessed March 28, 2012. http://www. ReasonableFaith.org/.

Craig, William L. "Hawking and Mlodinow: Philosophical Undertakers." ReasonableFaith.org. Accessed December 28, 2012. http://www.reasonablefaith.org/ hawking-and-mlodinow-philosophical-undertakers.

Craig, William L. "Is There Evidence For God?" A Debate between Krauss and Craig. October/November 2011. Accessed December 28, 2012. http://www.reasonablefaith.org/ the-craig-krauss-debate-at-north-carolina-state-university.

Craig, William L. "Theistic Critiques Of Atheism." ReasonableFaith.org. Accessed December 28, 2012. http:// www.reasonablefaith.org/theistic-critiques-of-atheism.

Craig, William Lane., and James Porter Moreland. *The Blackwell Companion to Natural Theology*. Chichester, U.K.: Wiley-Blackwell, 2009.

Craig, William Lane., and Quentin Smith. *Theism, Atheism, and Big Bang Cosmology*. Oxford [England: Clarendon Press, 1993.

Craig, William Lane. *Philosophy of Religion: A Reader and Guide*. New Brunswick, NJ: Rutgers University Press, 2002.

Crowther, Robert. "Academic Freedom Expelled from Baylor University–Evolution News & Views." Evolution News & Views. November 2007. Accessed December 28, 2012.

http://www.evolutionnews.org/2007/09/academic_freedom_expelled_from004189.html.

Crowther, Robert. Evolution News & Views. Fall 2007. http://www.evolutionnews.org/2007/09/academic_freedom_expelled_from004189.html.

"The Crux." Discover Magazine. Accessed December 28, 2012. http://blogs.discovermagazine.com/crux/2012/09/07/the-limits-of-science-and-scientists/.

"CSC–Discovery Institute's Science Education Policy." CSC–Discovery Institute. February 09, 2012. Accessed December 28, 2012. http://www.discovery.org/a/3164.

Davies, P. C. W. *The Physics of Time Asymmetry*. Berkeley: University of California Press, 1974.

Dawes, Gregory W. *The Historical Jesus Quest: Landmarks in the Search for the Jesus of History*. Louisville, KY: Westminster John Knox Press, 2000.

Dawkins, Richard. "Edge 53." Accessed December 28, 2012. http://www.edge.org/documents/archive/edge53.html.

Dawkins, Richard. *River out of Eden: A Darwinian View of Life*. New York, NY: Basic Books, 1995.

D'Costa, Gavin. *Resurrection Reconsidered*. Oxford, England: Oneworld Publications, 1996.

Dembski, William A., and Sean McDowell. *Understanding Intelligent Design*. Eugene, Or.: Harvest House Publishers, 2008.

Dembski, William A. *Darwin's Nemesis: Phillip Johnson and the Intelligent Design Movement*. Downers Grove, IL: IVP Academic, 2006.

Dembski, William A. *The Design Inference: Eliminating Chance through Small Probabilities*. Cambridge: Cambridge University Press, 1998.

Dembski, William A. *The Design Revolution: Answering the Toughest Questions about Intelligent Design*. Downers Grove, IL: InterVarsity Press, 2004.

Dembski, William A. *No Free Lunch: Why Specified Complexity Cannot Be Purchased without Intelligence*. Lanham, MD: Rowman & Littlefield, 2002.

"Denial of Genocides." Enotes.com. Accessed December 28, 2012. http://www.enotes.com/denial-reference/denial.

Dennett, Daniel Clement. *Darwin's Dangerous Idea: Evolution and the Meanings of Life*. New York: Simon & Schuster, 1995.

Denton, Michael. *Evolution: A Theory in Crisis*. Bethesda, MD: Adler & Adler, 1986.

DeWolf, David, John West, and Casey Luskin. "Intelligent Design Will Survive Kitzmiller v. Dover." Winter 2007. Accessed December 28, 2012. http://www.discovery.org/scripts/viewDB/filesDB-download.php?command=download.

"Dictionary Used for Glossary." Dictionary.com. Accessed September 2012. http://dictionary.reference.com/.

Dictionary.com. Accessed September 15, 2012. http://dictionary.reference.com/.

"Discovery Institute Archives." Discovery Institute. Accessed December 28, 2012. http://www.discovery.org/.

Durrett, Rick, and Deena Schmidt. "Genetics, Vol. 180: 1501–1509." Waiting for Two Mutations: With Applications to Regulatory Sequence Evolution and the Limits of Darwinian Evolution. November 2008. Accessed December 28, 2012. http://www.genetics.org/content/180/3/1501.short.

Ehrman, Bart D. *Misquoting Jesus: The Story behind Who Changed the Bible and Why*. New York: HarperSanFrancisco, 2005.

Engels, Donald W. *Alexander the Great and the Logistics of the Macedonian Army*. Berkeley: University of California Press, 1978.

Evans, Richard J. *In Defense of History*. New York: W.W. Norton, 1999.

"Evolution and Functional Impact of Rare Coding Variation from Deep Sequencing of Human Exomes." Evolution and Functional Impact of Rare Coding Variation from Deep Sequencing of Human Exomes. Accessed December 28, 2012. http://www.sciencemag.org/content/337/6090/64.abstract.

Finkelstein, Israel, and Neil Asher Silberman. *The Bible Unearthed: Archaeology's New Vision of Ancient Israel*. New York: Touchstone, 2002.

Fisher, Mary Pat, and Lee Worth. Bailey. *An Anthology of Living Religions*. Upper Saddle River, NJ: Prentice Hall, 2000.

Flint, Peter W., and James C. VanderKam. *The Dead Sea Scrolls after Fifty Years: A Comprehensive Assessment*. Leiden: Brill, 1998.

Flood, Gavin D. *An Introduction to Hinduism*. New York, NY: Cambridge University Press, 1996.

Froese, Paul. "Forced Secularization in Soviet Russia: Why an Atheistic Monopoly Failed." *Journal for the Scientific Study of Religion* 43, no. 1 (March 2004): 35–50. doi:10.1111/j.1468–5906.2004.00216.x.

Gamow, George. *One, Two, Three ... Infinity; Facts & Speculations of Science,*. New York: Viking Press, 1947.

Garstang, John, and John Garstang. *The Story of Jericho,*. London: Marshall, Morgan & Scott, 1948.

Gascoigne, Mike. *Forgotten History of the Western People: From the Earliest Origins*. Camberley: Anno Mundi, 2002.

Gauger, Ann. "Adam and Eve Redux." CRI Christian Research Journal (pgs 26–29). July/August 2012. Accessed December 28, 2012. http://www.equip.org/christian-research-journal/.

Gauger, Ann, Douglas Axe, and Casey Luskin. *Science and Human Origins*. Seattle, WA: Discovery Institute Press, 2012.

Geisler, Norman L., and Frank Turek. *I Don't Have Enough Faith to Be an Atheist*. Wheaton, IL: Crossway Books, 2004.

Geisler, Norman L., and Ronald M. Brooks. *When Skeptics Ask*. Wheaton, IL: Victor Books, 1990.

Geisler, Norman L. *Baker Encyclopedia of Christian Apologetics*. Grand Rapids, MI: Baker Books, 1999.

Geisler, Norman L. *Creating God in the Image of Man?* Minneapolis, MN: Bethany House, 1997.

Geisler, Norman L., Francis Beckwith, William Lane. Craig, and James Porter Moreland, (ed). *To Everyone an Answer: A Case for the Christian Worldview : Essays in Honor of Norman L. Geisler*. Downers Grove, IL: InterVarsity Press, 2004.

Geivett, R. Douglas., and Gary R. Habermas. *In Defense of Miracles: A Comprehensive Case for God's Action in History*. Downers Grove, IL: InterVarsity Press, 1997.

Giblin, Peter, and Michael Scullion. *Sumeria*. Adelaide: [s.n.], 1969.

Gitt, Werner. *In the Beginning Was Information*. Bielfeld: Christliche Literatur-Verbreitung, 1997.

Gould, Stephen. "Evolution's Erratic Pace, Volume 86, No. 5, Pg 14 (1977)." Accessed December 28, 2012. http://www.eric.ed.gov/ERICWebPortal/search/detailmini.jsp?_nfpb=true.

Grabbe, Lester L. *Ahab Agonistes: The Rise and Fall of the Omri Dynasty*. London: T&T Clark, 2007.

Grant, Frederick C., Rudolf Bultmann, and Karl Kundsin. *Form Criticism, a New Method of New Testament Research,*. Chicago: Willett, 1934.

Griffith, F. L. *Archaeological Survey of Egypt*. London: Regan Paul, 1905.

Habermas, Gary. "Philsophia Christi–EPS Article Library." Antony Flew's Deism Revisited. 2007. Accessed December 28, 2012. http://www.epsociety.org/library/articles.asp?pid=28.

Habermas, Gary R., and Gary R. Habermas. *The Historical Jesus: Ancient Evidence for the Life of Christ*. Joplin, MO: College Press Pub., 1996.

Habermas, Gary R., and Mike Licona. *The Case for the Resurrection of Jesus*. Grand Rapids, MI: Kregel Publications, 2004.

Haldane, J. B. S. *Possible Worlds*. New Brunswick, NJ: Transaction Publishers, 2000.

Hancock, Graham. *Fingerprints of the Gods*. New York: Crown Publishers, 1995.

Hancock, Graham. *Underworld: The Mysterious Origins of Civilization*. New York: Crown Publishers, 2002.

Harrison, Everett Falconer. *Introduction to the New Testament*. Grand Rapids: Eerdmans, 1964.

Harrison, R. K. *Introduction to the Old Testament; with a Comprehensive Review of Old Testament Studies and a Special Supplement on the Apocrypha,*. Grand Rapids: Eerdmans, 1969.

Hartwig, Mervyn, and Jamie Morgan. *Critical Realism and Spirituality: Theism, Atheism, and Meta-reality*. Abingdon, Oxon: Routledge, 2012.

Hawking, S. W., and Leonard Mlodinow. *The Grand Design*. New York: Bantam Books, 2010.

Hawking, S. W., and Roger Penrose. *The Nature of Space and Time.* Princeton, NJ: Princeton University Press, 1996.

Head, Jonathan. "Turkey p.m. Says French Bill on Genocide Denial 'racist'" BBC News. January 24, 2012. Accessed December 28, 2012. http://www.bbc.co.uk/news/world-europe-16695133.

Hebberd, S. S. *The Philosophy of History.* La Crosse, WI: S.S. Hebberd, 1901.

Hegel, Georg Wilhelm Friedrich, Georg Wilhelm Friedrich Hegel, and Irwin Edman. *Hegel: Introduction to the Philosophy of History.* [Whitefish, MT]: Kessinger Publishing, 2005.

Hemer, Colin J., and Conrad H. Gempf. *The Book of Acts in the Setting of Hellenistic History.* Tübingen: J.C.B. Mohr, 1989.

"The History of the Ancient World: From the Earliest Accounts to the Fall of Rome." PublishersWeekly.com. November 2006. Accessed December 28, 2012. http://www.publishersweekly.com/978-0-393-05974-8.

"History.com Arhives." History.com. Accessed December 28, 2012. http://www.history.com/.

Howell, Martha C., and Walter Prevenier. *From Reliable Sources: An Introduction to Historical Methods.* Ithaca, NY: Cornell University Press, 2001.

Hoyle, Fred. *The Nature of the Universe.* New York: Harper, 1960.

Ingold, Tim. "On the Distinction between Evolution and History." Accessed December 28, 2012. http://www.socionauki.ru/journal/articles/130380/.

Jastrow, Robert. *God and the Astronomers.* New York: Norton, 1978.

Jenkins, Philip. *The Lost History of Christianity: The Thousand-year Golden Age of the Church in the Middle East, Africa, and Asia-and How It Died.* New York: HarperOne, 2008.

Joannès, Francis. *The Age of Empires: Mesopatamia in the First Millennium* Bc. Edinburgh: Edinburgh University Press, 2004.

Judson, Lindsay. *Aristotle's Physics: A Collection of Essays*. Oxford [England: Clarendon Press, 1991.

Kaiser, Walter C., and Lyman Rand. Tucker. *Toward Rediscovering the Old Testament*. Grand Rapids, MI: Zondervan, 1987.

Kang, C. H., and Ethel R. Nelson. *The Discovery of Genesis: How the Truths of Genesis Were Found Hidden in the Chinese Language*. St. Louis: Concordia Pub. House, 1979.

Keller, Werner, and Joachim Rehork. *The Bible as History*. New York: Morrow, 1981.

Kido, Elissa. "For Real Education Reform, Take a Cue from the Adventists." The Christian Science Monitor. November 15, 2010. http://www.csmonitor.com/Commentary/Opinion/2010/1115/For-real-education-reform-take-a-cue-from-the-Adventists?sms_ss=email.

Kitchen, K. A. *On the Reliability of the Old Testament*. Grand Rapids, MI: W.B. Eerdmans, 2003.

"Kitzmiller vs. Dover." CSC–Intelligent Design Will Survive Kitzmiller v. Dover. June 08, 2007. Accessed December 28, 2012. http://www.discovery.org/a/3877.

LaFay, Howard. "Ebla: Splendor of an Unknown Empire." National Geographic. December 1978. Accessed December 28, 2012. http://photography.nationalgeographic.com/photography/enlarge/saint-simeon-church_pod_image.html.

Largent, Mark A. *Sourcebook on History of Evolution*. Dubuque, IA: Kendall/Hunt Pub., 2002.

"Leading Biochemistry Textbook Author: Pro-ID Undergraduates "should Never Have [been] Admitted"–Evolution News & Views." Evolution News & Views. Fall

2006. Accessed December 28, 2012. http://www.evolution-news.org/2006/11/author_of_leading_biochemistry.html.

Lemley, Brad. "November 2000." Discover Magazine. http://discovermagazine.com/authors/brad-lemley.

Lewis, C. S. *Miracles: A Preliminary Study.* New York: Macmillan, 1947.

Lewis, Gwynne. *The French Revolution: Rethinking the Debate.* London: New York, 1993.

Licona, Mike, and Pieter Craffert. "Earliest Christianity and the Resurrection." Earliest Christianity. January 12, 2012. Accessed December 28, 2012. http://earliestchristianity.wordpress.com/2012/01/12/pieter-craffert-on-jesus-resurrection-liconas-summary-and-evaluation.

Licona, Mike. *The Resurrection of Jesus: A New Historiographical Approach.* Downers Grove, IL: IVP Academic, 2010.

"The Limits of Complex Adaptation: An Analysis Based on a Simple Model of Structured Bacterial Populations | Axe | BIO-Complexity." BIO-Complexity, Vol. 2010(4):1–10. 2010. Accessed December 28, 2012. http://bio-complexity.org/ojs/index.php/main/article/viewArticle/BIO-C.2010.4.

Lüdemann, Gerd, and Alf Özen. *What Really Happened to Jesus: A Historical Approach to the Resurrection.* Louisville, KY: Westminster John Knox Press, 1995.

Mader, Slyvia. *Biology–Origins of Life Textbook.* 7th ed. ISBN 0-07-118080-X. McGraw-Hill Higher Education, 2005.

Mayr, Ernst. *What Makes Biology Unique?: Considerations on the Autonomy of a Scientific Discipline.* New York: Cambridge University Press, 2004.

McCall, Thomas S. *The Bible Jesus Read Is Exciting!: A Popular Introduction to the Old Testament, Featuring Scripture's "hidden Plot"* Garden City, NY: Doubleday, 1978.

McCullagh, C. Behan. "Bias in Historical Description, Interpretation and Explanation." History and Theory 39 (1):39–66. 2000. Accessed February 06, 2013. http://philpapers.org/rec/MCCBIH.

McCullagh, C. Behan. *Justifying Historical Descriptions.* Cambridge: Cambridge University Press, 1984.

McDowell, Josh, and Josh McDowell. *The New Evidence That Demands a Verdict.* Nashville, TN: T. Nelson, 1999.

McDowell, Josh. *Evidence for Christianity.* Nashville, TN: Nelson Reference & Electronic, 2006.

Mendenhall, George E., and Gary A. Herion. *Ancient Israel's Faith and History: An Introduction to the Bible in Context.* Louisville: Westminster John Knox Press, 2001.

Meyer, Stephen C. *Signature in the Cell: DNA and the Evidence for Intelligent Design.* New York: HarperOne, 2009.

Meyer, Stephen. "CSC–New Film Examines the Cambrian Explosion, Biology's Big Bang, 530 Million Years in the Past." CSC–New Film Examines the Cambrian Explosion, Biology's Big Bang, 530 Million Years in the Past. September 09, 2009. Accessed December 28, 2012. http://www.discovery.org/a/12421.

Meyer, Stephen. "SIGNATURE IN THE CELL by Stephen C. Meyer." Accessed December 28, 2012. http://www.signatureinthecell.com/about-the-book.php.

Miller, Brett. "Complexity and Specified Complexity." Accessed December 28, 2012. http://www.evidentcreation.com/DE-Spec.html.

Mindy, Belz. "Kangaroo Court." WORLD NEWS. February 2007. Accessed December 28, 2012. http://www.worldmag.com/2007/02/kangaroo_court.

Montgomery, John Warwick. *Christianity for the Tough-minded; Essays in Support of an Intellectually Defensible Religious Commitment.* Minneapolis: Bethany Fellowship, 1973.

Montgomery, John Warwick. *History, Law and Christianity.* Edmonton, Alta.: Canadian Institute for Law, Theology & Public Policy, 2002.

Monton, Bradley. "Is Intelligent Design Science? Dissecting the Dover Decision." Online Research in Philosophy. January 3, 2006. doi:http://www.arn.org/docs/monton/is_intelligent_design_science.pdf.

Monton, Bradley John. *Seeking God in Science: An Atheist Defends Intelligent Design.* Peterborough, Ont.: Broadview Press, 2009.

Moreland, James Porter, and John Mark Reynolds. *Three Views on Creation and Evolution.* Grand Rapids, MI: Zondervan Pub., 1999.

Moreland, James Porter, and William Lane. Craig. *Philosophical Foundations for a Christian Worldview.* Downers Grove, IL: InterVarsity Press, 2003.

Moreland, James Porter. *An Apologetic Critique of the Major Presuppositions of the New Quest of the Historical Jesus.* 1979.

Morris, Henry M. *The Genesis Record: A Scientific and Devotional Commentary on the Book of Beginnings.* Grand Rapids: Baker Book House, 1976.

Moser, Paul K., and Paul Copan. *The Rationality of Theism.* London: Routledge, 2003.

Muller, Herbert Joseph. *The Uses of the Past; Profiles of Former Societies.* New York: Oxford University Press, 1952.

Muncaster, Ralph O. *A Skeptic's Search for God.* Eugene, Or.: Harvest House Publishers, 2002.

Nagel, Thomas. *The Last Word.* New York: Oxford University Press, 1997.

Nagel, Thomas. *Mind and Cosmos: Why the Materialist Neo-Darwinian Conception of Nature Is Almost Certainly False.* New York: Oxford University Press, 2012.

"Nature Archives." Nature.com. Accessed December 28, 2012. http://www.nature.com/nature/index.html.

Nayeh, Joseph, and Seymour Gitin. Special Report: Ekron Identity Confirmed. Accessed December 28, 2012. http://www.archaeology.org/9801/abstracts/ekron.html.

Nayeh, Joseph. "Canter Bridge." Accessed December 28, 2012. http://canterbridge.org/2007/11/18/reviewing-joseph-naveh-the-development-of-the-aramaic-script.

niv *Archaeological Study Bible: An Illustrated Walk through Biblical History and Culture.* Grand Rapids, MI: Zondervan, 2005.

Oard, Michael, and Ken Ham. "Answers in Genesis–Creation, Evolution, Christian Apologetics." Genesis. Accessed December 27, 2012. http://www.answersingenesis.org/.

O'Brien, Joan, and Wilfred Major. *In the Beginning: Creation Myths from Ancient Mesopatamia, Israel and Greece.* [Atlanta, Ga.]: Scholars Press, 1982.

Osanai, Nozomi. "Chapter 7: A Comparison from Secular Historical Records." Answers in Genesis. Accessed December 28, 2012. http://www.answersingenesis.org/articles/csgeg/comparison-secular-historical-records.

Ostling, Richard N., and Billy Graham. "Breaking News, Analysis, Politics, Blogs, News Photos, Video, Tech Reviews." Time. November 15, 1993. Accessed December 28, 2012. http://www.time.com/time/magazine/article/0,9171,979587,00.html.

Overbye, Dennis. "Zillions Of Universes? Or Did Ours Get Lucky?" The New York Times. October 28, 2003. Accessed December 28, 2012. http://www.nytimes.com/2003/10/28/science/zillions-of-universes-or-did-ours-get-lucky.html.

Pandit, Subodh K. *Come Search with Me: Let's Look for God.* [Longwood, Fla.]: Xulon Press, 2008.

Pannenberg, Wolfhart. *Jesus, God and Man.* Philadelphia: Westminster Press, 1968.

Peckham, Brian, Wood Joyce Louise. Rilett, John E. Harvey, and Mark Leuchter. *From Babel to Babylon: Essays on Biblical History and Literature in Honour of Brian Peckham.* New York: T & T Clark, 2006.

Peterson, Kevin J., Michael R. Dietrich, and Mark A. McPeek. "MicroRNAs and Metazoan Macroevolution: Insights into Canalization, Complexity, and the Cambrian Explosion." BioEssays, 31 (7):736–747. 2009. Accessed December 28, 2012. doi:http://www.dartmouth.edu/~peterson/46-Bioessays.pdf.

Philip, Neil. *Mythology of the World.* Boston, MA: Kingfisher, 2004.

Philips, John Edward. *Writing African History.* Rochester, NY: University of Rochester Press, 2005.

"Philosophia Christi." Evangelical Philosophical Society. http://epsociety.org/philchristi/past-issues.asp.

"Picture Credits–GNU Free Documentation License, Public Domain, and NASA (Credit Given)." Wikipedia. Accessed December 28, 2012. http://www.wikipedia.org/.

Plantinga, Alvin. "Books and Culture | A Christian Review." March/April 2007. Accessed December 28, 2012. http://www.booksandculture.com/.

Plantinga, Alvin. "Methodological Naturalism?" *Perspectives on Science and Christian Faith* 49 (September 1997): 143–54.

Plantinga, Alvin. "Welcome to the EPS–Evangelical Philosophical Society." Welcome to the EPS–Evangelical Philosophical Society. September 12, 2012. Accessed December 27, 2012. doi:www.epsociety.org/philchristi.

Powell, Bonnie A. "'Explore as Much as We Can': Nobel Prize Winner Charles Townes on Evolution, Intelligent Design, and the Meaning of Life." UC Berkeley News Center. June 2005. Accessed December 28, 2012. http://www.berkeley.edu/news/media/releases/2005/06/17_townes.shtml.

Pradhan, R. C., and K. S. Prasad. *Language and Mind.* New Delhi: Decent Books, 2006.

Price, Randall. *Searching for the Original Bible.* Eugene, Or.: Harvest House Publishers, 2007.

Price, Randall. *The Stones Cry out.* Eugene, Or.: Harvest House Publishers, 1997.

"Prof Dan Robinson."–Faculty of Philosophy. Accessed December 28, 2012. http://www.philosophy.ox.ac.uk/members/senior_research_fellows/dan_robinson.

"Public Domain Images, Royalty Free Stock Photos, Copyright Friendly Free Images. Not Copyrighted, No Rights Reserved. All Pictures on This Site Are Explicitly Placed in the Public Domain, Free for Any Personal or Commercial Use." NASA, STScI, And/or ESA (for All Space Oriented Images). Accessed December 28, 2012. http://www.public-domain-image.com/.

Puech, Emile. "BAR 38:06 | The BAS Library." Accessed December 28, 2012. http://members.bib-arch.org/publication.asp?PubID=BSBA.

Ramsay, William Mitchell. *The Bearing of Recent Discovery on the Trustworthiness of the New Testament*. Grand Rapids: Baker Book House, 1953.

Roberts, J. M. *A Short History of the World*. New York: Oxford University Press, 1997.

Robinson, James M. *A New Quest of the Historical Jesus*. London: SCM Press, 1959.

Rogerson, J. W., and Philip R. Davies. *The Old Testament World*. Englewood Cliffs, NJ: Prentice-Hall, 1989.

Rosenberg, Alexander. *The Atheist's Guide to Reality: Enjoying Life without Illusions*. New York: W.W. Norton, 2011.

Rosenberg, Donna. *World Mythology: An Anthology of the Great Myths and Epics*. Lincolnwood, IL: NTC Pub. Group, 1994.

Ross, Hugh. *The Creator and the Cosmos: How the Greatest Scientific Discoveries of the Century Reveal God*. Colorado Springs, CO: NavPress, 1993.

Ross, Hugh. Reasons To Believe : Where Modern Science & Faith Converge. Accessed December 28, 2012. http://www.reasons.org/.

Ross, Marcus. "Intelligent Design and Young-Earth Creationism—Investigating Nested Hierarchies of Philosophy and Belief." Accessed December 28, 2012. http://gsa.confex.com/gsa/2003AM/finalprogram/abstract_58668.htm.

Ruse, Michael, and Ernst Mayr. *Darwinism Defended*. Reading, MA: Addison-Wesley, Advanced Book Program/World Science Division, 1982. Print.

Ruse, Michael. *The Darwinian Paradigm: Essays on Its History, Philosophy, and Religious Implications*. London: Routledge, 1993. Print.

Schaeffer, Francis A. *The Complete Works of Francis A. Schaeffer: A Christian Worldview*. Westchester, IL: Crossway Books, 1982.

Schaeffer, Francis A. *Genesis in Space and Time; the Flow of Biblical History*. Downers Grove, IL: Inter-Varsity Press, 1972.

Schaeffer, Francis A. *The God Who Is There: Speaking Historic Christianity into the Twentieth Century*. Chicago: Inter-varsity Press, 1968.

Schweitzer, Albert, W. Montgomery, and James M. Robinson. *The Quest of the Historical Jesus: A Critical Study of Its Progress from Reimarus to Wrede*. New York: Macmillan, 1968.

Selig, Abe. "First Temple Period Archeological Site Unveiled in J'lem." Www.JPost.com. February 23, 2010. Accessed December 28, 2012. http://www.jpost.com/NationalNews/Article.aspx?id=225957.

Shaw, David G. "Volumes 36–40, 1997–2001." Volumes 36–40, History and Theory. Accessed December 28, 2012. http://www.historyandtheory.org/archives/archives8.html.

Simpson, George Gaylord. *The Meaning of Evolution*. [New York]: New American Library, 1951.

Skilton, Andrew. *A Concise History of Buddhism*. Birmingham: Windhorse Publications, 1994.

Sowell, Thomas. *Inside American Education: The Decline, the Deception, the Dogmas*. New York: Free Press, 2003.

Spencer, Robert. *Did Muhammad Exist?: An Inquiry into Islam's Obscure Origins*. Wilmington, DE: ISI Books, 2012.

"Stanford Encyclopedia of Philosophy." Accessed December 28, 2012. http://plato.stanford.edu/.

Stanford, Michael. *An Introduction to the Philosophy of History*. Cambridge, MA: Blackwell, 1998.

Strauss, Mark L. *Four Portraits, One Jesus: An Introduction to Jesus and the Gospels*. Grand Rapids, MI: Zondervan, 2007.

Strobel, Lee. *The Case for a Creator: A Journalist Investigates Scientific Evidence That Points toward God*. Grand Rapids, MI: Zondervan, 2004.

Strobel, Lee. *The Case for Christ: A Journalist's Personal Investigation of the Evidence for Jesus*. Grand Rapids, MI: Zondervan, 1998.

Stroud, James E. *Christianity in the 22nd Century: Darwin, Jihad and Church-ianity*. Xulon Press, 2010.

Sumer: Cities of Eden. Alexandria, VA: Time-Life Books, 1993.

Surburg, Raymond F. *Introduction to the Intertestamental Period*. St. Louis: Concordia Pub. House, 1975.

Swinburne, Richard. *Miracles*. New York: Macmillan, 1989.

Taylor, Vincent. *The Formation of the Gospel Tradition*. London: Macmillan, 1964.

Terrien, De Lacouperie. *The Languages of China before the Chinese. Researches on the Languages Spoken by the Pre-Chinese Races of China Proper Previously to the Chinese Occupation*. Taipei: Ch'eng-wen Pub., 1966.

Thiele, Edwin Richard. *The Mysterious Numbers of the Hebrew Kings;*. Grand Rapids: W.B. Eerdmans Pub., 1965.

Thomas, Brian. "Human Origins." Acts and Facts Journal. Autumn 2012. Accessed December 28, 2012. http://www.icr.org/icr-magazines.

Tiwari, Kedar Nath. *Comparative Religion*. Delhi: Motilal Banarsidass, 1987.

Tucker, Aviezer. *Our Knowledge of the Past: A Philosophy of Historiography*. Cambridge: Cambridge University Press, 2004.

"Understanding Evolution." Understanding Evolution. Accessed December 28, 2012. http://www.evolution.berkeley.edu/.

"University of Haifa." Most Ancient Hebrew Biblical Inscription Deciphered. Accessed December 28, 2012. http://newmedia-eng.haifa.ac.il/?p=2043.

Van, Voorst Robert E. *Anthology of World Scriptures*. Belmont, CA: Wadsworth Pub., 1994.

Varghese, Roy Abraham. *The Christ Connection: How the World Religions Prepared the Way for the Phenomenon of Jesus*. Brewster, MA: Paraclete Press, 2011.

Vilenkin, Alexander. "Did the Universe Have a Beginning? Alexander Vilenkin." YouTube. June 19, 2012. Accessed December 28, 2012. http://www.youtube.com/watch?v=NXCQelhKJ7A.

Voltaire. *The Philosophy of History*. London: Printed for I. Allcock, 1766.

Walls, Jerry L. *The Oxford Handbook of Eschatology*. Oxford: Oxford University Press, 2008.

Walsh, W. H. *Philosophy of History, an Introduction*. New York: Harper, 1960.

Wellhausen, Julius. *Prolegomena to the History of Israel*. Atlanta, GA: Scholars Press, 1994.

Wells, Jonathan. *Icons of Evolution: Science or Myth? : Why Much of What We Teach about Evolution Is Wrong*. Washington, DC: Regnery Pub., 2000.

Wells, Jonathan. *The Politically Incorrect Guide to Darwinism and Intelligent Design*. Washington, DC: Regnery Publishing, 2006.

West, John Anthony. *Serpent in the Sky: The High Wisdom of Ancient Egypt*. Wheaton, IL: Quest Books, 1993.

West, John G., ed. *The Magician's Twin: C.S. Lewis on Science, Scientism, and Society.* Seattle, WA: Discovery Institute Press, 2012.

Westermann, Claus. *The Genesis Accounts of Creation.* Philadelphia: Fortress Press, 1964.

Wexler, Jay D. "'Is It Science?' Question," First Amendment Law Review, 5:90, 93." 2006. Accessed December 28, 2012. https://litigation-essentials.lexisnexis.com/webcd/app?action=DocumentDisplay.

White, Jerrell G. *First Century Palestine : The Land, People, Places, and Events of the New Testament.* St.Louis: Sain, 1978.

White, Timothy P. "Letter to the University of Idaho Faculty, Staff and Students." October 4, 2005. Accessed December 28, 2012. http://www.president.uidaho.edu/default.aspx?pid=85947.

Whitesides, George M. "Revolutions In Chemistry: Priestley Medalist George M. Whitesides' Address,." Chemical and Engineering News, 85: 12–17. March 26, 2007. Accessed December 28, 2012. http://pubs.acs.org/cen/coverstory/85/8513cover1.html.

"Why Do Creatures in Ancient Amber Look So Modern?'"" The Institute for Creation Research. Accessed December 28, 2012. http://www.icr.org/.

Wilford, John Noble. "'House of David' Inscription: Clues to a Dark Age." The New York Times. November 1993. Accessed Winter 2012. doi:http://www.nytimes.com/1993/11/16/science/house-of-david-inscription-clues-to-a-dark-age.html.

Williams, Peter S. "The Definitional Critique of Intelligent Design Theory Â–Lessons Fromthe Demise of Logical Positivism–Peter S. Williams." Accessed December 28, 2012. http://www.arn.org/docs/williams/pw_definitionalcritique.htm.

Witherington, Ben. *The Jesus Quest: The Third Search for the Jew of Nazareth*. Downers Grove, IL: InterVarsity Press, 1995.

Witherington, Ben. "Religion at the Dawn of Civilization." *Biblical Archaeology Review* 39, no. 1 (January/February 2013): 57–60.

Wright, N. T. *The Challenge of Jesus: Rediscovering Who Jesus Was and Is*. Downers Grove, IL: InterVarsity Press, 1999.

Wright, N. T. *The New Testament and the People of God*. Minneapolis: Fortress Press, 1992.

Wright, N. T. *The Resurrection of the Son of God*. Minneapolis, MN: Fortress Press, 2003.

Wright, NT. "The New Unimproved Jesus." *Christianity Today*, September 13, 1993, 26.

Young, Rodger C. "Inductive And Deductive Methods As Applied To OT Chronology." Masters Seminary Journal. Accessed December 28, 2012. http://www.galaxie.com/article/11507.

Zacharias, Ravi K. *Beyond Opinion: Living the Faith That We Defend*. Nashville: Thomas Nelson, 2007.

Zammito, JH. "Discipline, Philosohpy, and History." Accessed Summer 2012. doi:http://onlinelibrary.wiley.com/doi/10.1111/j.1468-2303.2010.00544.x/abstract